HOCKWORTHY HEADSTONES

NOTES ON A
DEVON COUNTRY CHURCHYARD
AND THOSE WHO LIE THERE

HOCKWORTHY HEADSTONES
NOTES ON A
DEVON COUNTRY CHURCHYARD
AND THOSE WHO LIE THERE

Susan Maria Farrington

Colden
Publications
2014

Published by
Colden Publications
P O Box 22
Wiveliscombe
TA4 2ZH

Copyright Susan Maria Farrington, 2014

All rights reserved. No part of this publication may be reprinted or reproduced or utilised in any form or by any electronic, mechanical, or other means, now known or hereafter invented, including photocopying or retrieval system, without permission in writing from the copyright owner.

ISBN: 978-0-9540992-3-7

Printed by
Short Run Press Limited
Exeter
Devon
EX2 7LW

CONTENTS

ILLUSTRATIONS	vii
PREFACE	ix
ACKNOWLEDGEMENTS	xi
INTRODUCTION	1
HOCKWORTHY CHURCH HISTORY	3
WAR MEMORIAL	15
CHURCH PORCH MEMORIAL	21
HOCKWORTHY CHURCHYARD	31
PLANS	33
INSCRIPTIONS	38
Appendix A Incumbents and Patrons	102
Appendix B Church Rebuilding Faculty	104
Appendix C Church Tablets	107
Appendix D Churchwardens	109
Appendix E Parish Farms and Houses	110
Appendix F Monument Designs	112
Appendix G Burial Registers 1578-2014	113
Burial Registers Index	149
BIBLIOGRAPHY AND SOURCES	165
GENERAL INDEX	167
NUMERICAL INDEX	177

Hockworthy Church, 1906

ILLUSTRATIONS

The front cover and drawings on *pp. 30* and *112* are by
Diana Farrington.

The churchyard plans *pp. 33-37* were designed by Naveen Anandakumar.

The map on *p. x* by The Ordnance Survey (David & Charles, 1980 re-print).

Images have been kindly loaned by
Tony Redwood *[p.59]*; Charles Doble *[p.75]* and Jean Goddard *[p.100]*.

The badge on *p.18* is courtesy of the Royal Military Police Museum.

Extracts from
A Map of the County of Devonshire, 1765 by Benjamin Donn *[p. x]*,
Hockworthy Tithe Map *[p.2]*
and the Hockworthy Burial Registers on
pp. 43, 95, 113, 114, 115, 116 and 164
are by kind permission of the Devon Heritage Service.

Articles are reproduced from the
Taunton Courier [p.13] and *Western Times [p.26]*

All other photographs by the author
(and her grandmother Dorothy Farrington *p.vi*)

For

all those from Hockworthy who have gone before;
especially in memory of the men and boys of Hockworthy who
went to fight for their country, their village and their homes.

PREFACE

As one of the two churchwardens of Hockworthy, it had long been on my conscience that we had no churchyard plan, as is required, showing burials. I had envisaged a single sheet of paper. She claims that I had asked her to do this even before asking her to marry me; but when Susan Farrington joined me at Hole Farm after our marriage in September 2009, she kindly agreed to help and the project developed. She brought with her skills honed in cemeteries in the Indian Sub-Continent and other ex-colonial countries, unique skills, but much needed, as many of our headstones are illegible, or seemed so to those of us unpractised in such matters.

Concurrently, since arriving in the parish, Sue has initiated what has now become an annual tradition. This is to research the life of one of those recorded on the parish War Memorial, which is read out after the roll call at our Remembrance Day service in November.

In the Devon Heritage Centre, she found the manuscript archive of Major Jack Daniell, churchwarden from 1979-1986. Mrs Mary Daniell, his widow, was happy for this material to be brought to public notice, and the depositor, the Borden Gate Parish Council, has kindly granted permission for Sue to use this research for her survey.

These strands have now been drawn together, with additional information about the church, the recollections of local people and biographical details of those commemorated, to create this ecclesiastical history of Hockworthy.

From close involvement, I can testify to how much time and research this has taken. But I hope readers will agree that it has been worth the wait, as those who created our enchanting village are recalled within these pages.

John Doble

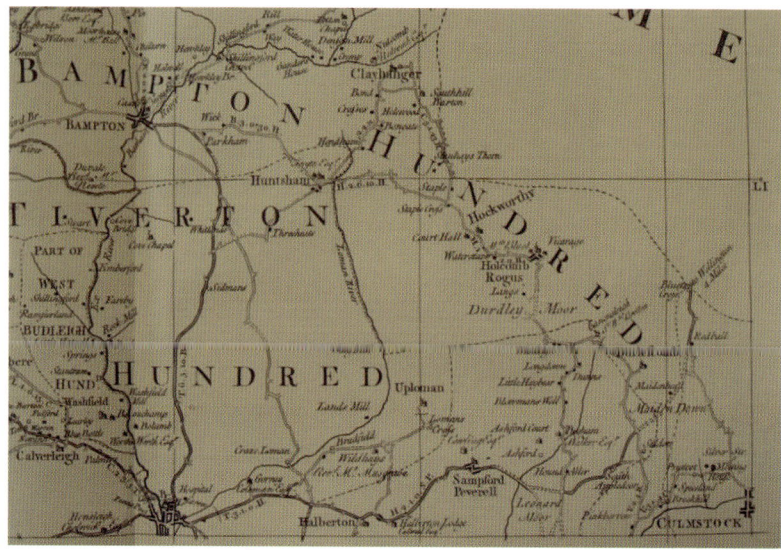

Benjamin Donn's *A Map of the County of Devonshire, 1765*

The first Ordnance Survey map of Hockworthy. Using a plate engraved in 1809, it was based on surveys dating from 1796 and 1801.

ACKNOWLEDGEMENTS

My heart sank somewhat when a survey of the Hockworthy parish churchyard was suggested by my husband, John Doble. Although not large in number, many headstones were quite challenging to read. But a chance browsing through my grandmother's photograph album made the decision for me. My grandfather came home on leave from India and they married in Devon in 1906. A contemporary newspaper account describes them taking a tour of Dartmoor for their honeymoon, "... putting up each night at wayside inns". In their album of a mere half dozen images of the wedding and honeymoon, by an extra-ordinary coincidence there is one of Hockworthy church.

What chance that over a hundred years ago my grandparents, with no obvious links, should have climbed the same steep ascent to the church and looked at the same headstones? There was no doubt now that work should begin immediately on John's request. The photograph has become the *Frontispiece*, to remember them, and all who have shared the same glorious outlook from the steps of the church in our unspoilt and hidden gem of a Devon valley.

However, being new to the parish, I was dependent on the help and input of a number of people with long-standing connections with the village: Sarah Baker, Jean and Malcolm Goddard, Mary and Richard Heywood, Joyce Norman, Keith Prescott, Tony Redwood, Robie Reed and Sylvia and Henry Stevens, who all generously shared their knowledge. Mary Daniell kindly approached Borden Gate Parish Council who agreed to the use of her husband's papers, and the Rector, the Reverend Sue Blade, gave her blessing to the project.

I am indebted to all descendants, too many to name individually, who have provided much very helpful information. One major, as yet unresolved, mystery concerns the three members of the Mewett family who are commemorated on the two parish war memorials. Many have assisted in the quest to find the link between these three brothers from Sussex and Hockworthy. I am most grateful for your help; the church bells will peal loud and long when this baffling riddle is solved.

For war memorial and other research, my thanks go to Charles Doble, Rosalind Hodge, Renée Jackaman, Roger Perkins and Michael Rose; also to those who helped at the Commando Veterans Association, the Devon Heritage Centre and St Nazaire Society, and at the following museums: London Scottish Regiment, Royal Military Police and Tiverton Museum of Mid Devon Life.

Naveen Anandakumar, Frances Dransfield, Giles Edmonston-Low, David Hawkings, Jess Maltby, Caroline Seymour, Katriona Smith and the team at Short Run Press assisted with preparing the material for publication, while my sister-in-law Diana Farrington wove her magic with her drawings. To everyone, my heartfelt thanks, and most especially to Glenda Anderson who has been there from the outset: at the end of a telephone, or in The National Archives (TNA), churchyard surveying or burning much midnight oil. And last, but certainly not least, to my husband John for writing the history of the church and for his forbearance and support throughout.

smf
Hockworthy
2014

INTRODUCTION

The initial purpose of this publication was to put on record a survey of the headstones around Hockworthy parish church. This evolved and expanded once we realised what an opportunity there was to shed light on those buried here from this small, largely unchanging, rural community. Study of publically accessible archives and web-sites began to reveal how interwoven the families were; these biographical details are included within the inscription transcriptions *[pp.38-99]*. Likewise, where possible, biographical information has been included for those commemorated on the two war memorials *[pp.15-30]*.

The author would welcome any additional details readers may wish to share, and also wishes to apologise should there be any inaccuracies or misinterpretations. As very few headstones have survived from before the rebuilding of the church in the mid-19th century, in order to complete the story, the extant burial registers have been transcribed and are included at *Appendix G [p.113]*. But the story begins with a history of the church.

HOCKWORTHY TITHE MAP EXTRACT
1842

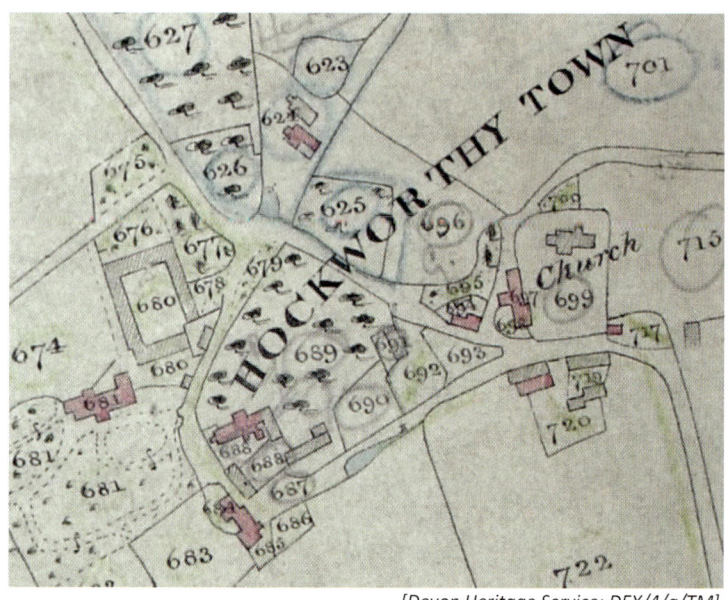

[Devon Heritage Service: DEX/4/a/TM]

KEY
Tithe Apportionments - 8 March 1842

624 Herds: House, Buildings & Yard
625 Herds: Young Orchard
626 Herds: Little Orchard
680 Court Hall: Barn, Linhay & Yard
681 Court Hall: House & Lawn
684 Court Hall: 3 Cottages & Garden
685 Court Hall: Plot
686 Court Hall: Garden
687 Glebe: Waste
688 Glebe: Vicarage House & Garden
689 Glebe: Orchard
690 Glebe: Garden
691 Glebe: Linhay & Yard

692 Court Hall: Garden & Plantation
693 Lady Lands: Garden
694 Lady Lands: Cottage & Garden
695 Court Hall: Plantation
696 Glebe: Half Acre
697 The Poor House
698 Court Hall: Cellar & Garden
699 Church & Yard
715 Glebe: Higher Barns Close
717 Court Hall: Cottage & Garden
719 Court Hall: Linhay & Yard
720 Court Hall: House & Garden
722 Court Hall: Hurfords Mead

*[For further study of buildings and field names,
see Devon Heritage Service: DEX/4/a/TA/210/Hockworthy]*

HOCKWORTHY CHURCH HISTORY

Hockworthy is a Devon parish on the border of Somerset covering a large area (some 3 x 2 miles) mainly steep pasture-land including Chimney Down (851ft) one of the highest points in the area between Wellington, Tiverton, Bampton and Wiveliscombe. Stallenge Thorne, Hockford Waters and Lea Barton were mentioned in Domesday Book (1086). In the old days Lea, Staple Cross and Waterslade were hamlets within the parish.

It is not known when Christian worship started here. The history of Hockworthy Church is uncertain, partly because of its antiquity and sparse documentary evidence, then because all the old wall plaques and monuments disappeared when the church was rebuilt in the 19th century. Domesday Book does not mention a church. But that does not mean that none existed. With several farms recorded in the parish at the time, it seems likely that their inhabitants had somewhere to worship.

The first indication of a church is the signature of Arnald "Priest of Hockworthy" witnessing the 1166 charter, when Walter de Claville gave land for the foundation of the Augustinian Priory of Canonsleigh. In 1184 Henry de Berneville and Walter de Chevithorne transferred their role as Patrons of Hockworthy (the right to appoint the priest) to the Prior of Canonsleigh.

Church interior

Three Thomas Bilbie of Cullompton bells dating from 1808, engraved with the name of churchwarden Edward Darby

In 1202 the Bishop of Exeter confirmed the gift of the church to Canonsleigh. The Exchequer Fee list of 1242/3 shows Hugo de Bynnewill as feudal lord of Hockworthy. By 1284 there were only seven Canons at Canonsleigh, when a Papal Bull accused them of neglect. They were evicted and the Priory with all its estates was made an Abbey for nuns headed by an Abbess who, for the next 250 years till the Reformation, was the Patron of Hockworthy church. [*Appendix A*]

Hockworthy's size then is indicated by the taxation list of Pope Nicholas IV in 1288-91, when it was assessed at £2.10.0 compared with £3 for Burlescombe and £6 for Holcombe Rogus. The surviving burial registers, which start in 1578, give an indication of how the population has fluctuated over the centuries (the full list of burials is at *Appendix G*); now it is about 150.

Burials in each century	Parish population at each census		
1600s – 344	1801 - 283	1841 - 369	1881 - 304
1700s – 480	1811 - 324	1851 - 400	1891 - 308
1800s – 466	1821 - 354	1861 - 375	1901 - 252
1900s – 177	1831 - 335	1871 - 377	1911 - 373

The first church could well have been made of wood, perhaps before the Norman Conquest. The Norman feudal lords, the de Bernevilles, probably built the original stone church, of which the only Norman relic is the font. The tower has a medieval core with a c. 15th century window on the south side. It was largely rebuilt in 1848.

The tower contains three bells by Thomas Bilbie of Cullompton, whose name, with the date 1808, is cast on the bells along with the name of the churchwarden, Edward Darby. The Bilbies were long-established West Country bell-makers of great renown. The original mechanism for pealing the bells, including big elm wheels, is all still there and considered important by the Council for the Care of Churches. By 2000 the bell chamber was choked with sticks and excrement from generations of jackdaws; this was cleared by voluntary labour and the openings made bird-proof with wire. In 2008 the existing clapper mechanism for chiming the bells was restored. To swing them for pealing is impossible, as the wheels were considered too fragile to restore and too valuable historically to be replaced. At the foot of the right-hand side of the door to the tower there is an Ordnance Survey bench-mark denoting a spot-height on

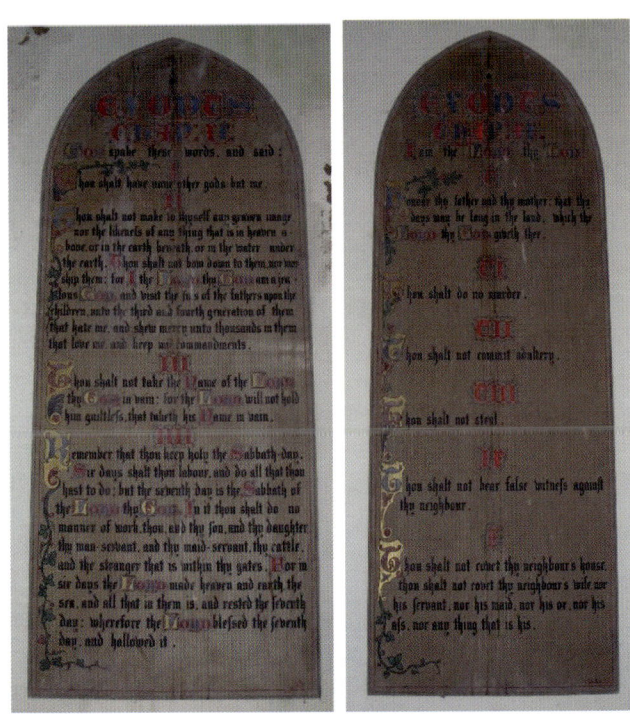

The Ten Commandments

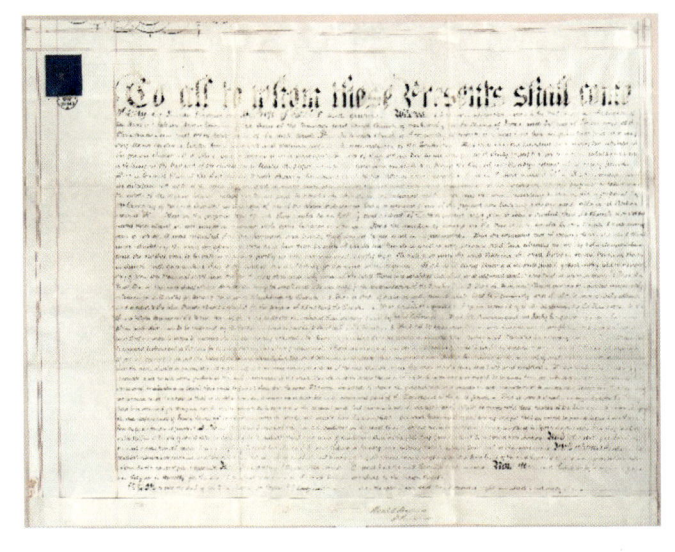

The Bishop's faculty for the rebuilding of the church, 1863

the map of 663½ feet (202m) above sea level. Painted on boards, the Ten Commandments (6' x 2'6") are on the west wall. The original 1852 bill from John Toms of Wellington was for £7.10.0. *[c. £800 in today's prices]*.

By 1863 the main body of the church was considered to be "in a very dilapidated condition" and it was rebuilt in 1863-65 at the initiative and presumably mainly at the expense of the Newman family, who were by then the main landowners and who provided the two vicars between 1852 and 1920. However, two grants totalling £60 were also received from the Incorporated Society for Promoting the Enlargement, Building and Repairing of Churches and Chapels.

The gallery at the west end and the high box pews were removed and the seating increased from 120 to 174. A north aisle, porch and vestry were added. The work done by Davis of Taunton cost about £1,500.

The Bishop's "faculty" (permission) for the rebuilding survives; a facsimile hangs on the south wall, the text being recorded at *Appendix B*. This enjoined "... the greatest care ... in the removal of ... tablets and monuments and that the same should be preserved and ... affixed in some convenient part of the new church." Most sadly this was not done. No pre-1863 memorials remain, although there are five later memorials or inscriptions to the Newmans *[Appendix C]*.

However, in the steps up to the tower (added at the re-building; previous access to the tower was probably from inside the church) are fragments of two memorial stones: Elizabeth Morse who died in 1770, and Dorothy, wife of Revd John Catford, vicar of Hockworthy from 1640-1672, who lived at Court Hall. The lack of respect in not re-erecting the memorials, even using two as building stone, is regretted. Hope remains that other similar fragments will be found.

Remains of Dorothy Catford's C17th memorial set into the lintel over the tower staircase

The Victorian organ built by Vowles of Bristol

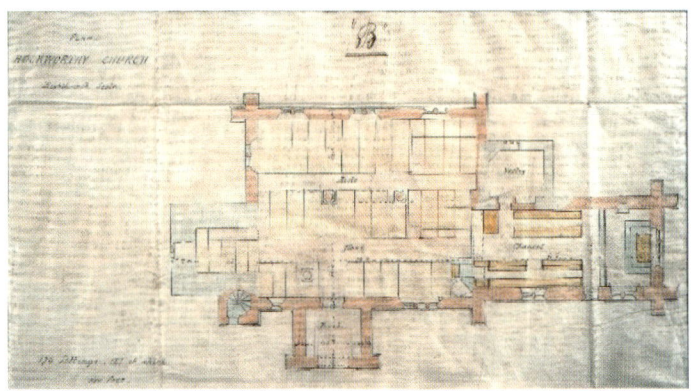

The plan accompanying the rebuilding faculty, 1863

It is not known if there were any vaults under the church; they too are something that might, or might not, be uncovered at a later date. Part of a window from the old church was used as an arch over the gate between the churchyard and the Newmans' garden *[see p.93]*.

The attractive new church rededicated to St Simon and St Jude is in the Early English style with unusually the chancel being nearly as long as the rest of the church. A Gothic arch divides the chancel from the remainder. There are two columns of grey/pink marble. Of the four lovely stained-glass windows, two are by John Hardman of Birmingham, A W N Pugin's favourite stained-glass maker. The other in the chancel is by Atkins & Co of Tottenham. Mercifully the Norman font was retained.

The plan accompanying the faculty (also on the south wall) *[see preceding page]* confirms that the tower was retained from the previous building. It also indicates that parts of the walls in the vestry/organ area are from the original church. In 1986-7 the roof of the tower was repaired, when Major Jack Daniell and Merlin Heywood were churchwardens.

The tower stairwell

The architect was Charles Durnford Greenway of Warwick; he died tragically young aged 31 in 1870 in Exeter. This is believed to be his only church. The window on the south wall nearest the altar, depicting the rebuilding of the temple in Jerusalem, is dedicated to Greenway, paying tribute in an inscription below to his "gratuitous services" in rebuilding the church. Presumably he did not charge for his work: he was a first cousin of Reverend William J Newman, the incumbent.

The organ, one of the finest in the area, is believed to have been made by Vowles of Bristol, and was installed in 1884. A plaque on the side records the devoted service to the church generally of 'Molly' Heywood (1918-2005) organist for sixty-five years. The striking altar cloth was weaved and donated by churchwarden Lavinia Elvy in 2001. The exterior doors have magnificent wrought iron-work, which, it has been said by an architectural expert, "is one of the unique glories of this fine church".

View from the church tower, 2013

Candelabra above the chancel

One of the four light-holders

In 2009 the pews near the font were rearranged to create a corner seat and a space for Christenings and for children to play. Under the tower, cupboards and a serving table have been erected in keeping with the woodwork elsewhere in the church.

The churchyard is a bit over one acre bounded by ancient stone walls to the south and west, and by hedges to the north and east. There are five fine old yews and some holly trees. In the spring there is a profusion of primroses, and of ox-eye daisies in the summer. The oldest stone marks the grave of Sarah Bucknell, who died in 1725 aged 22. A host of other Hockworthy people lie there from many centuries before, their spirits pervading and, one hopes, appreciating these lovely, well-cared-for surroundings. Most were engaged in the same farms, quarries and lime-kilns that are still such important features in our parish today, as can be seen in the brief biographical notes on the tomb-stones that follow.

The Church is listed Grade 2 Star with English Heritage; the 1725 grave-stone is Grade 2 listed. It is in the Diocese of Exeter and, since 1964, has been part of the Sampford Peverell team of six parishes. A list of clergy from 1166 until today is on a board on the south wall *[see Appendix A]*.

The Church registers of baptisms, banns, marriages and burials from 1577 have been transferred to the Devon Heritage Centre for safe-keeping. They also hold a 1525 church document granting land in the SW corner of the churchyard for a "church house". This later became the location for the "poor-house". In 1866 the site was chosen for the school, which closed in 1950. The building has now become the Village Hall *[see p.85]*. The Wesleyan Methodist Preaching Room that was established at Staple Cross in 1883, reverted to being a house in 1926.

So this beautiful church stands, where one has stood for about a thousand years, in its lovely position on a hill-side with wide views set in the heart of the village. That it remains in good condition, is thanks to the devoted care of generations of Christians and indeed non-Christians, who continue to value its presence, as well as to the generosity of the Newman family, who saved it from near-collapse in the 19th century, thus bequeathing to the people of Hockworthy a structure, which should last for centuries to come.

John Doble

12

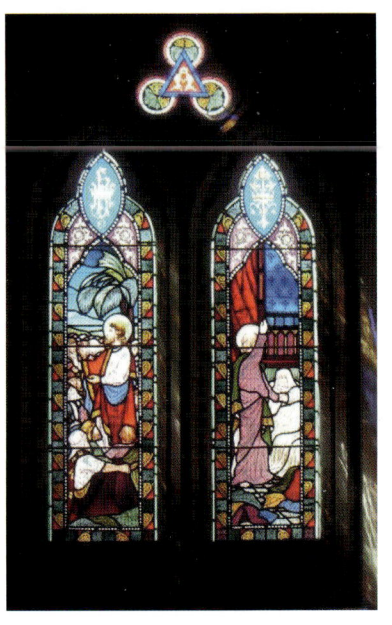

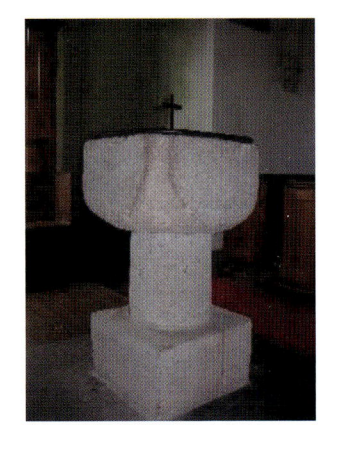

CONSECRATION OF THE PARISH CHURCH AT HOCKWORTHY.

On Saturday last the church of this parish, after having been entirely rebuilt with the exception of the tower, was consecrated for divine service. The old fabric was in the year 1863 found to be in a very dilapidated condition, and it was resolved to pull it down, and erect a new and commodious edifice (capable of accommodating an additional number of worshippers) on its site. On the 26th of June in that year the work was accordingly commenced, and at the present time the parishioners of Hockworthy possess a neat and substantial structure in the place of an old and ruined fabric. The church is situated on a gentle elevation commanding a lovely picturesque view of the surrounding country. It is built in the Early English style by Mr Davis, of Taunton, and contains a nave and side aisle, with oak pews, stained and varnished. The roof is light and elegant, and the chancel is divided from the body of the church by a Gothic arch. At the east end is a beautiful stained glass window, on which are pourtrayed scenes in the life of the Saviour, the centre piece representing the crucifixion. The communion table is covered with a richly worked altar cloth, with gilt fringes. On it are placed the altar candlesticks, communion service, &c., and above is some elegantly carved mosaic work, with the letters I H S and K I P. The pulpit is of stone, inlaid with marble mosaics, and supported on a marble pillar. The reading desk is also of stone, and tastefully carved. The tower is open to the body of the church, and the whole of the edifice presents a neat and substantial appearance.

Hockworthy being in the diocese of Exeter, the consecration of the church would have been performed by the Lord Bishop of that Diocese, but owing to advanced age and bodily infirmity, his lordship was unable to be present, and he deputed the Right Rev. the Bishop of Colombo to perform the office of consecration in his stead.

The service was choral throughout, and the usual form of consecration having been gone through, the lessons, &c., for the day were proceeded with, and were taken part in by the Vicar of Hockworthy and several local clergy. The sermon was preached by the Rev. Chas. Newman, of Truro.

During the collection, the Bishop of Colombo read the offertory sentences, and his lordship subsequently administered the holy communion.

Taunton Courier   8 November 1865

A hatchment has been installed on the north wall, to mark Queen Elizabeth II's Golden Jubilee

WAR MEMORIAL

W Lewis,
   AB, Royal Navy
W Burston,
   Pte, 2nd Devonshire Regt
W H Cockram,
   Pte, 9th Devon Regt
F J Cockram,
   Pte, 3rd Berks Regt
A G Mewett,
   Pte, 12th Royal Sussex Regt
W Mewett,
   Cpl, 2nd Royal Sussex Regt
G G Northam,
   Lce Cpl, 2nd Glostr Regt
P Prescott,
   Gunner, R. Garrison Artillery
F Thomas,
   Pte, 3rd Devon Regt
A J Troake,
   Pte, 10th Devon Regt
G Kidley,
   Pte, Wilts Regt

There are brass plaques in the church, located near the organ on the north side of the arch leading to the chancel, which pay tribute to the men of Hockworthy who died in the two World Wars. The *Exeter and Plymouth Gazette* of Friday 23 April 1920 reported:

Hockworthy – The unveiling of the war tablet will take place today, the ceremony being followed by a dinner for returned soldiers and sailors. A most enjoyable dance took place here the night before last.

A further tablet in the church porch *[see p.21]* commemorates those who served, and returned. Unfortunately no first names or regiments were recorded, which makes identification more complicated. The biographical details which follow, therefore, have not always been verified by personal memories and there may be inaccuracies.

Around 1,100,000 British and Empire personnel died in the Great War. Ten are commemorated on the tablet here, although a further three are known to have been born in Hockworthy who died but are not on the memorial. Added to the thirty-eight who also served, this represents a large proportion of the male population of the parish. With so many away at war, the impact on the community must have been significant. During the period of the war, civilian burials in the parish numbered fourteen.

They died on the Western Front, the Balkans, while serving with the Egyptian Expeditionary Force and in Mesopotamia, all so far from their families and homes in the peaceful hills of Devon. One young sailor died in the Orkneys, others in hospital in England. Although none died on the 1st July 1916, the opening day of the Battle of the Somme, the day with the highest toll of casualties, one was killed on 30th June, another on the 2nd July. Two are commemorated on Commonwealth War Grave Commission (CWGC) memorials near where they fell as they have no known grave.

1914 –1918 WAR MEMORIAL BIOGRAPHIES

[Badges reproduced from the war memorial]

J/58860 Ordinary Seaman Walter LEWIS
Royal Navy

Walter's family were agricultural labourers from East Somerset. His father, Sidney, a waggoner, came to Lea Barton after his marriage to Mary Blackmore in 1890. Walter was born on 9th November 1897 in Holcombe Rogus, and his three sisters in Hockworthy. He was a cowman when he enlisted at Devonport on 19 Sept 1916. Walter served on *HMS Vivid*, and transferred to *HMS Valiant*, dying on 25th November from meningitis aged 19 years after only sixty-eight days in uniform. He is buried at Lyness Royal Naval cemetery, Isle of Hoy, in the Orkney Islands where the author and her husband visited his grave in 2014. His brother John is on the memorial tablet in the church porch *[p.24]*.

8741 Private Walter BURSTON
2nd Battalion, The Devonshire Regiment

Born on 12th June 1889 on a farm near Stogumber, Walter's family moved frequently following available work, as was typical of agricultural labourers. They lived at Staple Cross but were at Ham's Cottage, Petton when Walter died in 1914. The eldest of four daughters and two sons, Walter had enlisted into the Devonshire Regiment at Exeter as a professional soldier before the war. He was stationed in Egypt but, in November 1914, landed at Le Havre in the British Expeditionary Force. On 18th December, Walter's 'C' company took part in an attack on the German lines near Neuve Chappelle. With no known grave, he is commemorated on the CWGC Memorial at Le Touret, which records more than 13,000 men who died in the area within the first year of the war.

23098 Private Frederick John COCKRAM
The Royal Berkshire Regiment, later The Labour Corps

Born in 1895 in East Anstey, the eldest of the three sons of Alice and Frederick Cockram who served in the Great War. His father was an agricultural labourer living at Lea Cottage, while Fred worked as a gardener. He transferred from the Royal Berkshires to the Labour Corps (Regt No: 245375) and died on 14th November 1918, just after hostilities ended. He was buried in the civic cemetery at Efford, Plymouth. His brother William died in 1916 *[q.v.]*, and his younger brother Sydney is recorded on the porch memory *[see p.22]*.

20929 Private William Henry COCKRAM
9th (Service) Battalion, The Devonshire Regiment

The second of Alice and Frederick Cockram's three sons to serve in the Great War. William was born 1897 in Oakford and in 1911 was a cowman at a farm at Exebridge. His elder brother Frederick *[q.v.]* also died, but his younger brother Sydney survived *[see p.22]*. William was wounded in the Battle of the Somme and died on 2nd July 1916. He is buried in the Corbie Communal cemetery extension.

SD/1407 Private Alexander George MEWETT
12th (Service) Battalion, The Royal Sussex Regiment

Alexander (Alec) is one of three sons of Alfred & Emily Mewett, from Willingdon, near Eastbourne, Sussex, recorded on memorials in Hockworthy. None of the brothers is on the Willingdon church memorial, and no link has yet been found between the family and Hockworthy. Before the war, Alec was working at the Sussex Grand Parade Club, Eastbourne together with his younger brother Reginald. Alec enlisted in Eastbourne into the Royal Sussex Regiment. He was killed in action on 30th June 1916, aged 26, and is buried in the CWGC Guards Cemetery, Windy Corner, Cuinchy.

Acting Sergeant Walter W MEWETT
1120 Military Foot Police

The eldest son of Alfred & Emily Mewett from Willingdon, Eastbourne, Walter is one of three Mewett brothers commemorated in Hockworthy with no obvious link with the parish. The youngest brother, Reginald, survived the war *[see p.24]*. In 1914 Walter married Florence Blake and they had a daughter. He had joined the R. Sussex Regiment in 1900, but transferred to the Military Foot Police before war broke out. He fought on the Western Front ('mentioned in dispatches') until March 1916 when he was invalided home. He died from consumption on 22nd July 1916, is buried in Southampton Old Cemetery, and appears on the Southampton Cenotaph. *[Badge courtesy of RMP Museum]*

11309 Private Gilbert George NORTHAM
2nd Battalion, The Gloucestershire Regiment

The Battalion war diary records the death on 5th July 1915 when aged twenty-two of Pte Northam, and his burial at Chapelle d'Armentieres. Gilbert was born at Upottery, Devon in 1893, the fifth of William and Isabella's sons. He was an assistant blacksmith at Cockington, near Torquay before the war. In 1911, Frederick, one of Gilbert's seven brothers was working as a farm labourer at Dares Down. The family later moved into Hockworthy, where five other Northams are commemorated on the porch tablet. Four of these were Gilbert's brothers.

36655 Gunner Percy PRESCOTT
206th Siege Battery, The Royal Garrison Artillery

Percy's father William was born in Bampton, his mother, Lucy Vickery in Raddington. William was a carpenter, and the family lived at Borden Gate. Percy was the seventh of twelve children, all born in Hockworthy. He served in the 206th Siege battery, Royal Garrison Artillery and died of wounds 25 July 1917 aged 23. His headstone is in the CWGC cemetery at Lijssenthoek, near Ypres in Flanders. Five of his nine brothers are commemorated on the porch tablet and the family's service was publically recognised *[see p.26]*. For many years, Percy's great grandson, Keith, has kept the church at Hockworthy in the best possible order.

7897 Private Frederick THOMAS
16TH Battalion (Royal Devon Yeomanry and Royal North Devon Yeomanry), The Devonshire Regiment

Born in 1886, the fourth son of William and Louisa Thomas who lived at Roundmoor Cottage on the Huntsham estate. He joined the Devon Yeomanry and by 1911 Frederick was in Malta with the 2nd Battn Devonshire Regt. He fought at Gallipoli and then joined the Egyptian Expeditionary Force. He was killed in action on 3rd Dec 1917. He is buried in the Jerusalem CWGC cemetery. In 1913, he had married Nellie, daughter of Henry Hicks of Uplowman, and they had a daughter.

26071 Private Albert John TROAKE
10th (Service) Battalion, The Devonshire Regiment

Albert was born and was living in Hockworthy when he enlisted in Tiverton. The son of John and Mary Troake, both gardeners, he had three brothers and a sister. In 1913 he married Elizabeth Foxford who was living at Russells in Wiveliscombe when her husband died. Albert served in the Salonika campaign, arriving in the Balkans in late 1915 to fight the army of Bulgaria. He was killed in action on 25th April 1917. With no known grave, he is commemorated on the CWGC memorial at Doiran in Macedonia, Greece in a cemetery where there are a total of 1,138 burials.

There may be others, but at least three more Hockworthy-born soldiers are known to have died, who are not commemorated on the Memorial.

[See p.177 for the churchyard plot numbers Index]

28961 Private Frank BROOMFIELD
10th (Service) Battalion, Gloucestershire Regiment

Born in Hockworthy, Frank was the son of Emma **B-42** and Henry **B-39** Broomfield and nephew of Elizabeth Sprague **B-40**, all of whom predeceased him. He was married and working as a house and ship painter when he enlisted in Bristol. He died in Flanders on 19th November 1916 and is buried in Warlencourt British cemetery.

27849 Guardsman Albert Jesse FORGAN
Grenadier Guards

Born in Hockworthy in 1891, Albert was the son of Edith and Tom Forgan, a butcher from South Staple (once the Turks Head pub), and grandson of Jesse and Elizabeth Talbot **A-14**. Albert was a journeyman butcher living in Weston-super-Mare. He enlisted in Cardiff and died in Flanders on 12th October 1917. He is commemorated on the Tyne Cot Memorial.

15940 Private Walter SHEPHERD
Dorsetshire Regiment

The son of William and Ann Shepherd, Walter was born in Hockworthy, and was a dairy worker before the war. He enlisted in Exeter into the Devonshire Regiment, before transferring to the Dorsets. He drowned on service in Mesopotamia on 17th June 1916.

1939–1945 WAR

5679508 Private Samuel Frederick Gerald KIDLEY
2nd Battalion, The Wiltshire Regiment (Duke of Edinburgh's)

Born 1914 at Langford Budville, Gerald was the elder of Alfred and Rhoda Ann Kidley's three sons and two daughters. He served in Operation Husky (the invasion and occupation of Sicily). He was killed in action 18th July 1943, the eighth day of the campaign, and is buried at the Catania war cemetery in Sicily. His youngest brother Walter married Freda (née Lee) in 1948 and they came to Staple Cross in 1952. Walter died in 1999, Freda in 2014, and they are buried behind the church at Hockworthy.

CHURCH PORCH MEMORIAL
COMMEMORATING
THOSE WHO SERVED AND SURVIVED

ERNEST VICTOR CARR
Born in 1892 at Cove, near Tiverton, one of Charles and Edith Fanny Carr's five children. Both father and son were blacksmiths, living at Borden Gate. Ernest enlisted into the West Somerset Yeomanry (Regt no: 830), transferring to the Somerset Light Infantry (Regt no: 295107). He first saw service in the Balkans on 23 Sep 1915 and was discharged as Lance Corporal on 8 Feb 1919. Brother of Gilbert Henry Carr *[q.v.]* He married Florence Coles from Ashbrittle in 1922, and died in 1975.

GILBERT HENRY CARR
Born 1895 at Cullompton, Devon, one of Charles and Edith Fanny Carr's five children. As did his elder brother Ernest Victor Carr *[q.v.]*, Gilbert enlisted into the West Somerset Yeomanry (Regt No: 731), transferring to Somerset Light Infantry (Regt No: 295068). He entered the war 23 Sep 1915 in the Balkans and was discharged 10 Feb 1919 with the rank of Sergeant. In 1921, he married Ethel Lilian Wood and died 27 July 1950, when living at Landboat Farm, Cheriton Fitzpaine, Devon.

Thomas Henry CHIDGEY
Born 14 March 1896 in Pontyprid, Glamorgan, the son of Charlotte and William J Chidgey, a rabbit trapper with five children. In 1911 the family were at Turnham Farm, Hockworthy. Brother of William John Chidgey *[q.v.]* A farm labourer before the war, he served in the home-based Royal Defence Corps (RDC) and was discharged sick in June 1918. In June 1920 he joined the Royal Navy (No: K/58899), serving with David Ware *[q.v.]*. He was a stoker and later became a Chief Petty Officer. Unmarried, he lodged with his sister at Holcombe Rogus.

William John CHIDGEY
Born 1892 in Glamorgan, the son of Charlotte and William J Chidgey, a rabbit trapper who had five children. In 1911 the family were at Turnham Farm, Hockworthy. Brother of Thomas Henry Chidgey *[q.v.]* William continued in the army after the war and was a Sergeant in the 2nd Somerset Light Infantry when he married Alice Ruth Perry in Wellington in 1920. He died in 1971.

Sydney COCKRAM
Born 1899 at Oakford, the third son of Frederick and Alice Cockram who lived at Luckleys. Of their eight children, two are commemorated on the war memorial having died in the Great War. Another son is buried in the churchyard **A-16,** as is one of their two daughters **E-4.** Sydney married in 1921 Elizabeth Bessie, daughter of John Hawkins, believed to be the sister of J Hawkins *[q.v.]*. A farmer, Sydney died in 1955 in hospital in Exeter.

Lawrence Frederick CROOK
Born 1903 at Sampford Peverell, son of Eli and Lydia Crook, who had four other children. Eli was a waggoner at Lea Cottage. Lawrence was a sailor serving at the Royal Naval Barracks, Devonport when he married Daisy C Dunn in 1937. He died in Exeter in 1959.

Frank DARBY
Born 13 March 1884 in Huntsham, third son of Louis and Mildred Darby **A-10** of Kerswell. Brother of **A-11**, grandson of **A-12**, great grandson of **A-13** and great great nephew of **C-4.** Prior to enlisting in Tiverton into the Canadian Forces (Regt No: 3404) in October 1916, he had served three years in 1st Devon Yeomanry. He built Hillside, Ashbrittle, where he died on 13 May 1953. He is buried in Ashbrittle with his eldest sister Mabel (1878-1974).

John Montague DESTER

Born 1881 in Hockworthy, second son of William and Anne Dester **B-46** of Staple Court. He married Ethel Jane Goddard in 1907 who died in Kent in 1932. John died in Perth, Australia 14 Oct 1949 where members of his family had emigrated. He served in the Royal Garrison Artillery (Regt no: 116167) in the Great War.

J Hawkins

It has been difficult to fully identify 'J Hawkins' as inscribed on the tablet. The most likely appears to be William James, son of John and Mary Hawkins. Born in 1893, in the 1901 census his name is given as James; in 1911 he is William James, doing general farm work at Tiverton. William James has a sister Elizabeth and the family lived at Daggeridge. An Elizabeth Hawkins married Sydney Cockram *[q.v.]*, who lived next door at Lea Cottage. After the war he worked at a coal yard in Wellington where he married Edith Ferris in 1924.

Cecil Charles HEDGELAND

Born 1899 in Dittisham, Devon, son of Frederick and Fanny Hedgeland **B-13**. He served in the Hampshire Regiment (Regt no: 42743), and then the Royal Berkshire Regiment (Regt no: 44937). In 1917 he was severely wounded and suffered until his death in 1934. In 1920 he married Hilda Brock. A carpenter, he lived at West End, next to Glebe Cottage, in Hockworthy.

Charles Herbert HILTON

Born in 1895 in Whitfield, Lancashire, he was the son of James and Alice Hilton **A-9**. They had four children (one had died before 1911) and lived at Dares Down. Charles's father was a teacher who came to the West Country for his health. Not verified, but Charles is believed to have served in the Manchester Regiment during the war.

William George HOBBS

Born 1890 at the Workhouse in Tiverton, the son of Mary Jane, described in the census as "a charwoman from Bampton", and William Hobbs, a labourer. They also had two daughters, Rosa and Bertha. Before the war he worked for William and Louisa Thomas at Roundmoor Cottage, Huntsham, parents of Frederick Thomas on the war memorial *[p.19]*. William George Hobbs married their daughter Louisa Thomas in 1911. Latterly he was a postman who did his deliveries on a bicycle. He lived at Holcombe Rogus with his sister Bertha who taught the piano, and died in 1949.

John LEWIS
Born in 1894 at Pitminster, near Taunton. Son of Sidney and Mary Lewis, who married in 1890 and came to Hockworthy from near Chard. His brother Walter, listed on the war memorial *[p.16]*, served in the Royal Navy and died in 1916. John worked as a farm boy at Lea Barton before the war. An internet website suggests he married Gladys May Goodhind in 1921, that they had two children and that he died in 1963.

Reginald MEERS
Reginald John Meers was the surviving child of William and Frances Meer's five children. He was born in 1890 in Dalwood, Axminster. Both his father and grandfather were thatchers and, before the war, Reginald was a groom. He later was a garage proprietor at Chelston, and died on 25 Dec 1960 in Wellington. In 1915 he married Laura Tooze, great great granddaughter of **A-29**, and great great niece of **A-28**. Before her marriage she worked for the Desters **B-46**, and as a cook for the Newmans **B-48**.

Reginald MEWETT
Born in Sussex in 1894, the third son of Alfred and Emily Mewett. It is as yet not known why he and his two brothers are commemorated on the Hockworthy war memorials *[see p.18]*. Reginald was in the Sussex and Middlesex regiments. He remained in the army, serving in the 1939-45 war, and obtained the rank of Sergeant. He and his wife Helena (née Southcoat) had a son and daughter. They settled in Yorkshire, where he died in 1968.

Frederick NORTHAM
Born 1887 at Luppitt near Honiton, son of William Northam and Isabella, later known as 'Granny Northam'. Before the war he was a farm labourer at Dares Down. Brother of William J *[q.v.]*, Elias E *[q.v.]*, and Henry *[q.v.]* on the porch memorial, and Gilbert Northam on the war memorial *[p.18]*. In the war he served as an Able Seaman on *HMS Drake*. After the war he was a postman and, in 1928, married May Marke. He died in Taunton in 1962.

Elias Eli NORTHAM
Born 1889 in Buckerell, near Exeter, he was the son of William and Isabella Northam, and brother of William J *[q.v.]*, Frederick *[q.v.]*, and Henry *[q.v.]* on the church porch memorial *[p.24]*, and Gilbert Northam on the Hockworthy war memorial *[p.18]*. He married Ethel Woodbury in 1917 and died in 1959. He was a Corporal in the South Wales Borderers and became a gardener when he retired from military service.

Henry NORTHAM

Born 4 March 1896 at Awliscombe, near Honiton, the sixth son of William and Isabella Northam. Brother of William J *[q.v.]*, Frederick *[q.v.]*, and Elias *[q.v.]* on the porch memorial, and Gilbert Northam on the Hockworthy war memorial. He married Ivy D Wright in 1926 in Rockwell Green, where he died in 1975. He worked in a brickworks after the war.

Walter NORTHAM

Born at Highweek, Devon in 1889, Walt was the twin son of John and Jessie Northam of Hurds, Hockworthy. He married Almira Pepperell, the village schoolmistress, in 1915. Their son Leslie W D Northam (1918-2003) of the Dorsetshire Regiment won a Military Medal in December 1944. Walter died in 1968, his wife in 1966; they are buried in Hockworthy in an unmarked grave, as is their daughter Ruby Preston. His family is not closely related to the other Northam family on the war memorials. Walter's first cousin twice removed, Roderick Northam, farms at South Staple.

William J NORTHAM

The eldest of the five sons of Isabella and William Northam who served in the war. He was born in 1884 at Luppitt and served with the Inniskillen Fusiliers, obtaining the rank of Lance Corporal. Brother of Frederick *[q.v.]*, Elias Eli *[q.v.]* and Henry *[q.v.]* on the porch memorial, and Gilbert Northam on the war memorial. He became a small-holder near West Buckland and married Annie May Coles in Wellington in 1921.

Edward 'Ted' PRESCOTT

Born in 1893, Ted was fifth of ten sons (and two daughters) of Lucy and William Prescott, carpenter at Borden Gate. Five of his brothers served in the war (Gilbert, Henry, John and Robert, and Percy who died). Ted, a carpenter, married Mildred Pearce in 1925. Her sister Betty married Lionel Redwood **D-4**. A Gunner in 19th Coy, RGA, Edward was wounded in the Persian Gulf in March 1916. He died in 1963 in Halse, Somerset.

Gilbert Victor PRESCOTT

Born in 1896, Gilbert Victor Prescott was seventh of ten sons (and two daughters) of Lucy and William Prescott, a carpenter who lived at Borden Gate. Five of his brothers served in the war (Edward, Henry, John, Robert, and Percy who died). He worked as a cowman at Bences Farm, Hockworthy before serving in the Royal Garrison Artillery, becoming a Lance Corporal, and was wounded twice. He married Bessie Avery in Hastings in 1918. He stayed in the army after the war and died in 1967 in Sussex.

WILLIAM AND LUCY PRESCOTT AND THEIR FAMILY

The Western Times   Friday 13 Oct 1916

"These are (l-r): Pte F J Prescott formerly of the Coldstreams, and now discharged through ill-health; L/Cpl Robert Prescott SLI who went through the fighting in China in 1912 and is now in India; Gnr Edward Prescott RGA who is now in Bombay hospital with fever – he was also wounded in the Persian Gulf in March; Gnr Percy Prescott RGA who recently returned from Jamaica for the Front; Bmdr Gilbert Prescott RGA who is now in France – he has been twice wounded, and has recently recovered from the effects of sunstroke; Tpr Harry Prescott of the West Somerset Yeomanry. He has been in the Dardanelles, has suffered from severe frostbite, and is now with his regiment in Egypt. By the way, Mr and Mrs Prescott have another son residing at Hockworthy on a farm. A week or two ago he received his papers from the military, thus adding another name to the already remarkable list.

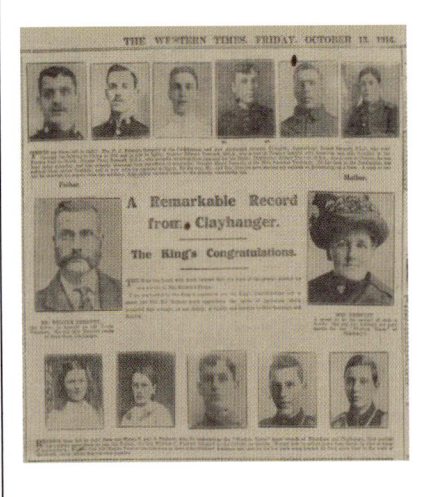

THE KING'S CONGRATULATIONS

The King has heard with much interest that you have at the present moment six sons serving in His Majesty's Forces. I am commanded by the King to express to you The King's congratulations and to assure you that His Majesty much appreciates the spirit of patriotism which prompted this example, in one family, of loyalty and devotion to their Sovereign and Empire.

Reading from left to right these are Misses F and O Prescott, who, by undertaking the *Western Times* paper rounds at Huntsham and Clayhanger, have enabled our regular agent there to join the Forces; the late William J Prescott belonged to the Coldstream Guards. Having been invalided home from Egypt, he died at home of consumption; Masters Jim and Reggie Prescott are following in their elder brothers footsteps, and have for the last three years devoted all their spare time to the work of the Scouts, among whom they are very popular."

Henry 'Harry' Prescott

Eighth of ten sons (and two daughters) of Lucy and William Prescott, carpenter at Borden Gate. Born 1898, Harry joined the West Somerset Yeomanry. He suffered from severe frostbite in the Dardanelles, and later served in Egypt. He transferred to the Royal Engineers (Regt. No: 233598) and was demobbed in July 1919. He was a wheelwright/ carpenter. He married Edith Shepherd in 1935. Five of his brothers served in the war (Edward, Gilbert, John and Robert, and Percy who died).

John Prescott

Born 1885, John 'Jack' Prescott was the eldest of William and Lucy Prescott's family of ten sons and two daughters. Both Jack and his father were carpenters. In 1908, he married Eva Ellen 'Emma' Goss and they lived at Staple Cross. He served in the Royal Engineers in the Great War, where he was injured, and died in 1968. Five of his brothers served in the war (Edward, Gilbert, Henry and Robert, and Percy who died).

Robert How 'Bob' Prescott

Born 1891, the fourth of ten sons (and two daughters) of Lucy and William Prescott, from Borden Gate. Like his father, Bob was a carpenter. Five of his brothers served in the war (Edward, Gilbert, Henry and John, and Percy who died) Bob was a Lance Corporal in the Somerset Light Infantry, serving in China in 1912, and in India 1916. In 1921 he married Bessie Hurford and they lived at Trace Bridge where he had an ancient water-powered woodworking mill. He died in 1979.

Frederick James Prescott

Another of Lucy and William Prescott's ten sons, Frederick joined up in 1905, but was invalided out of the army as reported in the *Western Times* of 13 Oct 1916: "... Formerly of the Coldstream Guards and now discharged through ill-health." His name does not appear on the porch memorial.

John Redwood

Born in 1873, and raised at Morles Farm, John was the second son of Hugh and Mary Ann Redwood's 10 children. John married Alice Annie Salisbury in 1897, and they held the license for the Staple Cross pub for 50 years. He was also a carpenter, as was his father. He enlisted 13th Nov 1914 into the Royal Defence Corps and served until Feb 1919. He died in 1949 and is buried in Hockworthy **A-3**. Father of Lionel **D-4** and first cousin of Jesse *[q.v.]* and Ernest *[q.v.]*. John's grandson, Anthony 'Tony' Redwood lived for many years at Staple Cross and has generously and enthusiastically shared his wide knowledge of Hockworthy and his memories of its residents.

Arthur Henry REDWOOD

Born Huntsham in 1899, son of John and Alice Redwood **A-3,** who had the licence for the Staple Cross inn. He had two brothers **D-4** and three sisters. He served in the Royal Air Force for the last year of the war. He then held the tenancy of the White Horse hotel in Tiverton. He and Violet (née Berry), whom he married in 1939, had one son. They retired to Sampford Peverell where he died in 1983.

Ernest REDWOOD

Ernest and his brother Jesse *[q.v.]* were sons of William and Martha Redwood, of Luckleys, and first cousins of John Redwood **A-3.** Born Hockworthy in 1890, the youngest of 13 children, Ernest was a carpenter like his father. He served in the Cheshire Regt in the war and, after his marriage to Hilda M Guscott in 1920 at Cruwys Morchard, they lived in The Wirrall where he had two daughters. He died in Cheshire in 1969.

Jesse REDWOOD

Jesse and his brother Ernest *[q.v.]* were sons of William and Martha Redwood, of Luckleys, and first cousins of John Redwood **A-3.** Born Hockworthy in 1883, Jesse enlisted into the Marines in 1904 and served until 1922. In 1923 he married Emily Cawsey, who died in 1944. He retired to Hockworthy and lodged with Edith May (née Aldridge), widow of Mark Tooze *[q.v.]* at Lake Cottage. A carpenter, he died in 1973.

Samuel SHOPLAND

Son of James and Mary Ann Shopland **B-31**, of Court Hall, who moved to the village between 1891 and 1901 from Rose Ash in Devon where Samuel was born in 1880. He served in the Royal Devon Yeomanry and, during the war, in the Durham Light Infantry and the Labour Corps. In 1924 he married Rosina, daughter of Samuel and Ellen Dart **B-18**. They lived at The Villa and both are buried in the churchyard **B-32**.

W THOMAS

It has not been possible to confirm the identification of W Thomas. Frederick Thomas of the Devonshire Regiment who died in 1917 and is commemorated on the war memorial *[p.19]* had two brothers, both born in Sampford Peverell, either of whom may be 'W Thomas': Walter in 1886, and William in 1889. Their parents were Louisa and William Thomas, a farm labourer.

~~

Identifying the four Toozes has been complicated by there being several Tooze families in the area in the early 20th century. In addition, over seventy of that name served in the Great War, thirteen of whom died.

F TOOZE
Believed to be Frederick Tooze, the son Eliza and Samuel Tooze, a farm labourer. He was born in Hockworthy in 1900 but, by 1911, the family had moved to Court Cottage, Ashbrittle. He enlisted in Aug 1917 into the Wiltshire Regiment and suffered severe leg wounds in October the following year. He was de-mobbed on 1 Mar 1919. These details are given but without firm confirmation that it is the correct 'F Tooze'.

JAMES 'JIM' TOOZE
Born 1894 in Holcombe Rogus, he was the first son of Mark and Mary Tooze of Fenton Farm, Holcombe Rogus. Two of his brothers, Mark and 'Jack', are also commemorated. Jim lived at Ashbrittle and went to Canada in 1923. Later he worked for Mr Burnell on a farm in Ashbrittle.

JOHN 'JACK' TOOZE
Born 1896 in Holcombe Rogus, Jack Tooze was the second of eight children of Mark and Mary Tooze of Fenton Farm, Holcombe Rogus. He was a shepherd at Ramsey Farm, Holcombe Rogus before the war, and later lived at Staple Cross. He died in Exeter in 1941.

MARK TOOZE
Born 1898 in Holcombe Rogus, the son of Mark and Mary Tooze. He used to live at Burnt House (a farm cottage to Court Hall) and then moved to Huntsham where he died on 17 Oct 1951, aged 53. He married Edith May Aldridge in 1928. He went to Canada with his brother Jim in 1923, and returned in 1926. He was a farm worker and died in 1951.

~~

ROBERT THOMAS VICKERY
Born 1889 at Holcombe Rogus, younger of two sons of John and Elizabeth Vickery. In 1911 he was a farm labourer at Quarry Hockford. He worked as a labourer at Brompton Ralph where he married Harriet Lee in 1920.

DAVID ALFRED WARE

Born 29 Sep 1897 in Hockworthy, the son of Elizabeth and Thomas Ware **B-44**, a carpenter and sub-postmaster in the village. His elder brother Harold Edgar Ware *[q.v.]* is also commemorated on the porch memorial. In 1916 David enlisted into the Royal Navy, and then continued in the Service for a further 12 years after the war (no: 1034911). In 1923 he married Elsie Taylor in Devonport. He was a keen cyclist and died in 1981.

HAROLD EDGAR WARE

Born 15 Sep 1896 in Hockworthy, Harold was the elder of two sons of Elizabeth and Thomas Ware **B-44**, the village sub-postmaster. Harold served in the Royal Navy and was invalided out in 1920. He followed in his father's footsteps, becoming a postman after the war. He married in 1940 Phyllis I M Dinham and they had three daughters. He died in Cornwall in 1991; Phyllis died there in 2006.

Whilst every attempt has been made to trace descendants of those who died or served during the Great War, many of the above biographies have been prepared using publically available web-sites and other genealogical sources, such as newspapers, burial registers and census returns. Apologies are due should there have been any inaccuracies in identification – the hope was, and is, that we may now know a little about those from our village who left our valleys to answer the call.

"We will remember them".

HOCKWORTHY CHURCHYARD

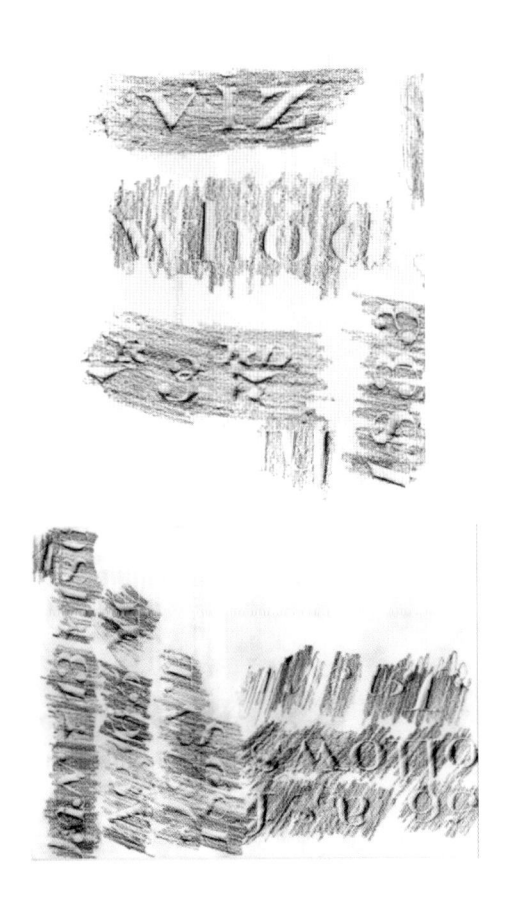

As will be seen in the following plans, only the surviving headstones have been plotted. It has not been possible to identify any of the bumps or outlines of graves, particularly noticeable as they are in this view from the church tower. However, the full burial registers, dating from 1578, have been transcribed *[Appendix G]*. The same family names appear across the centuries, and this is endorsed by the linkages which emerged as the biographies of those interred were prepared. The inscriptions are listed alphabetically with their individual identifying plot numbers which may be found on these plans *[see p.177]*. Spelling of names and places is as engraved; a / indicates the end of a line of text, and a name in *[italics]* after an inscription is the engraver of the headstone *[see p.112]*.

Only one headstone survives from before the rebuilding of the church in the mid-19th century (Sarah Bucknell, who died in 1725). Other than the Newmans **B-48** and **B-50**, the four clergymen known to have been buried in the churchyard have no surviving stones:

    Revd John NORRIS. Buried 21 March 1639. Aged 41 years
    Revd John SHARPE. Buried 24 January 1700
    Revd Thomas THORNE. Buried 1731 (or 1732)
    Revd Joseph JONES. Buried 1749 (or 1750)

CHURCHYARD PLANS & INSCRIPTIONS

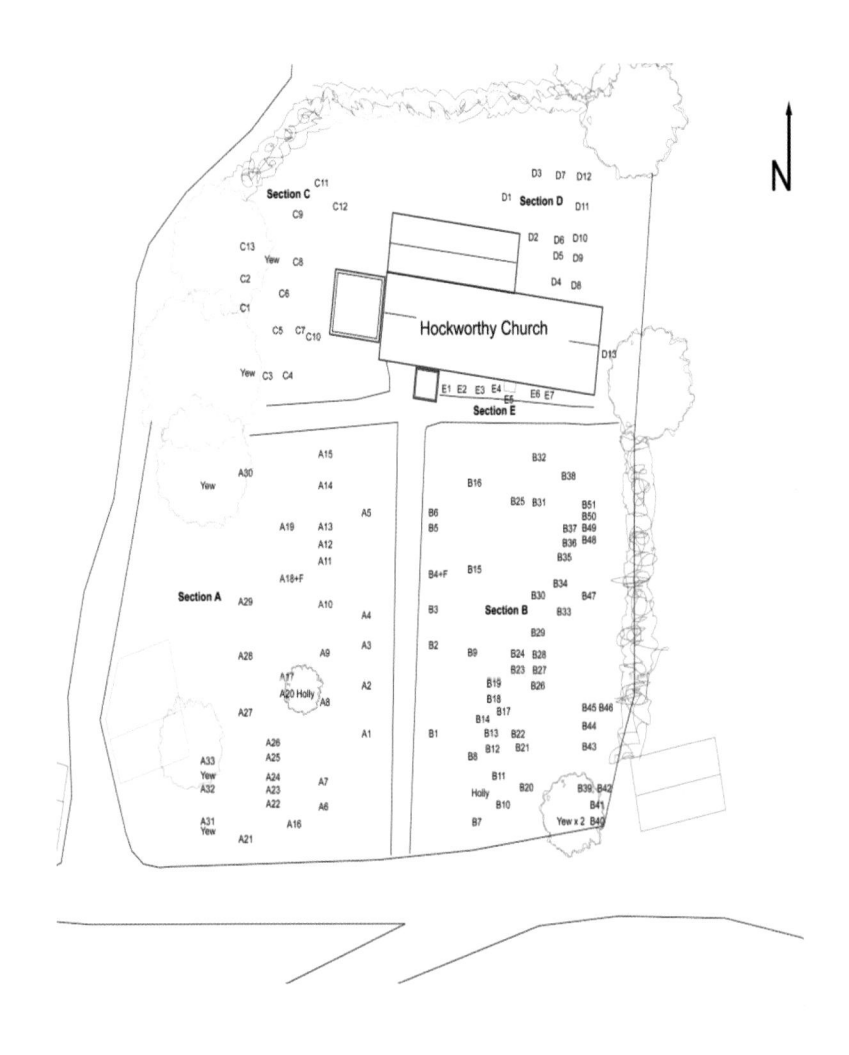

For larger scale section plans, see following pages

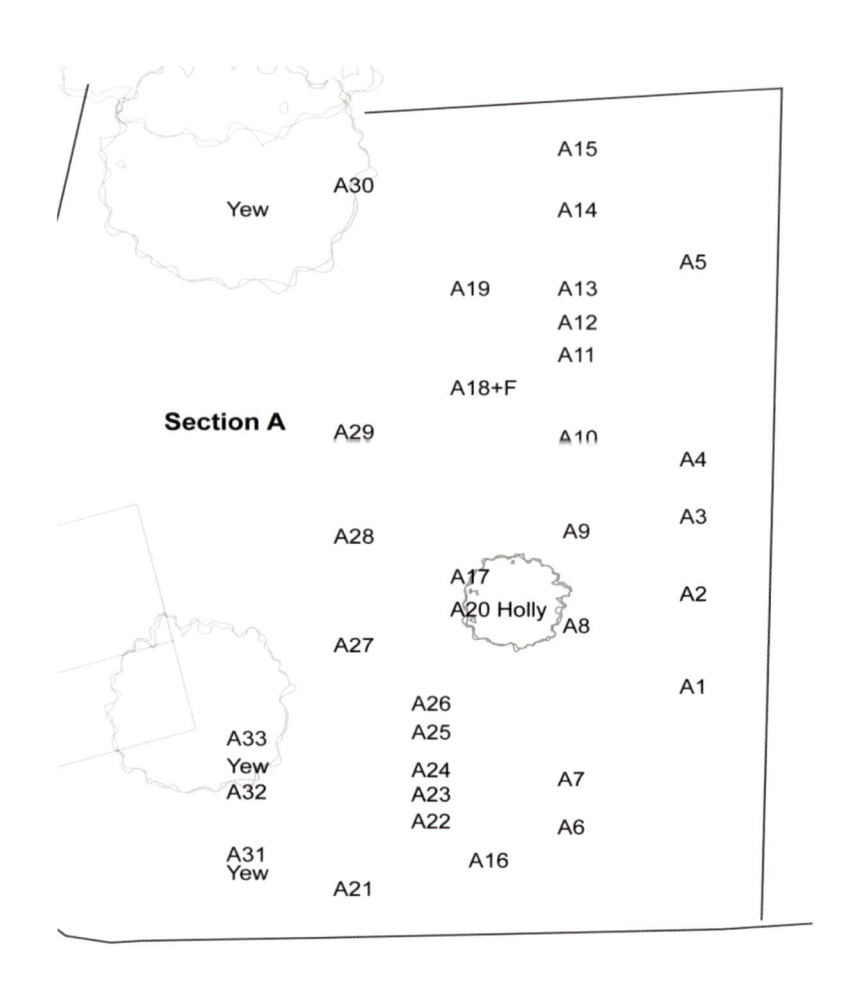

Section A

```
                                A15
                A30             A14
     Yew
                                              A5
                    A19    A13
                           A12
                           A11
                    A18+F
Section A   A29             A10
                                        A4
                                        A3
            A28             A9
                       A17              A2
                       A20 Holly
                       A27      A8
                                        A1
                        A26
                        A25
  A33                   A24     A7
  Yew                   A23
  A32                   A22     A6
  A31              A16
  Yew      A21
```

N ↑

Section A

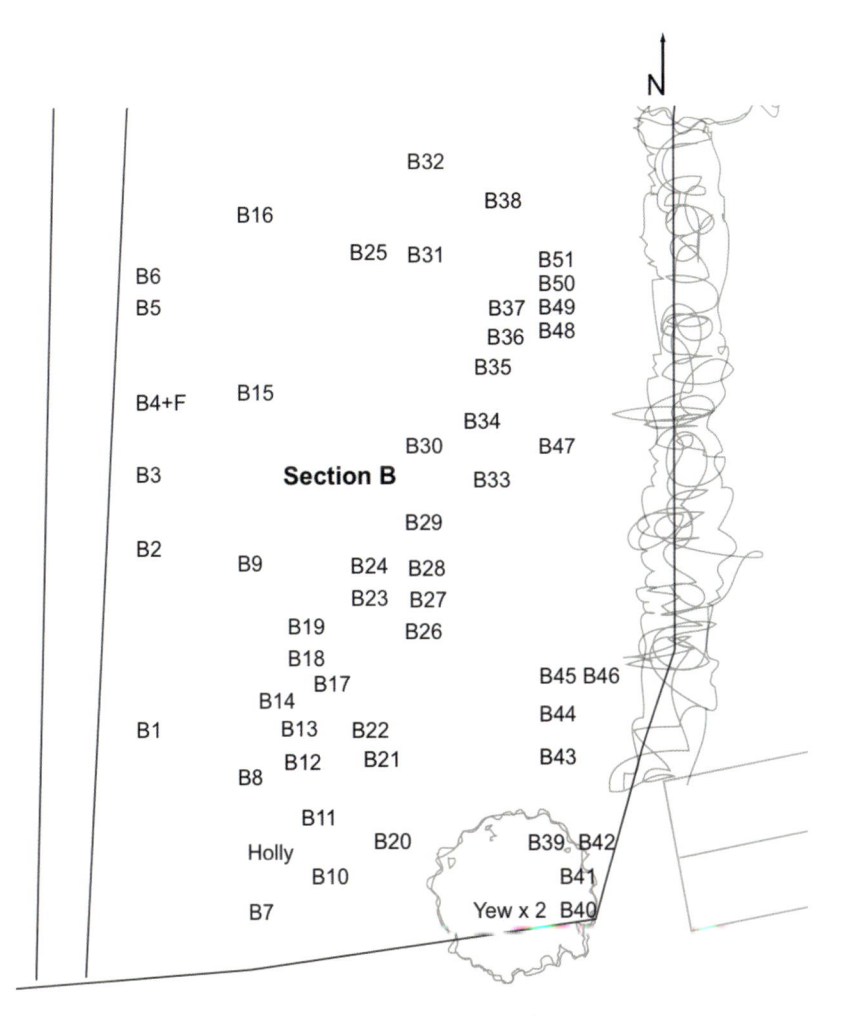

Section B

Section C

C11
C9 C12
C13
Yew C8
C2
C6
C1
C5 C7 C10
Yew C3 C4

Section C

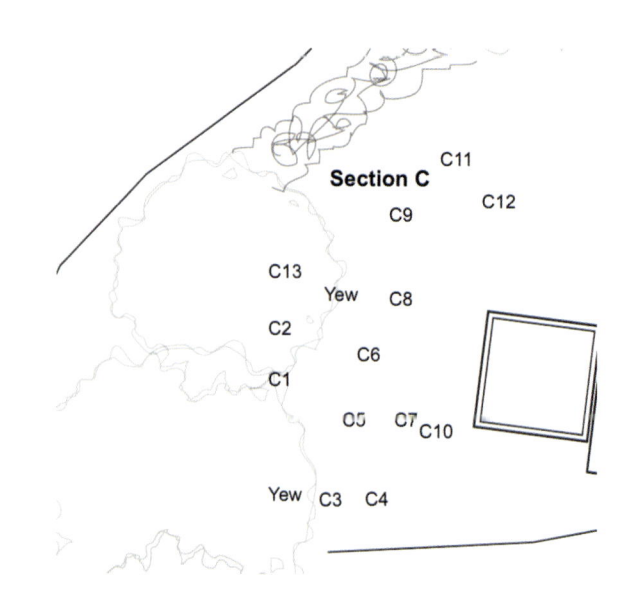

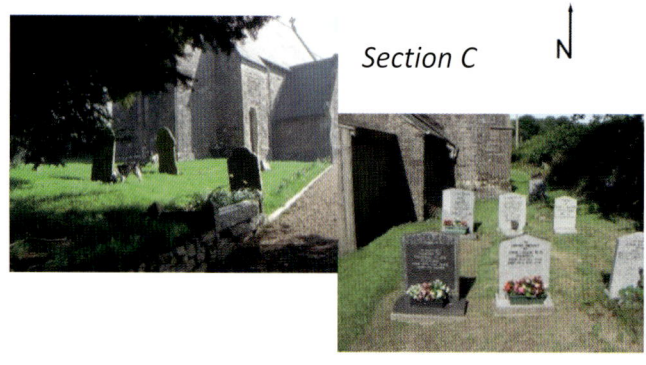

N ↑

Section D

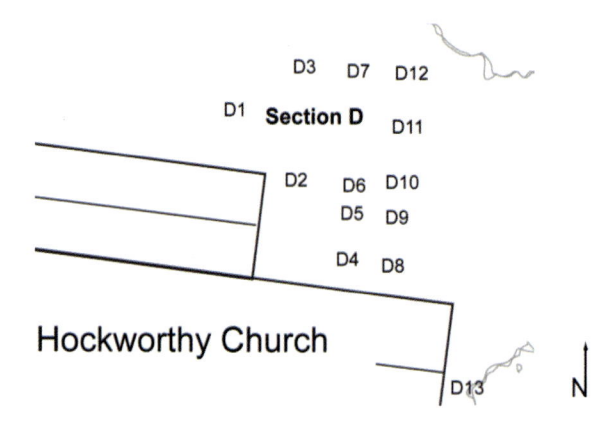

D3 D7 D12
D1 **Section D** D11
D2 D6 D10
    D5 D9
    D4 D8

Hockworthy Church

D13

N ↑

Hockworthy Church

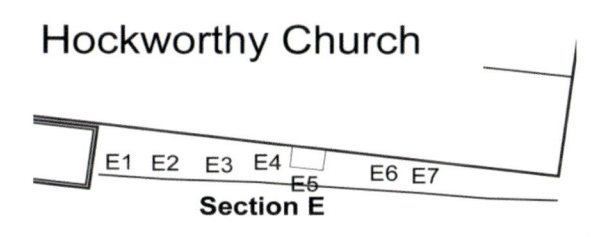

E1 E2 E3 E4   E6 E7
             E5
Section E

N ↑

Section E

*Looking south from
the church tower*

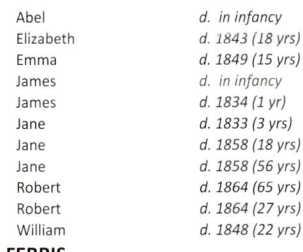

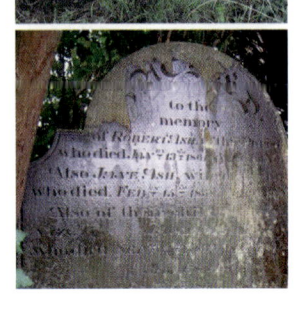

ASH	**A-31**
Abel	d. in infancy
Elizabeth	d. 1843 (18 yrs)
Emma	d. 1849 (15 yrs)
James	d. in infancy
James	d. 1834 (1 yr)
Jane	d. 1833 (3 yrs)
Jane	d. 1858 (18 yrs)
Jane	d. 1858 (56 yrs)
Robert	d. 1864 (65 yrs)
Robert	d. 1864 (27 yrs)
William	d. 1848 (22 yrs)
FERRIS	
Emma	d. 1909 (74 yrs)
John	

Transcription

Sacred / to the / memory / of Robert ASH of this Parish / who died Janry 13th 1864 Aged 65 years / also Jane ASH, wife of the above / who died Febry 15th 1858 Aged 56 years / Also of their children as follows / viz. Jane ASH / who died Septer 3rd 1833 Aged 3 years / James ASH / who died Febry 6th 1834 Aged 1 year / Abel and James ASH / died in their infancy / Elizabeth ASH / who died Febry 4th 1843. Aged 18 years / William ASH / who died Novr 17th 1848. Aged 22 years / Emma ASH / who died Novr 5th 1849 Aged 15 years / Jane ASH / who died June 4th 1858. Aged 18 years / Robert ASH / who died Decr 20th 1864. Aged 27 years / He taketh away who can hinder him / Also Emma wife of the above Robert / secondly of John FERRIS of this parish / April 27th 1909. Aged 74 years. Thy will be done.

Description	Measurements
Rounded top with square and scotia shoulders. Engraved lettering.	h-140cm w-99cm d-8cm

Born in Milverton c. 1799, Robert was the son of William and Elizabeth Ash **A-32**. In 1841 he is recorded as a cordwainer *[a worker in leather]* living at Green House, Hockworthy, later becoming a master boot and shoe maker employing two men and a boy. He married 27 March 1822 Jane Cooksley (1799-1858) and moved to Rose Cottage. Of his known ten children, only two survived to marriage; Caroline who married James Wensley, son of **A-17**, and Robert, who trained as a shoemaker, became a policeman at Bathwick, in East Somerset, but returned to Hockworthy on the death of his father in January 1864 to resume his earlier trade of cordwainer. He died eleven months later aged only 27 years. His wife Emma, who he had married in Bathwick, then married John Ferris (son of John and Sarah Ferris **A-20**).

ASH A-32

Betty	d. 1820 (45 yrs)
Joan	d. 1860 (74 yrs)
William	d. 1853 (80 yrs)

Transcription

Sacred / to the memory of / Betty ASH of this Parish / who departed this life / August 1st 1820 / Aged 45 years / William ASH husband of / the above who died Feb 28th 1853 / Aged 80 years / Also Joan ASH his second wife / who departed this life / March 22nd 1860 / Aged 74 years / Blessed are the dead / which die in the Lord

Description
Stone Gothic
[buried in a holly bush under the yew trees]

Measurements
h-73cm w-58cm d-7cm

Buried are William Ash with his two wives Elizabeth (Betty) and Joan. He married Betty in 1797 in Milverton, Somerset and Joan in Exeter, Devon in 1822. Both Joan and William were born in Milverton. The family lived in Huntsham until c. 1812, when they moved to Ham Mills, Hockworthy where William was a master butcher. William and Betty's eldest son was Robert Ash **A-31**. Of thirteen children, two daughters were from his second marriage.

AUTON E-4

Herbert James	d. 1992 (82 yrs)
Nora Mary	d. 2003 (89 yrs)

Transcription

In loving memory of / Herbert James / AUTON / died 15th March 1992 / aged 82 years / and his wife / Nora Mary / died 15th May 2003 / aged 89 years

Description
Cremation stone; polished granite dark grey; engraved silver letters.

Measurements
h-31cm w-46cm

Herbert was a butcher in Wellington, who later had a small holding at Sampford Moor. He married Nora Cockram at Hockworthy and their ashes lie at the spot where their wedding photographs were taken in 1932. Two of Nora's brothers are on the Hockworthy war memorial *[p.17]*, and a third brother, Sydney, is commemorated on the porch memorial *[p.22]*. Her parents, Frederick and Alice Cockram, are buried in Hockworthy in an unmarked grave.

BOWERMAN B-7

Sarah — *d. 1935 (78 yrs)*
William — *d. 1932 (76 yrs)*

Transcription

In / loving memory / of / William BOWERMAN / who died Sept 6th 1932 / aged 76 years. / Also of Sarah / wife of the above / who died Feb 11th 1935 / aged 78 years / "Peace perfect peace"

Description
Marble scroll on base. Flower pot. Square kerbs. Lead lettering. *[fallen over]*

Measurements
Total: h-92cm w-50cm d-14cm
Base: h-26cm w-56cm d-24cm
Kerbs: 197cm x 162cm

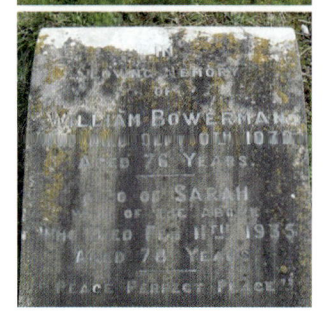

Sarah and William were married for forty years. They farmed at Brockhole Farm, Morebath and at the time of his death William was at Hockford, Hockworthy. He was born in Bampton, his wife in Clayhanger. The *Western Times* of 22 Feb 1935, in reporting her death, described her as being "devoutly attached to the little church at Hockworthy". Their only child, Sarah, married William James Greedy **B-10** in 1927.

BREWER B-13

Francis — *d. 1921 (36 yrs)*

Transcription

Francis BREWER / Died March 4, 1921 / Aged 36

Description
Grey polished granite flower pot. Lead lettering.

Measurements
h-16cm w-23cm d-20cm

Francis Brewer was born in Bampton 1885, and married Lena Aldridge in 1907 (she was born in Huntsham in 1888). Their two daughters were both born in Hockworthy, Eva in 1908, and Ellen in 1910. In 1911 the family were living at Staple Cross, and Francis worked as a farm labourer.

Alongside is another flower holder **B-14** inscribed with *In loving memory* but it is not known to which grave it belongs.

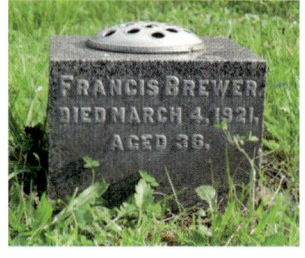

40

BROOMFIELD   B-42

Emma   *d. 1915 (71 yrs)*

Transcription

Until the day break / and the shadows flee away / In loving memory / of / Emma BROOMFIELD / who fell asleep / May 5th 1915 / Aged 71 years

Description	Measurements
Metal open wheel cross above shield.	h-89cm w-43cm d-2cm

Hockworthy-born Emma was the second of four daughters of Henry and Elizabeth Tarr. A laundress, in 1866 she married Henry Broomfield **B-39**. They lived at Staple Cross, by 1881 had moved to Burnt House Cottage and in her widowhood, Emma lived in Huntsham. They had six sons and two daughters; one, Sarah Ann, married William Vickery, a builder in Taunton, with whom Emma was living at the time of the 1911 census.

BROOMFIELD   B-39

Henry   *d. 1887 (46 yrs)*

Transcription

In the midst of life / we are in death / In memory of / Henry BROOMFIELD / who died / March 7th 1887 / aged 46 years

Description	Measurements
Metal open wheel cross above shield.	h-101cm w-43cm d-2cm

Henry Broomfield was a stone quarryman, the son Henry Broomfield, an agricultural labourer from Burlescombe. His mother Johannah was born in Sampford. Henry was born in Hockworthy, and married Emma Tarr **B-42** in 1866. Their fourth son, Frank Broomfield, died in the Great War in 1916. *[see p.20]*. Henry's sister, Elizabeth, married Robert Sprague, both of whom are buried nearby **B-40**.

BROWNE		**C-13**
	Peter Finlay	*d. 2014 (83 yrs)*
MAX		
	Hannah Rose	*d. 2013 (15 yrs)*

Transcription

Dr Peter Finlay BROWNE 2 November 1930 - 27 February 2014
In memory of Hannah Rose MAX 9 January 1998 – 11 August 2013

A theoretical physicist and author specialising in astro nuclear physics, Dr Browne was born in Belfast and was a scholar of Trinity College Dublin. He lived in Manchester, the Lake District and Cornwall, latterly moving to Taunton to be near the youngest of his three daughters, Alison Mundy, in Hockworthy. Also commemorated nearby is his granddaughter Hannah Rose May, daughter of Rachel Browne and Randy Max. Though she was born and died in Rotterdam, Holland, she spent happy days at Court Hall with her cousins when living in Holcombe Rogus, where she attended the primary school.

BUCKNELL		**B-6**
	Eliza	*d. 1871 (2 yrs)*
	John	*d. 1856 (53 yrs)*

Transcription

Sacred / to the memory of / John BUCKNELL / of this parish / who departed this life / December the 27th 1856 / aged 53 years / also of / Eliza BUCKNELL / grand daughter of the above / who departed this life / July 17th 1871 aged 2 years

Description
Half round with square and scotia shoulders. Stone.

Measurements
h-107cm w-60cm d-8cm

Born in Hockworthy, John Broome Bucknell was named after his father and was baptised in Uplowman. He married Anne Besley from Thorne St Margaret in 1829. John farmed 45 acres at Durley, near Redwoods Farm, with three labourers; after his death, his son Arthur Besley Bucknell expanded the holding to 86 acres. Arthur married Hannah Pring in 1857, and they moved to Beer Down Farm, Uplowman, where their daughter Eliza, buried here, was born on 30 May 1869. Sarah Bucknell, **B-5**, was John's great great aunt. After John's death, his widow Anne married Henry Lucas **B-4**.

BUCKNELL   B-5

Arthur — Father
Hannah — Mother
Sarah — d. 1725 (22 yrs)

Transcription

Here lyeth the body / of Sarah ye daughter / of Arthur BUCKNELL / and Hannah his wife / of this parish who / departed this life / November ye 5th 1725 / Being aged 22 years / My dear friends / Mourn no more / it's all the odds / I am gone before

Description
Small stone upright rectangular shape with engraved perimeter line with copperplate engraved lettering.

Measurements
h-69cm w-43cm d-6cm

This, the oldest headstone surviving in Hockworthy churchyard, has been listed Grade II by English Heritage. Sarah's brother Jacob was great grandfather of John Bucknell **B-6**, who lies in the grave beside Sarah.

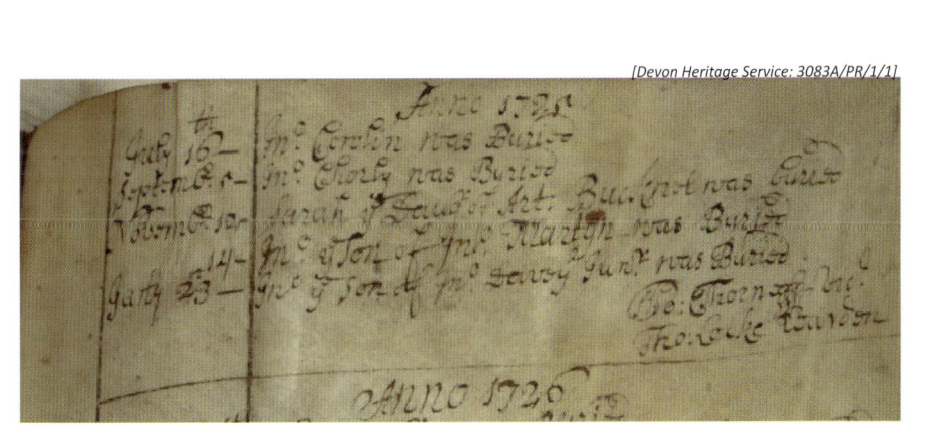

[Devon Heritage Service: 3083A/PR/1/1]

Sarah Bucknell's burial entry in the Hockworthy registers

BURNETT		B-8
Henry (Harry)	d. 1946 (66 yrs)	
PENN		
Lilian Rose	d. 2001 (92 yrs)	

Transcription

In / loving memory of / a dear father / Henry "Harry" / BURNETT / 1879-1946 / Also his daughter / Lilian Rose / PENN / 1908 – 2001 / Ashes interred St Leonards / Bucks / God bless
[Paul Fudge]

Description	Measurements
Light grey polished granite ogee top with base on concrete plinth. Flower pot. Engraved black lettering.	Total: h-78cm w-53cm d-10cm Base: h-10cm w-61cm d-18cm

The son of George (a gardener) and Sarah Burnett from Brompton Ralph, Henry was born there on 6 Nov 1879. A coal miner (hewer) in Porth, Glamorgan, he married Eliza Jane Day in Wedmore on 23 Dec 1906. After her death, in 1919, the family moved to Hockworthy, where Henry lived at Stuckleys and died on 10 June 1946. Lilian Rose was born on 13 March 1908 in Glamorgan and married in 1931 Stanley Harold Penn (1905-1984) in Buckinghamshire. She died on 8 May 2001 in Amersham, Buckingham, where her ashes are interred. She requested to be commemorated on her father's headstone in Hockworthy.

BUTT		A-6
George	d. 1942 (78 yrs)	
Hannah	d. 1938 (87 yrs)	

Transcription

RIP / In ever loving memory of / our dear mother / Hannah BUTT / fell asleep Oct. 19. 1938. Aged 87. / Also our dear father / George BUTT / fell asleep Jan. 6. 1942. Aged 78. / + Ever in our memory +

Description	Measurements
Maltese cross on tapered base on slab with square kerbs and with pyramid top wing posts. Stone. Flower pot. Lead lettering.	Total: h-125cm Cross: h-92cm w-46cm d-11cm Base: h-32cm w-49cm d-55cm Kerbs: 188cm x 196cm

George was born at Cheriton Fitzpaine in 1862. In 1884, he married Hannah (née Goslin), born at Templeton, Tiverton. Her first husband, Joseph Masland, died in 1882 leaving her with five children. A farm labourer, George later lived at Hockford, working at the stone quarry. They had three more children. Hannah later lived at Bray's Cottage, and was the oldest Hockworthy resident when she died aged 87.

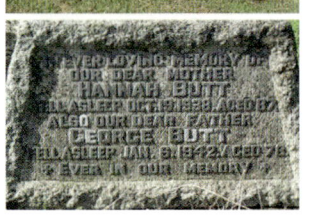

CLEEVE B-19

William   d. 1837

Transcription
W.C. /1837
Believed to be William CLEEVE d.1837

Description
[Possibly a foot stone - very small white stone on the north side of the Samuel DART surround]

Measurements
h-39cm w-32cm d-6cm

Parish Registers suggest this unidentified footstone may belong to yeoman farmer William Cleeve who was buried on 20th April 1837 aged 48 years.

COCKRAM A-16

Dickie   d. 1993 (89 yrs)
Dora   d. 1969 (62 yrs)

Transcription
In / loving memory of / Dora COCKRAM / 1906 – 1969 / Dickie COCKRAM / 1904 – 1993 / Rest in peace / together

Description
Flat ledger. Grey speckled granite. Engraved black lettering.

Measurements
h-46cm w-56cm

The son of Alice and Frederick, agricultural labourer Alfred (Dickie) Cockram was born in Oakford. He joined up in 1921 and was in the Somerset Light Infantry for seven years, serving in Ireland, India, Sudan and on Salisbury Plain. He married Dora, Huntsham-born Margaret Jane Hardacre in 1931. Dickie lived at Burnt House, and worked for Mr Stone **B-25** at Court Hall. Two of his brothers are on the parish war memorial *[p.17]* having died in the 1st World War, and a third, who survived the war, is commemorated on the tablet in the church porch *[p.22]*. His sister, Nora Auton, is buried in the churchyard **E-4,** as are his parents in an unmarked grave.

45

COTTRELL		A-7
James	*d. 1881 (50 yrs)*	
William Walter	*d. 1863 (4 yrs)*	

Transcription

In memory of / William Walter COTTRELL / who died Septr 17th 1863. / Aged 4 years. / The days of his youth hast been / shortened. / Also of / James COTTRELL / father of above / who died June 19th 1881 / Aged 50
Footstone: W.W.C / 1863

Description	Measurements
Stone trefoil shape with carved cross with sloping shoulders. Narrow kerbs. Footstone. Engraved lettering.	h-120cm w-52cm d-8cm Footstone: h-36cm w-26cm d-7cm Kerbs: 215cm x 165cm

William Walter Cottrell's father, grandfather and great uncle were all stonemasons. His father James was born c. 1831 in Stawley, and in 1857 he married Mary (née Lovell) from Burlescombe (1837-1917). They had seven children as well as young William Walter, all of whom were born in Hockworthy. They lived at both Burnt House and then The Villa.

DANIELL		D-9
John (Jack) N.A.	*d. 1988 (73 yrs)*	

Transcription

In / loving memory / of / John (Jack) N. A. / DANIELL / born 11th Dec. 1914 / Died 12th May 1988

Description	Measurements
Polished light grey granite ogee with rounded corners integrated flower pot. Base on concrete plinth. Black raised lettering.	Total: h-39cm w-32cm d-6cm Base: h-8cm w-61cm d-30cm

Major John "Jack" Ninian Averell Daniell joined the Royal Artillery in 1935, and served on the North-West Frontier of India before the war. He married Mary (née Manning) in 1942 and had three sons. After retirement, he co-founded West Dean College of Arts in Sussex, before taking up a post at Relyon in Wellington. They moved to Glebe Cottage, Hockworthy in 1972 and he served as churchwarden 1979-86. His research notes on the history of Hockworthy were deposited in the Devon Heritage Centre and have been drawn on for this publication.

DARBY   C-4
William   d. 1859 (72 yrs)

Transcription
Sacred / to the memory of / William DARBY late of this / Parish who departed this / life Octr 21st 1859 / Aged 72 years

Description
Stone rounded top with square and scotia shoulders. Hole drilled in top. Engraved perimeter line. Decorative engraving under text. Engraved lettering.

Measurements
h-94cm w-57cm d-9cm

Husband of Susannah (née Pavey), William was born c. 1787 in Uplowman. He farmed Morrells (Morles) from the 1820s and *The Huntsham Book* reproduces an interesting cutting from *The Exeter Flying Post* of 25 May 1820 describing Morles as "… a good farm-house, barn, stable, and linhays, and about 100 acres (within a ring fence) of good meadow, pasture, arable, orchard, and woodland, now in the occupation of Mr William Darby." Within ten years he had moved to Great Staple, where he farmed 220 acres with five labourers. Unconfirmed, but he may have been the brother of Edward Darby **A-13** who farmed at Kerswell.

Survey mark beside tower door    *External porch light*

DARBY		**A-13**
Edward		*d. 1837 (61 yrs)*
Loveday		*d. 1851 (80 yrs)*

Transcription

Sacred / to the / memory of / Edward DARBY of This Parish / who departed this life / March 14th 1837 Aged 61 years / Behold all ye that come to see / Who in this grave is laid / Death is your lot; forget it not / A debt that must be paid. / Also Loveday DARBY wife of the above / Who died October 10th 1851. Aged 80 years

Description	Measurements
Rounded top with prominent humps and shoulders. Stone. Engraved lettering.	h-141cm w-78cm d-8cm

Edward (born c. 1776) and Loveday (born Dulverton c. 1774) were the first of the known members of the Darby family to farm Kerswell on the Huntsham estate. It would appear that Edward was the "Edward Darby" described as churchwarden in 1808 on the Bilbie bell in the church tower. His son William Edward Darby **A-12** took on Kerswell after his father's death.

DARBY		**A-12**
Jane		*d. 1894 (82 yrs)*
William Edward		*d. 1875 (65 yrs)*

Transcription

In memory of / William Edward DARBY / of Kerswell, Hockworthy / who died August 2nd 1875 / aged 65 years / The just man walketh in his integrity / His Children are blessed after him. / Proverbs XX Chap. 7 Ver. / Also of Jane / Wife of the above / Who died August 10th 1894. Aged 82.

Description	Measurements
Stone round top with accentuated point. Engraved lettering.	h-137cm w-66cm d-9cm

The son of Edward and Loveday Darby **A-13**, William Edward was born and died at Hockworthy. In March 1839 he married Jane, the daughter of Ann and William Sweet, landowner in Stawley, Somerset where Jane was born in 1812. She was baptised at Kittisford in January 1813. They had three children and farmed 320 acres at Kerswell.

DARBY A-10

Louis	d. 1923 (76 yrs)
Mildred	d. 1922 (66 yrs)

Transcription

In / Loving memory / of / Louis DARBY / of Kerswell / who entered into rest / Jan 22nd 1923, Aged 76. / also of / Mildred / wife of the above / who entered into rest / Oct 5th 1922, Aged 66
[Fewings, Tiverton]

Description
Polished pink granite half round top on base with stone plinth. Decorative engraved design. Lead lettering.

Measurements
Total: h-151cm
Top: h-118cm w-62cm d-15cm
Base: h-33cm w-77cm d-28cm
Plinth: h-10cm w-85cm d-38cm

The son of William Edward **A-12** and grandson of Edward **A-13**, Louis was the last of the Darby family to farm Kerswell on the Huntsham estate. As his father, Louis was born and died at Hockworthy. In 1876 he married Mildred, daughter of Richard and Jane Heard, of Cowlings Farm, another Huntsham estate property. Indeed, Kerswell and Cowlings were adjacent properties. They had six children. Their eldest son Edward is buried in the next grave **A-11**.

DARBY A-11

Edward	d. 1919 (39 yrs)
Louis	Father *(A-10)*
Mildred	Mother *(A-10)*

Transcription

In / loving memory / of / Edward / eldest son of / Louis & Mildred DARBY / of Kerswell / who died July 16th 1919. Aged 39. / Until the day break and the shadows flee away.

Description
Granite cross on three bases on stone plinth. Lead lettering.

Measurements
Total: h-139cm
Cross: h-84cm w-45cm d-10cm
1st base: h-13cm w-30cm d-25cm
2nd base: h-15cm w-40cm d-35cm
3rd base: h-17cm w-55cm d-48cm

The eldest son of Louis and Mildred Darby **A-10**. A farmer, he died at Kerswell.

DART		B-18
Ellen	d. 1949 (80 yrs)	
Samuel	d. 1920 (66 yrs)	

Transcription

In / loving memory of / Samuel DART / who died 4th March 1920 / Aged 66 / Also of / Ellen DART / his beloved wife / who died 21st April 1949 / aged 80
[Fewings & Co. Tiverton]

Description

Grey polished granite with peon top and square shoulders. Engraved perimeter line and "never-ending knot". Square kerbs with wing posts and chippings. Lead lettering.

Measurements

Total: h-91cm w-61cm d-9cm
Base: h-20cm w-76cm d-31cm
Kerbs: 200cm x 202cm

Samuel Dart was born in 1855 at Hockworthy. Son of John and Charlotte Dart, an agricultural labourer, who lived at Little Hocktord. Samuel had three sisters, and three brothers. In 1885 he married Ellen, the daughter of William and Ann Morrell, farm labourer at Hockworthy, but from a Morebath family. Ellen was born in Uplowman in 1868 and died at South Coombe Farm, Morebath. Samuel was an agricultural labourer who, for a while, was employed by Robert Shattock **B-33.** They had four children, one of whom, Rosina, married Samuel Shopland **B-32.** It is believed that Ellen's sister was Elizabeth Hawkins **C-7.**

DESTER B-46

Anne	d. 1926 (75 yrs)
Mary Grace	d. 2002
William	d. 1917 (89 yrs)

Transcription

[west] IHS / In loving memory of / William DESTER J.P. / of Staple Court / born July 24th 1827 / died April 28th 1917 / Also of Anne / born October 24th 1850 / died February 12th 1926 / Until the day break / and the shadows flee away. / *[inscribed twice]* *[south]* Eternal joy / Mary Grace / only daughter of / John and Ethel / (Western Australia / 18.9.2002)

Description	Measurements
White marble cross on square tapered base with inscriptions in lead lettering on polished granite panels attached to the base.	Total: h-187cm Cross: h-122cm w-53cm d-10cm Base: h-6cm w-77cm d-62cm

William & Anne (née Hall) came here from Warwickshire after their marriage in 1874. William was active into old age, engaged in many local organisations, including being Chairman of Tiverton Rural District Council for 16 years. Their four children were all born here. The family continued to farm Staple Court until the death in 1955 of their third son, Cecil **B-45**. Known as "Squire", Cecil was a character in the area. After his death, his unmarried sister Lilian **B-45** moved to Taunton where she died in 1972 aged 87. Cecil's brother John emigrated to Australia; he, and several members of his family, are commemorated on the family grave. The eldest brother, William Staple Dester, was a grocer in Taunton where he used his mother's maiden name to trade as William Henry Hall.

DESTER B-45

Cecil Bates	d. 1955 [70 yrs]
Ethel	d. 1932
John Montague	d. 1949
Lilian Ann (Nancy)	d. 1972 [87 yrs]
Maud Blanche	d. 1931 [56 yrs]
Montague Howse	d. 1941
William Staple	d. 1943 [65 yrs]

Transcription

[west] Lead kindly light / Cecil Bates DESTER / 1. 10. 55.
[north right] Rock of ages / John Montague DESTER / died Perth, Australia. / 14.10.49 / Also his wife Ethel / died in Kent 1932.
[north left] Fight the good fight / Montague Howse DESTER / only son of J. M. DESTER / Died Queensland, Australia / 29.5.41. *[1941]*
[east] peace perfect peace / Lilian Ann / DESTER / "Nancy" / only daughter of / William & Anne 2.10.72 *[1972]*
[south left] Abide with me / William Staple DESTER / 6.1.43 *[1943]*
[south right] Home at last thy labours done / Maud Blanche DESTER / wife of W. S. DESTER / 25.6.31. *[1931]*

Description	Measurements
Large grey speckled polished granite chest tomb with six columns within square kerbs with bevelled edges and ornate metal posts with linking chain. Lead lettering.	Tomb: h-72cm w-75cm l-67cm Kerbs: 184cm x 490cm Railings: h-43cm

Cecil was the last member of his family to farm Staple Court. Several of his family who emigrated to Australia are commemorated on this chest tomb.

Section A

Section B

DINHAM B-43

Albert   d. 1865 (10 mths)
Charles   d. 1884 (76 yrs)

Transcription

In affectionate remembrance / by the wife and children of / Charles DINHAM / born June 6th 1807 / died March 28th 1884 / I was weary and he gave me rest / Also Albert DINHAM / son of the above / born July 31st 1864 / died June 10th 1865 / "Sleeping in Jesus"

Description
Round top with open cross. Bevelled edge. Engraved lettering.

Measurements
h-129cm w-56cm d-8cm

Charles, who was born at Burlescombe in 1807, was the son of William and Agnes Dinham. Father and son were both farm labourers. Jane, daughter of John and Mary Burnell of Woodend, Huntsham, was his second wife, who he married in 1856, after his first wife Mary died in 1855. The family lived variously at Loudwells Cottage in Holcombe Rogus, and Slantycombe and Lea Cottage in Hockworthy. Albert was their second-born child. Another of their eight children, Mary Ann, born Hockworthy 1870, was a domestic servant of Charles and Charlotte How **B-30**.

DOBLE E-5

Marcella   d. 2003 (90 yrs)

Transcription
Marcella DOBLE 1912-2003

Description
Bench outside south of church wood with engraved lettering.

Measurements
h-78cm w-161cm d-59cm

Wife of Commander Douglas Doble, RN, Mrs Doble was born in Sherborne St John, Hants on 15 April 1912, the elder daughter of Harold and Marjorie "Bobbie" Cowan. In 1966 they moved to Ashbrittle where their son Charles is now churchwarden. Their elder son, John, is churchwarden of Hockworthy. Marcella moved to Hole Farm in 1982 and died in Wellington on 25 January 2003, and is buried with her husband at Ashbrittle.

DUNN B-21

John	d. 1875 (70 yrs)
Mary	d. 1879 (70 yrs)

Transcription

In memory of / John DUNN / of this parish / who died Octr 5th 1875 / aged 70 years / also Mary his wife / who died April 23rd 1879 / Aged 70 years / The Lord gave and the Lord / hath taken / away

Description
Stone Gothic shape. Engraved lettering. *[leaning backwards]*

Measurements
h-86cm w-44cm d-7cm

John was a farm labourer at Stuckleys, although in later life lived at Lower Lea Cottage. Mary his wife is described as a nurse in the 1871 census. Their son William and two grandsons are buried in **B-20**. In view of the proximity of the headstones, it is probable that John is the elder brother of William **B-22**, but this is unverified.

DUNN B-20

Jesse	d. 1899 (25 yrs)
John	d. 1898 (21 yrs)
William	d. 1897 (64 yrs)

Transcription

In loving memory / of William DUNN / who died Octr 11th 1897 / Aged 64 years / His end was peace / Also John / son of the above / who died April 19th 1898 / Aged 21 years / (buried at Netley cemetery) / Gone but not forgotten / Also Jesse / Son of the above / who died Jany 15th 1899 / aged 25 years / Blessed are the dead who / die in the Lord.

Description
Stone Gothic top with rounded shoulders. Engraved lettering.

Measurements
h-99cm w-50cm d-5cm

William was baptised at Uplowman on 23 Dec 1832, the son of John and Mary Dunn **B-21**. He was an agricultural labourer. He and his wife Susan lived at Kittisford, where their last two children were born, both of whom are buried here. Jesse worked on the land, while his younger brother John served in the Devon Regiment. He died at the Royal Victoria Hospital, Southampton.

DUNN B-22

| Harriet | d. 1848 (36 yrs) |
| William | d. 1895 (89 yrs) |

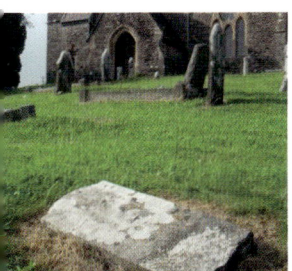

Transcription

In memory / of / Harriet wife of / William DUNN / of this Parish / who died July 31st 1848 / Aged 36 years / also of William DUNN / who died March 27th 1895. Aged 89 years / Parish clerk for 50 years

Description
Stone round top with square shoulders. Engraved lettering.
[fallen and lying on the ground]

Measurements
h-83cm w-37cm d-9cm

William was born in Hockworthy c. 1806. In 1836 he married Harriet Vickery, from Ashbrittle. William and Harriet had eight children, and he spent his whole life at Staple Cross working as a boot and shoe maker and serving as parish clerk for nearly fifty years. After the death of Harriet in 1848, in 1866 he married Mary Gamlin, daughter of Thomas Lucas, and widow of Robert Gamlin who had died in 1859.

FALLS C-12

Janet d. 1968 (72 yrs)

Transcription

Janet Margaret / Godelena FALLS / (née TWYSDEN) / 18th August 1895 / 29th May 1968

Description
Granite tablet on ground with bevelled edge and lead lettering.

Measurements
h-54cm w-44cm

Janet married widower Lieutenant Commander John Blyth Falls, RN in London in 1921. Son of Thomas Falls, he was born in S. Ireland in 1892, and died in 1934 in London. Janet was born at Thurlestone, in South Devon, the daughter of Captain James Stevenson Twysden, RN, JP, and Aileen Frances Mary daughter of Sir William Henry Wilson-Todd, Bt, MP, of Halnaby Hall, Yorks. Her sister Anne **C-11** married Captain Thomas Balfour Fellowes, RN. Her daughter Flavia was born in 1923. Mrs Falls built the bungalow "Staple Well" at Staple Cross, replacing an old stone cottage owned by the Desters **B-46** from Staple Court. She died in a car accident at Durston near Taunton.

FARLEY		A-21
Fred	d. 1978 (81 yrs)	
Kay	d. 1976 (77 yrs)	

Transcription

In / loving memory / of / Fred FARLEY / 1894-1978 / Also his wife / Kay FARLEY / 1899–1976

Description
Grey speckled granite peon shape on slab. Granite flower holder. Lead lettering.

Measurements
h-62cm w-41cm d-75cm

The Farleys lived in London but for many years they rented half of Lea Cottage, where they were befriended by their next-door neighbours Jack and Minnie Yarde. Fred was blind and particularly enjoyed hearing the birdsong at Lea. They wished to be commemorated after their death in Hockworthy, as they were so fond of the village. Jack (Andrew Joseph Yarde, died 1962, aged 66) worked at Lea and he and his wife Minnie (died 1972, aged 69) are buried, as they wished, beside their friends the Farleys in an unmarked grave.

FELLOWES		C-11
Anne	d. 1986 (88 yrs)	
Thomas Balfour	d. 1974 (82 yrs)	

Transcription

Thomas Balfour / FELLOWES / Captain Royal Navy / 13th July 1891 / 11th February 1974 / also his beloved wife / Anne (née TWYSDEN) / 26th July 1898 / 30th December 1986 / RIP

Description
Light grey half round upright with black engraved lettering.

Measurements
h-63cm w-46cm d-8cm

The sister of Janet Margaret Godelena Falls **C-12,** Anne Evelyn Frances (née Twysden- see **C-12**) married Captain Thomas Balfour Fellowes, RN, the son of Rear Admiral Sir Thomas Butler Fellowes, KCB, in 1921. Captain Fellowes had an illustrious career, serving in both world wars, and being awarded, amongst others, the Russian Order of St Stanislaus, and a rare German Red Cross Honour Badge. He was invalided out of the Navy and lived at Milton Abbas, Dorset before moving to Court Hall c. 1947, bringing all his staff with him. He later lived at Hurfords Mead.

FERRIS		**A-20**
John		
Sarah		d. 1863 (71 yrs)
FROST		
Mary		d. 1863 (77 yrs)

Transcription

In / memory of / Mary FERRIS / of this Parish / who departed this life / January 19th 1863 / Aged 77 years. / Always suppose thy death is nigh / and seek to be prepared to die / Also Sarah FERRIS / sister of the above / who died December 28th 1863. / Aged 71 years. / Also John FERRIS / who departed this life *[no date inscribed]*

Description	Measurements
Stone. Peon top splayed sides to hipped lower section. Engraved lettering. Two peon shaped footstones M.F. / 1863 and S.F. / 1863	h-102cm w-70cm d-8cm Footstone 1: h-23cm w-30cm d-7cm Footstone 2: h-22cm w-34cm d-8cm

Of the two of Henry and Frances Frost's daughters commemorated here, Mary was the elder. The two sisters ran a grocer shop at Staple Cross and, in the 1857 Billings *Directory of Devonshire*, Mary is also described as a "beer waiter". She was unmarried, but her sister Sarah (also known as Sally) married John Ferris, a wheelwright. The curious lack of death date on the headstone may be explained by the following Burial Register entry although it may not be the same John Ferris: "John Ferris of Hockworthy but died at the Union at Tiverton. Buried 1 Dec 1861 aged 67"

FERRIS		**A-18 A-18F**
Edward Tom		(1 yr)
Elizabeth		d. 1866 (36 yrs)
John		d. 1890 (67 yrs)
Mark		(1 yr)
Mark		(2 yrs)
Martha Sarah		(1 yr)
Tom		(1 yr)

Transcription

She hath given up the ghost. Her sun is gone down. While it was yet day. / In affectionate / remembrance of / Elizabeth wife of / John FERRIS of this parish / died July 22nd 1866. Aged 36 years / Also of their children as follows / Edward Tom died aged 16 months / Mark died aged 16 months / Martha Sarah died 1 year and 11 months / Tom died aged 14 months / Mark died aged 2 years and 8 months / Also of John FERRIS who departed this life / March 4th 1890. Aged 67 years / Footstone: 1866

Description	Measurements
Bevelled edge. Engraved lettering.	h-170cm w-87cm d-8cm

Elizabeth was the eldest daughter of Henry **B-4** and Martha Lucas. The children buried here died: Edward Tom in 1858; Mark 1860; Martha Sarah 1861; Tom 1864 and Mark 1864. Her husband John, a blacksmith, was the eldest son of John & Sarah Ferris **A-20**. After Elizabeth died, John married Emma (née Naish), widow of Robert Ash **A-31**. He died at Chipstable but is buried here with Elizabeth and their children. Emma died in 1909.

Section C

Section D

FILMER D-7

George Henry   d. 1992 (79 yrs)

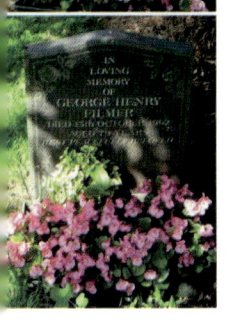

Transcription

In / loving / memory / of / George Henry / FILMER / died 15th October 1992 / aged 79 years / Rest peacefully beloved

Description	Measurements
Ogee dark grey polished granite. Base on concrete plinth. Engraved roses at top. Integral flower pot in base. Engraved silver lettering.	Total: h-72cm w-54cm d-3cm Base: h-8cm w-62cm d-31cm

Born in London, George was a stockbroker in the City of London. He and his wife Dawn retired to Staplemere at Staple Cross from Hertfordshire in the 1980s. They were the first people to live in the house, which was built by a developer on the site of a big shed, previously owned by Gerald Howe.

GAMLIN A-30

John   d. 1859 (53 yrs)

MARKS

John   d. 1864 (4 mnths)

FOWLER

Mary Ann   d. 1879 (42 yrs)
Robert

Transcription

Sacred / to the / memory / of John GAMLIN of this Parish / who departed this life July 17th 1859 / Aged 53 years / Also John MARKS, Grandson / of the above who died the 14th of / October 1864 Aged 4 months / Also Mary Ann Daughter of the above / the beloved wife of Robert FOWLER / of Court Place, Cove, Tiverton / who died January 10th 1879 / Aged 42 years

Description	Measurements
Half round top; square and scotia shaped shoulders. Engraved perimeter. Engraved lettering.	h-157cm w-79cm d-5cm

Born in Bathealton, John farmed over 200 acres at Bences. His wife Mary pre-deceased him by 13 years. At his death the farm was taken over by his eldest daughter Elizabeth and her husband John Marks. It is their son who is buried here with his grandfather and aunt, Mary Ann, Elizabeth's younger sister. In 1861 Mary Ann had married Robert Fowler, who farmed at Cove near Tiverton.

GODDARD		C-5
Edwin	d. 1915 (87 yrs)	
Sarah	d. 1896 (76 yrs)	
FOLLETT		
Charles	d. 1901 (53 yrs)	
REDWOOD		
Bessie	d. 1916 (57 yrs)	

Transcription

In / loving memory / of / Edwin GODDARD / of this parish / who died Nov 10th 1915 / aged 87 years / also Sarah wife of the above / who died Feb 27th 1896 / aged 76 years. / Also Charles FOLLETT / son-in-law of the above / who died June 28th 1901 / aged 53 years / In peace let me resign my breath. / And thy salvation see. / My sins deserve eternal death / But Jesus died for me / Also Bessie REDWOOD / second daughter of the above / who died at Sampford Peverell Novr. 26th 1916 / Aged 57 years

Description	Measurements
Gothic stone with bevelled edge. Engraved lettering.	h-134cm w-72cm d-7cm

Son of John & Mary of Gt Tadbeer, Ashbrittle, Edwin married Sarah Sayer in 1856, widow of Robert Venn. She had ten children, five with Edwin, and died in 1896. In 1897 Edwin married widow Emma Stephens (née May). Edwin & Emma moved to Staple Cross after farming Redwoods. Charles Follett, stockman at Slantycombe, was husband of Edwin's eldest daughter Clara. Edwin's second daughter, Bessie, married John Redwood.

GODDARD		C-9
Eveline	d. 1975 (80 yrs)	
Louis	d. 1969 (68 yrs)	

Transcription

In / loving memory / of / a dear husband & father / Louis GODDARD / who passed away / 10th November 1969 / aged 68 years / and of his wife / Eveline / 1st September 1975 / Aged 80 years / At Rest

Description	Measurements
Peon with double square shoulders. Light grey polished granite with black lettering. Oval front base on concrete plinth. Integral flower pot.	Total: h-78cm w-62cm d-9cm Base: h-10cm w-77cm d-20cm

Louis, who was born at Little Tadbeer, Ashbrittle, was the son of Edwin George Goddard and his wife Frances Ellen (née Redwood, whose brother was John Redwood **A-3**). Eveline and Louis first farmed at Wootton Courtenay but they came to Thornlands when Eveline's brother Frank Hussey **B-2** died. Louis's first cousin Gilbert **D-2** took on Thornlands when Louis and Eveline moved to Huntsham Barton. They retired to Dares Down in 1968. Their son Malcolm is married to Jean, daughter of Walter Lionel Thomas **C-8**; she made and donated beautiful replacement cushions in the chancel in 2013.

GODDARD   D-2

Mildred (Millie) Ruth   d. 2000 (93 yrs)
Gilbert James   d. 1996 (86 yrs)

Transcription

In / loving memory of / Gilbert James / GODDARD, / died 17th March 1996, / aged 86 years. / Also his beloved wife / Mildred (Millie) / Ruth, / died 19th September 2000, / aged 93 years / Reunited

Description	Measurements
Ogee light grey polished granite. Base on concrete plinth. Engraved black lettering. Integral flower pot in base.	Total: h-72cm w-54cm d-8cm Base: h-8cm w-62cm d-31cm

Gilbert, born 29 July 1909, was the son of Albert and Emily Goddard from Doble Farm, Ashbrittle. He was first cousin of Louis Goddard **C-9** and, in 1948, when Louis and Eveline moved to Huntsham Barton, Gilbert took on Thornlands. He married in 1935 Mildred (Millie) Heard from Clayhanger. Gilbert served as churchwarden at Hockworthy 1965-78. They bought land for their son Tom to build the bungalow Meadow View.

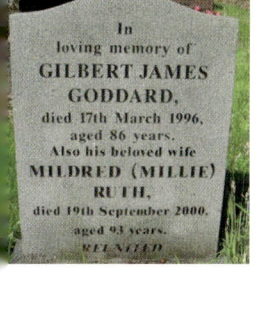

GOFFIN   C-1

Mary   d. 1871 (68 yrs)
William   d. 1869 (31 yrs)
William   d. 1888 (76 yrs)

Transcription

In / memory of / William GOFFIN / Died May 16th 1869 / Aged 31 / Mary GOFFIN / Died Novr 22nd 1871 / Aged 8 / William GOFFIN / Died June 17th 1888 / Aged 76 / Sexton of Hockworthy / We have laid you down to rest.

Description	Measurements
Gothic stone with bevelled edge. Engraved letters.	h-79cm w-50cm d-8cm

William and Mary Goffin and one of their six children are buried here. William junior, who was born in Hockworthy, had been working as a land drainer in South Wales before his early death from a lung disease. His father was born in Sampford Peverell on 17 Apr 1812, the son of George and Sarah Goffin. The family lived at Hockford, and William was a farm labourer. He was also church sexton for 37 years.

GREEDY   B-10

William James   *d. 1944 (64 yrs)*

Transcription

In loving memory of / William James GREEDY / who died Sept 26th 1944 / aged 64. / R.I.P.

Description	Measurements
Pink polished granite oval top with square shoulders. Lead lettering.	h-157cm w-79cm d-5cm

Francis and Sarah Greedy, William's parents, ran the post office in Huntsham where William was born in 1880. (Francis was also the sexton and a mason) William was a wheelwright who, in later life, is remembered as having been a large and jovial carpenter. In 1927 he married Sarah, daughter of William and Sarah Bowerman **B-7** from whom she inherited Quarry Hockford. She outlived her husband and, with no children, after her death, the farm was left to her nephew Eddie Harvey.

HAMILTON   C-10

Kathleen Munro   *d. 1939 (60 yrs)*

Transcription

Kathleen / Munro / HAMILTON / born St. Helena / 20. Sep. 1878. / Died 19. Feb. 1939.

Description	Measurements
Wood cross with wood roof and metal figure of Christ. Concrete splayed base. Bronze tablet with engraved inscription.	Total: h-142cm w-66cm d-27cm Base: h-33cm w-52cm d-56cm

Born in St Helena, in the South Atlantic, Kathleen (known as Kate) moved to Jersey, although her son, Stephen Heysham Hamilton, was born in Llandudno in 1910. She was living at Nicholashayne when she died. Stephen became a lay-reader at Hockworthy in June 1938. Ten years later he was ordained, and lived at Waterslade Cottage, Hockworthy. He is well-remembered in the village, and for cycling on a tandem with his wife Helen (née Evans) whom he had married in 1943.

HAWKINS   C-7

Nellie *[Ellen Lucy]*	d. 1895 (3 yrs)
Elizabeth	d. 1948 (86 yrs)
Freddie	d. 1893 (4 yrs)
William Thomas	d. 1932 (66 yrs)

Transcription

In / loving memory / of / William Thomas HAWKINS / who died Feb 10th 1932 / aged 66 years / also of Freddie / who died Nov 18th 1893 / aged 4 years / also of Nellie / who died Nov. 21st 1895 / aged 3 years / children of Wm & Elizth HAWKINS. Also Elizabeth HAWKINS his wife / who died Feb 14th 1948 / aged 86 years / rest in peace

Description

Gothic stone with double ornate shoulders. Bevelled edge to top. Engraved lettering.

Measurements

h-137cm w-70cm d-8cm

The son of James and Elizabeth Hawkins, William was born in Ashbrittle. He married Elizabeth Morrell in 1887 (born Uplowman) and was a private coachman and groom at the Vicarage, now Hockworthy House, living at The Lodge, Hockworthy. He had three daughters, and a son, all born in Hockworthy. He was involved with the church and a keen bell ringer. It is believed that Elizabeth's sister was Ellen Dart **B-18**.

HEDGELAND   B-12

Fanny Mabel	d. 1942 (69 yrs)
Frederick Charles	d. 1955 (80 yrs)

Transcription

In loving memory of / Fanny Mabel / beloved wife of / Frederick Charles HEDGELAND / Who fell asleep July 19th 1942 / Aged 69 years / Rest in peace. / Also of Frederick Charles / husband of the above / who died Jan. 28th 1955 / Aged 80 years / Peace, perfect peace.

Description

Art deco style rectangular stone with stepped shoulders and carved lily. Lead lettering.

Measurements

Total: h-65cm w-76cm d-7cm
Base: h-5cm w-92cm d-18cm

Born in 1874 in Exeter, he married in 1898 Fanny Mabel Westlake, who was born in Merton, near Torrington, as were her parents. Prior to her marriage, she cooked for a retired surgeon in Beaworthy. In 1901 Frederick was a policeman in Dittisham, where their son Cecil Charles was born *[see p. 23]*. Ten years later Frederick was a farm carter residing at Hockford and later he lived at West View, Hockworthy. Their daughter Violet Gwendoline was born at Clayhidon.

HEYWOOD　　　　　　　　　　　　　　　　　　　　A-2

Albert Tom　　　　d. 1944 (60 yrs)
Louisa　　　　　　d. 1973 (90 yrs)

Transcription

In / loving memory / of a dear / husband and father / Albert Tom HEYWOOD / of Lea Barton / fell asleep Nov. 10th 1944 / Aged 60 years. / "He giveth his beloved sleep" / Also of Louisa his wife / fell asleep Jan. 19th 1973. / Aged 90 years.

Description
Polished light grey granite cross on three bases on concrete plinth. Black lettering. Square kerbs with square posts. Granite chippings.

Measurements
Total: h-140cm
Cross: h-84cm w-49cm d-11cm
1st base: h-15cm w-31cm d-23cm
2nd base: h-18cm w-46cm d-36cm
3rd base: h-20cm w-61cm d-51cm
Kerbs: 208cm x 186cm

Tom's family had long farmed at Oakford, before moving to Lea Barton in 1919. In 1907 he married Louisa, daughter of John and Elizabeth Richards who farmed at East Anstey, where Louisa was born in 1882. He represented the parish on the Tiverton Rural District Council and was a school manager for Hockworthy. Tom's grandson and his family continue to farm Lea.

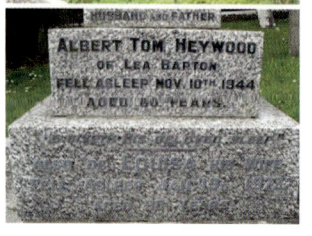

HEYWOOD　　　　　　　　　　　　　　　　　　　　E-7

Laura Mary　　　　d. 1995 (75 yrs)
Merlin John　　　　d. 1993 (79 yrs)

Transcription

In loving memory of / Merlin John HEYWOOD / who passed away / 12th March 1993 / aged 79. / Also his wife / Laura Mary / who passed away / 8th January 1995 / aged 75. Rest in peace

Description
Cremation stone; grey polished granite; engraved black lettering.

Measurements
h-31cm w-46cm

Merlin was the second son of Tom and Louisa Heywood **A-2**. He was aged six when the family moved to Lea Barton in 1919. As well as farming Lea, Merlin served for forty-five years as churchwarden. In 1946 he married Laura, daughter of James Griffin and his wife Florence (née White), of Steels Farm, Holcombe Rogus. His four sisters are all buried in the churchyard **D-1** and **D-11**.

HEYWOOD   D-11

Christine May   d. 2004 (93 yrs)
Edith Louise   d. 1987 (79 yrs)

Transcription

H / Loving / memories of / Edith Louise HEYWOOD / who passed away / 9th January 1987 / aged 79 years / Christine May HEYWOOD / who passed away / 13th December 2004 / aged 93 years / Peace, perfect peace

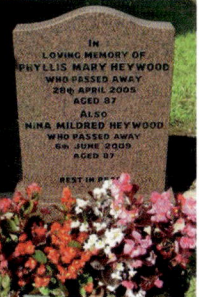

Description
Ogee shape, pink speckled polished granite with engraved gold H in leaf design at the top. Black lettering. Base with ogee front on concrete plinth.

Measurements
Total: h-73cm w-53cm d-10cm
Base: h-10cm w-61cm d-26cm

The eldest of four daughters of Tom and Louisa Heywood **A-2**, Edith worked at a boarding school in Reading before becoming House Matron at Wells Cathedral School and then at Blundell's in Tiverton. Christine, their second daughter, went to London to run a guest house in Holland Park owned by her mother's family. In retirement, they shared a house in Wellington.

HEYWOOD   D-1

Phyllis Mary [Molly]   d. 2005 (87 yrs)
Nina Mildred   d. 2009 (87 yrs)

Transcription

In / loving memory of / Phyllis Mary HEYWOOD / who passed away / 28th April 2005 / Aged 87 / also / Nina Mildred HEYWOOD / who passed away / 6th June 2009 / Aged 87 / Rest in peace
[Manning and Knight]

Description
Ogee pink speckled polished granite on concrete plinth. Black lettering.

Measurements
Total: h-77cm w-53cm d-10cm
Base: h-10cm w-6cm d-20cm

Phyllis Mary "Molly" was the third of four daughters of Tom and Louisa Heywood **A-2**, all of whom are buried in the churchyard. She spent all her life at Lea Barton and was a pillar of the church, organising the choir, serving as PCC secretary and, for sixty-five years, playing the organ. The youngest of the four sisters, Nina was Matron at the Somerset Farm Institute at Cannington, near Bridgwater, and retired to Wellington.

HILL	A-19
Betty	d. 1837 (72 yrs)

Transcription

Sacred / to the / memory / of Betty HILL / who departed this / life February 1st / 1837 aged 72 years / Tender mother when in life / Virtuous, an industrious wife / In peace she lived in love she died / She beg<u>d</u> for life but was denied

Description	Measurements
Half round with square and scotia shoulders. Stone. Engraved lettering.	h-126cm w-62cm d-9cm

With so little information, it has been impossible to add further detail to that given on the headstone: viz. that she was born c. 1765, was married and had children. However, the Burial Registers show a Thomas Hill, Parish Clerk, who was buried ten years earlier (7 Sep 1827). As he was aged 66, he could have been her husband. Likewise, the 1841 census records a John Hill at Slantycombe, and there are several other Hills listed in *The Huntsham Book*.

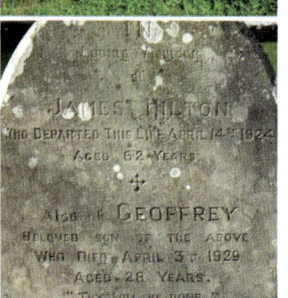

HILTON	A-9
Geoffrey	d. 1929 (28 yrs)
James	d. 1924 (62 yrs)

Transcription

In / loving memory / of / James HILTON / who departed this life April 14th 1924 / Aged 62 years / Also of Geoffrey / beloved son of the above / who died April 3rd 1929 / Aged 28 years / "Thy will be done"

Description	Measurements
Stone gothic with top 90cm front edges bevelled. Engraved lettering.	h-122cm w-69cm d-9cm

Both James and his wife Alice were born in Lancashire, James in Whitfield in 1862, Alice in Prestwich. Due to James's ill-health, they moved to Dares Down from Manchester in 1912 where he died aged 62 of a heart condition. James was a retired schoolteacher, and Alice was a confectioner/baker. Geoffrey died in hospital in Whitechapel, London. He was their second son who worked on the land. He was described in the *Western Times* of 19 Apr 1929 as "… a brilliant young man …who was held in the highest esteem. His unassuming and cheery manner assured him friendship wherever he went …". Another son, Charles Herbert, is included on the church porch tablet of those who served in the war *[see p.23]*.

HOCKING   D-8
Winifred Alice   d. 1989 (82 yrs)

Transcription

In loving / memory of / Winifred Alice / HOCKING / died 12th May 1989 / aged 82 years

Description
Polished dark grey granite. Integral flowerpot. Base on concrete plinth. Engraved lettering.

Measurements
Total: h-84cm w-60cm d-8cm
Base: h-9cm w-76cm d-30cm

Winifred, the daughter of John and Alice Redwood, **A-3**, was the sister of Lionel Redwood **D-4** and Vera Redwood **A-3**. She married Edgar John Hocking in 1942, a farmer from Brushford. He was a great horseman who was a leading point-to-point rider between the Wars, travelling as far as Dartmoor to race. Winifred moved to Crossways Cottage, Staple Cross after her husband died in 1986.

HOW   B-30
Charles   d. 1891 (76 yrs)
Charlotte   d. 1907 (85 yrs)
Frances Catherine   d. 1898 (5 yrs)

Transcription

[west] IHS / In / loving / memory / of / Charles HOW / who died December 11th 1891 / aged 76 years / "My God I leave to thee the rest" / "Thy will be done". *[south]* Charlotte wife of the above / who died April 11th 1907 / aged 85 years / "O Lord put forth thine hand / and take thy wanderers in". *[north]* Frances Catherine HOW / who died November 29th 1898 / Aged 5 years / Jesus called a little child unto him

Description
Stone cross on three tiered base. Lead lettering and square kerbs measuring 245cm x 256cm.

Measurements
Total: h-179cm
Cross: h-108cm w-51cm d-13cm
1st base: h-20cm w-45cm d-44cm
2nd base: h-20cm w-56cm d-56cm
3rd base: h-36cm w-77cm d-75cm

Son of John & Isabella who farmed near Brompton Regis, Charles was born at Knowstone in 1815. In 1852, he married Charlotte (née Stone), widow of John Rockett (d.1850) with whom she had two sons. Charles, churchwarden 1885-99, farmed at Court Hall. One daughter Charlotte married Robert W Shattock **B-33** followed, in 1894, by William J How. Another, Catherine, married Frank Kemp **B-34** followed by George Palfrey **B-37**. Frances, buried here, is daughter of their son Charles John How and his wife Harriet.

HUSSEY		B-3
Mary Ann	d. 1937 (77 yrs)	
William Robert	d. 1911 (24 yrs)	
William White	d. 1920 (59 yrs)	

Transcription

[west] In / loving memory of / William Robert HUSSEY / who departed this life / May 4th 1911 / aged 24 years. / "The Lord is my shepherd: I shall not want" / "Thy will be done"

[south] Also of / his father / William White HUSSEY / who died April 27th 1920 / Aged 59 years / "Peace perfect peace"

[north] In / loving memory of / Mary Ann / beloved wife of / William White HUSSEY / who died April 27th 1937 / aged 77 years

Description
Polished pink granite cross on tapered base and plinth. Engraved lettering. Surrounding square kerbs.

Measurements
Total: h-160cm
Cross: h-100cm w-51cm d-11cm
Base: h-62cm w-71cm d-67cm
Kerbs: 228cm x 183cm

William White Hussey and his wife Mary Ann (née Bucknell) were tenants of the Huntsham estate at Thornlands. Mary Ann never really recovered from William dying at such a young age as a result of a horse and cart accident at Stallenge Thorne Cross. Another son Frank **B-2** also pre-deceased her, at which time her daughter Eveline, and her husband Louis Goddard **C-9**, took on Thornlands. Mary Ann built Copper Ridge where she moved when her surviving son Maurice took on Hole Farm.

HUSSEY		B-2
Frank	d. 1933 (40 yrs)	

Transcription

[west] In loving memory of
[south] Frank HUSSEY / who passed away Feb 25th 1933 aged 40 years / He giveth his beloved sleep

Description
Polished pink granite chamfered kerbs with rough cut pyramid corner posts. Metal and second modern grey speckled ceramic flower pots. Engraved letterng.

Measurements
h-20cm w-94cm d-13cm l-162cm
Posts: h-31cm

Born at Uplowman, Frank was the son of William White Hussey and Mary Ann (née Bucknell) **B-3.** He was brother of William Robert Hussey **B-3**, and Eveline Goddard **B-9**. Frank was engaged to Edith Hill when he was tragically killed at Thornlands in an accident when his clothing caught in the revolving shaft of a corn grinding machine. Frank's surviving brother Maurice moved from Thornlands to Hole Farm c. 1935, at which time there were still people living in Hole Lane Cottage.

KEMP B-34
Frank — d. 1893 (41 yrs)

Transcription

In loving memory / IHS / Frank KEMP / of Cudmoor Bampton / who died July 28th 1893 / aged 41 years / In the midst of life we are in death

Description
Gothic stone with square and scotia shoulders and bevelled front edge within square kerbs with bevelled edges and metal posts and rods. Engraved lettering.

Measurements
h-127cm w-60cm d-9cm
Kerbs: 129cm x 249cm
Posts: h-40cm

Succeeding his parents, John Wallis Kemp and Frances (née Dinnicombe), as a tenant of the Huntsham estate, Frank farmed Cudmore, on which there was a Roman fort. He married in 1883; both he and his wife, Catherine How (daughter of **B-30**), were born in Hockworthy. Their three children were born in Bampton. Four years after Frank's death, Catherine married George Palfrey **B-37** who joined her farming at Cudmore.

LAMPREY B-11
Female — d. 1855 (infant)
Samuel — d. 1866 (24 yrs)

Transcription

In / memory of / Samuel LAMPREY / of this Parish / who departed this life / April 21st 1866 / Aged 24 years / Also of an Infant Sister / who died June 9th 1855 / Always suppose thy death is nigh / And seek to be prepared to die

Description
Stone Gothic shape. Engraved lettering.

Measurements
h-87cm w-51cm d-8cm

Samuel, an agricultural labourer, was the eldest son of Ann (née Davey and born in Milverton) and James, a lime burner although, in later life, he became a gardener in Yorkshire. They married in 1838 and lived at Waterslade. All seven of their known children were born in Hockworthy. Samuel's infant sister, Susan, died aged eleven months. It is possible that John Lamprey, who burnt to death with John Milton in a lime kiln accident at Hole Farm in 1863, was Samuel's uncle. [see *Wellington Weekly News* of 18 July 1863]

LOCK A-1

Maria   d. 1870 (43 yrs)
Thomas
Infants x 2

Transcription

In memory of / Maria / wife of Thomas LOCK / late of this parish / who died August 20th 1870 / aged 43 years / In the midst of life we are in death / Also two children who died in their infancy

Description	Measurements
Gothic stone with square and scotia shoulders and bevelled front edge within square kerbs with bevelled edges and metal posts and rods. Engraved lettering.	h-127cm w-60cm d-9cm Kerbs: 129cm x 249cm Posts: h-40cm

The family lived at Locks Cottage, Hockworthy, but moved to Tiverton after Maria's death. An agricultural labourer, Thomas was born in Ashbrittle, and Maria (née Quick) in Morebath. They married in 1849, and had six surviving children (Matilda, Thomas, Mary, John, Ann and Maria). In 1870 Thomas married Frances (Fanny) Collins. There is an anomaly: the death certificate and Burial Register give Maria's death as having been in 1868, whereas the gravestone is engraved with 1870. The two youngsters buried with their mother are John, who died in 1862 aged 3 years, and Bessie, who died in 1866 aged 1 year.

LONGMAN B-23

Anne *[Elizabeth]*   d. 1879 (67 yrs)
Samuel   d. 1881 (76 yrs)

Transcription

IHS / In / loving memory / of Anne wife of / Samuel LONGMAN / late of this village / who died at Wiveliscombe / April 5th 1879 aged 67 years / To die is gain Phil. 1, v.21. / Also of the above named / Samuel LONGMAN / who died Dec. 11th 1881 / in his 76th year / Rest for ever more

*[footstone **B-26**]* S.L. 18 ...
*[footstone **B-27**]* A.L. 18 ...

Description	Measurements
Stone Gothic shape. Engraved lettering.	h-105cm w-47cm d-7cm Footstones: h-36cm w-31cm d-8cm

Anne (née Rodgment) was born at East Down, near Barnstaple. Her husband Samuel was a master stone mason and builder, born at Shebbeare, Devon, the son of John and Martha (née Paige). They had four children, two of whom are buried in **B-24**. They lived at The Villa, Hockworthy, and both Samuel and Anne died at Wiveliscombe where his first born daughter Jessie was living, married to John Goddard.

LONGMAN   B-24

William *[Courtney]*   *d. 1852 (5 yrs)*
Elizabeth   *d. 1860 (21 yrs)*

Transcription

Sacred / to the memory of / William LONGMAN / who died May 6th 1852 / Aged 5 years / Ill is not here of our beloved and blessed / Gone is the sleeper in his God to rest. / Also Elizth R LONGMAN. / Sister of the above who died / Oct 24th 1860. Aged 21 years. / She faded jeully from the sight / As flowers in summer fade / And we have laid her in her resting place / To wait the coming of her Lord.
[footstone B-28] E.L
[footstone B-29] W.L. 1852

Description
Stone Gothic with carved cross.
Engraved lettering.

Measurements
h-158cm w-163cm d-9cm

Born in Holcombe Rogus, Elizabeth was the second daughter of Samuel and Anne Longman **B-23**. The "R" initial in her name is the maiden name of her mother, Rodgment. Her little brother William Courtney Longman was born in Hockworthy. Their elder sister Jessie married John Goddard, both of whom were buried in Wiveliscombe. Their surviving brother Samuel was a Surveyor of Customs in Kent where he died in 1933 in Sevenoaks. His daughters, Alice and Ethel, presented Hockworthy church with an altar book and cushion in his memory.

LUCAS   B-4

Henry   *d. 1874 (70 yrs)*

Transcription

In / memory of / Henry LUCAS / of this parish / who departed this life / the 9th October 1874 / Aged 70 years / Watch therefore for ye know not what hour / your Lord doth come.
St Matthew. Chap xxiv v.42
[footstone] H. L. / 1874

Description
Stone rounded top with accentuated point.
Engraved lettering. Gothic shaped footstone.

Measurements
h-146cm w-81cm d-9cm
Footstone: h-36cm w-29cm d-9cm

Born in Hockworthy, Henry farmed 160 acres at Thornlands, latterly with five men and a boy. After his first wife Martha Hill died in 1848, he married Anne (née Besley), the widow of John Bucknell **B-6**. His daughter Elizabeth (1830-66) was the first wife of John Ferris **A-18**. Henry Lucas was churchwarden 1854-58.

McCANCE   B-38
Joseph Bell   *d 1949 (49 yrs)*

Transcription

To the beloved memory of / Brigadier Joseph Bell McCANCE, O.B.E. / The Royal Scots (The Royal Regiment) / Born 19th September 1899 / Died 24th January 1949 / "I thank my God upon every / remembrance of you." / Phil. 1.3.

Description	Measurements
Rough granite cross on square base leaning heavily to the south. Lead lettering. Surrounding square kerbs.	Total: h-145cm Cross: h-100cm w-51cm d-10cm Base: h-45cm w-61cm d-44cm Kerbs: 212cm x 209cm

Joseph's grandfather was Joe Bell, a prominent Edinburgh Surgeon, on whom the Sherlock Holmes character was based. Joseph married Phyllis Adah (née Turner, born 1900 in Cumberland) who had previously been married to Ted Quilter, by whom she had one daughter. Phyllis and Joseph had twins born in 1928. Joseph returned from serving as Chief of Staff in Malta (1946-48) to take the duties of Deputy Commander, Lowland District, but died shortly afterwards in Tiverton hospital. After his death, his widow moved from Yew Tree House in Nicholashayne and, in 1958, married Hugh Cowan-Douglas in London.

MILTON   A-27
Charles   *d. 1850 (25 yrs)*

Transcription

Charles MILTON / died / 3rd April 1850 / Aged 25 years.

Description	Measurements
Stone round top. Engraved perimeter line and lettering.	h-25cm w-31cm d-10cm

In 1863 John Milton, together with John Lamprey *[see **B-11**]* was "burnt to death in a limekiln" at Hole Farm [*Wellington Weekly News* of 18 July 1863]. He was buried in Hockworthy, but it is not known if he was related to Charles, who was a labourer in a lime quarry. Charles's parents appear to be John (and his wife Ann Vickery) from a different Milton family in Ashbrittle. After Charles's death, they were living in the cottage in Hole Lane but, in 1841, they were in the "New Buildings" in Hockworthy, next to the Poor House; the "New Buildings" had been built by the Huntsham Estate for their employees in 1834 and are now Glebe Cottage and West End.

MOON C-2

Mary — *d. 1885 (84 yrs)*
Samuel — *d. 1875 (65 yrs)*

Transcription

In / memory of / Samuel MOON / died April 11th 1875 / Aged 65 years / Also / Mary MOON / wife of the above / Died October 23rd 1885 / Aged 84 years. / Them also which sleep in / Jesus will God bring with him.
[foot plate] S.M.

Description
Gothic stone with bevelled edge. Engraved lettering. Small metal cross in front with initials S.M.

Measurements
h-93cm w-49cm d-8cm
Cross: h-38cm w-30cm d-1cm

An agricultural labourer born in Cruwys Morchard, Samuel married Mary Sully in 1831. She was born in Dulverton. They lived at Higher Lea, Ham Mill, and Daggeridge Cottage, Hockworthy. Their eight children were all born in Hockworthy. After Samuel's death, Mary lived with Robert Sprague's widow Elizabeth at Hurford Cottage **B-40**.

MORRISH E-1

Derek John — *d. 1984*

Transcription

In memory / of a dear brother / Derek John MORRISH / fell asleep / 7th October 1984 / In God's keeping

Description
Cremation stone. Engraved slate.

Measurements
h-31cm w-43cm

From a Devon family, Derek was born in 1930, the son of Francis and Beatrice Morrish. He was an engineer who ran a number of light engineering enterprises in the barn to the south of the road at Waterslade, where he lived. His electrical company in Holcombe Rogus continues trading in Tiverton as Morrish Engineering.

Newman family plot, Hockworthy

NEWMAN
John
D-13

Transcription

To the Glory of God / and in memory of John NEWMAN of Dartmouth Esq. / the Patron of this living. This window and Reredos were placed / at the Restoration of this church on St Simon and St Jude's day 1861 by his son William James NEWMAN

Description
On outside wall of church

Measurements
h-40cm w-230cm

Although the Newmans, as a family, are remembered in Hockworthy for their long tenure as clergymen in the parish and for the rebuilding of the church in the 1860s, they had a much longer connection with South Devon. Originally from Totnes, from the late C14th they were in Dartmouth, where they still live. They were first involved in the wool trade and then, from the 1500s, in shipping, the wine trade and, in particular, the fisheries of Newfoundland with a flourishing business for 300 years. What brought them to Hockworthy is unknown, but their wealth clearly had an impact on the church and parish.

Revd William James Newman **B-50** was the only son of William Newman (1785-1862), a Dartmouth merchant. He graduated from Wadham College, Oxford in 1846 and became curate at Hockworthy in 1852. He was vicar from 1860 until his death in 1880, although a note in the burial register, the headstone and a memorial tablet state that he was vicar for 26 years. Whilst here, he oversaw the reconstruction of the church and the building of Hockworthy House, then known as the Vicarage. Catherine Durnford (1795-1858), the sister of his father's wife Harriet (1793-1868), married George C Greenway (1784-1851). Their son, Charles Durnford Greenway, who designed the new church, is commemorated under one of the windows *[see p.107]*.

Revd William James and Caroline's elder son, Revd William Frederick Newman **B-48** graduated from St John's College, Oxford in 1875. He succeeded his father as vicar in 1880 and remained until his death in 1920. His son, William Frederick Wyndham Newman **B-51**, served as churchwarden from 1922-46. His widow Nora (née Turner) continued as churchwarden until 1953, when she sold up and so ended a hundred years of Newmans in Hockworthy.

NEWMAN B-50

Caroline	d. 1883 (67 yrs)
Herbert Roope	d. 1891 (43 yrs)
William James	d. 1880 (60 yrs)

Transcription

[second one down from the church] [west] IHS / In memory of / Revd William James NEWMAN MA / Vicar of this parish for 26 years / Born at Dartmouth, Devon Oct 6th 1819 / Died Jany 5th 1880 / Aged 60 years / "Blessed are the dead which die in the Lord / from henceforth – that they may rest / from their labours" Rev. XIV.13. *[south]* Also of / Herbert Roope NEWMAN / younger son of / Revd W J and C NEWMAN / Obiit Novr 27th 1891 / Aged 43 years. / "And there was a great calm."/ St Matth. viii.26. *[north]* Caroline wife / of / Revd William James NEWMAN / Obiit July 9th 1883 / Aged 67 years. / "They that turn many to righteousness / shall shine as the stars for ever / and ever." Daniel xii.3.

Description	Measurements
Marble cross on two tiered base on concrete plinth. Lead lettering.	Total: h-143cm
	Cross: h-98cm w-51cm d-11cm
*[With three other family graves in metal fenced plot - see **B-51**, **B-49** and **B-48**]*	1st base: h-19cm w-43cm d-43cm
	2nd base: h-19cm w-71cm d-71cm

For Revd W J Newman, see p. 75. His wife Caroline Whitaker came from Oxfordshire. Graduating from Cambridge in 1867, Herbert then studied agriculture so he could farm the glebe for his brother **B-48**. The name Roope comes from a Dartmouth family with whom the Newmans were in business in Newfoundland.

NEWMAN B-51

Nora	d. 1970 (93 yrs)
William Frederick W	d. 1947 (74 yrs)

Transcription

[Nearest church] In / ever loving memory of / William Frederick Wyndham NEWMAN / Born Dec. 19th 1872 / Died April 18th 1947. / And his wife Nora / Born Aug. 21st 1876 / Died Mar. 17th 1970 / *Requiescat in pace.*

Description	Measurements
Rough granite cross on square block tapered base on concrete plinth. Lead Lettering.	Total: h-136cm
	Cross: h-92cm w-47cm d-12cm
*[With three other family graves in metal fenced plot - see **B-50**, **B-49** and **B-48**]*	Base: h-44cm w-62cm d-45cm

The third generation of Newmans to live at Hockworthy, he was not a clergyman. However, he served as churchwarden from 1922-46 and was a keen fox-hunter. His wife carried on as churchwarden after his death until 1953. She then sold Hockworthy House and farms (Waterslade, Turnham and Home Farm) and retired to London in the mid-1950s. Nora was born in Cumberland, the daughter of William Berrow Turner, a JP and mine owner.

NEWMAN B-49

Alice Susanna	d. 1864 (14 yrs)
Caroline Dumford	d. 1883 (39 yrs)
Frances Elizabeth	d. 1882 (26 yrs)

Transcription

[third down from the church]

[west] Frances Elizabeth NEWMAN / Obiit July 6th 1882. Aged 28 years. God is love.

[south] Caroline Durnford NEWMAN / Obiit March 27th 1883 Aged 39 years / I know that my Redeemer liveth.

[east] Alice Susanna / Died Dec 21 1864. Aged 14 years.

[north] daughters of the Revd William James / and Caroline NEWMAN.

Description
Flat marble ledger on base with engraved lettering.
[With three other family graves in metal fenced plot - see B-51, B-50 and B-48]

Measurements
Ledger: h-5cm w-65cm l-172cm
Base: h-19cm

Three unmarried daughters of Revd William James Newman and his wife Caroline **B-50**. All three sisters are buried here in Hockworthy, although Frances was living at South Town House, Dartmouth at the time of her death.

NEWMAN B-48

Frances Emma	d. 1933 (86 yrs)
William Frederick	d. 1920 (74 yrs)

Transcription

[furthest from the church]

[west] In fondest memory of / William Frederick NEWMAN, / M.A.Oxon. / (Vicar of this parish for 40 years) / who died at Hockworthy on June 19th. 1920 / in his 75th year. / This cross is erected / by his ever loving wife and children. / "Then shall the King say - 'Come ye blessed of / my father inherit the kingdom prepared for you / from the foundation of the world' " St Matt. XXV. 34.

[east] Also of / Frances Emma NEWMAN / (née WYNDHAM) widow of the Revd W F NEWMAN / born April 7th 1847, died July 6th 1933 / "But as for me, I will behold thy / presence in righteousness: / and when I awake up after Thy / likeness I shall be satisfied with it." / Ps.17.v.16. / "O may my soul on Thee repose".

Description
Rough granite cross with lily engraving on tapered base on concrete plinth. Lead lettering.
[With three other family graves in metal fenced plot - see B-51, B-50 and B-49]

Measurements
Total: h-163cm
Cross: h-117cm w-50cm d-17cm
Base: h-48cm w-59cm d-49cm
Kerbs: 468cm x 291cm
Railings: h-48cm

Elder son of Revd W J Newman & his wife Caroline **B-50**, Revd W F Newman became vicar of Hockworthy when his father died in 1880 *[see p.75]*. His wife Frances was born in Wiltshire.

77

NO NAME   A-8
?   d. 1882

Transcription

. . 1882
[Fragment which appears to be part of a headstone]

Description	Measurements
Square kerbs with fragment of a headstone.	Kerbs: 230cm x 290cm

A headstone fragment was found close by this grave, which appears to fit with what remains. Were this to be so, the following were buried in the churchyard in that year, 1882:
Jesse REDWOOD, Lucklies, Hockworthy. Buried 12 March 1882. Aged 2 yrs.
Jane JENNINGS, Hockworthy. Buried 10 June 1882. Aged 7 yrs.
Lily Laura SNOW, Hendom, Hockworthy. Buried 2 July 1882. Aged 2 yrs.
Elizabeth STEVENS, Hockworthy. Buried 13 November 1882. Aged 77 yrs.

PALFREY   B-36
Catherine   d. 1925 (65 yrs)

Transcription

[left hand page of open book tablet] In / loving memory / of / Catherine / PALFREY / who passed away / May 11th 1925 / aged 65 years.
[right hand page] 'Thy will be done'

Description	Measurements
Flat marble open book on ground. Lead lettering.	h-31cm w-39cm d-4cm

Catherine (née How) was born in Hockworthy in 1860. In 1883 she married Frank Kemp who died aged only 41 in 1893 and with whom she had three children. They farmed at Cudmore on the Huntsham estate. Catherine was married again in 1897 to George Palfrey **B-37** who took on the farming at Cudmore. They had one son. Catherine's sister, Charlotte Isabella, married firstly Robert White Shattock **B-33**, followed by William James How.

PALFREY   B-35

Francis J H	*d. 1919 (16 yrs)*
Herbert C	*d. 1905 (6 yrs)*

Transcription

[east] IHS / In / loving / memory of / Herbert C PALFREY / died December 4th 1905 / aged 6 years
[west] Also of / Francis J H PALFREY / who fell asleep March 6th 1919 / aged 16 years / "Behold I come quickly"
[south] "Suffer little children / to come unto me".

Description
Marble cross broken off and standing beside three tiered base on concrete plinth. Lead lettering.

Measurements
Cross: h-57cm w-33cm d-7cm
1st base: h-8cm w-19cm d-16cm
2nd base: h-11cm w-29cm d-26cm
3rd base: h-22cm w-38cm d-35cm

Herbert Charles was the second of four sons of George **B-37** and Catherine **B-36** Palfrey. He was born in Bampton in 1900. Also born in Bampton, in 1902, Francis James H was their fourth son.

PALFREY   B-37

George   *d. 1934 (63 yrs)*

Transcription

[left hand page of open book tablet] In / loving memory / of / George PALFREY / who passed away / Feb 26th 1934 / Aged 63 years.
[right hand page] 'Rest in the Lord.'

Description
Flat marble open book on ground. Lead lettering.
[top left hand corner broken off]

Measurements
h-32cm w-40cm d-4cm

George's family came from the Brendon Hills. He was born in Upton, the son of James and Elizabeth Palfrey, and married Catherine, the daughter of Charles and Charlotte How **B-30**. George was a well-respected sheep and cattle farmer and breeder who took on Cudmore when he married Catherine in 1897. They had four sons, all born in Bampton, two of whom are buried in **B-35**.

PARR   D-12

Frederick John — d. 1986 (67 yrs)
Mary — d. 1996 (75 yrs)

Transcription

Remembered / with love / Frederick John / PARR / Born 6th Sept. 1918 / died 5th March 1986 / also his wife / Mary / born 4th June 1921 / died 18th June 1996

Description

Ogee shape grey polished granite. Engraved silver lettering. Engraved flowers and book bottom left. Oval fronted base on concrete plinth. Integral flower pot.

Measurements

Total: h-71cm w-54cm d-8cm
Base: h-3cm w-62cm d-23cm

Frederick's father Frederick Richard Parr married a widow Florence Disney (née Simms) in 1918 whereupon they took on Turnham farm, as tenants of the Newmans at the Vicarage (which later became Hockworthy House). Frederick and Mary (née Snell) married in 1946 and purchased Turnham when the Newmans sold up in the 1950s. Their son Geoffrey and his family continue to farm here.

Section E

PAVEY   B-17

Henry Allen	d. 1851 (87 yrs)
Infants x 2	
Mary	d. 1831 (74 yrs)

Transcription

Sacred / to the / memory of Mary / wife of Henry Allen PAVEY / who departed this life May 9th / 1831 aged 74 years. / Also of / Henry Allen PAVEY / the above named who departed / this life October 17th 1851 / Aged 87 years / Also two infant grandsons. / Sons of William and / Mary PAVEY of Thornland / in this parish.

Description	Measurements
Stone round top with square and scotia shoulders. Engraved perimeter line. Engraved lettering.	h-121cm w-71cm d-7cm

A retired farmer born at Wambrook, Dorset, Henry went to live with his daughter and son-in-law at Staple Cross after the death of his wife Mary. Parish registers indicate the two grandsons to be: Joseph Pavey, who was buried 22 March 1834, aged 9 mths and Henry Pavey, buried 1 January 1822, aged ten days. The boy's parents, William and Mary, lived at Thornlands, a Grade II listed 17th century farmhouse.

PEPPERELL   C-3

| Sarah Mary | d. 1916 (43 yrs) |

Transcription

[south kerb] In loving memory of Sarah Mary PEPPERELL who died Jan 1st 1916, aged 43 years.
[east kerb] "At Rest"
[Fewings, Tiverton]

Description	Measurements
Granite kerbs with pyramid topped corner posts. Raised lettering on polished champhered face.	h-38cm w-92cm d-11cm l-187cm Posts: h-40cm

One of four daughters and two sons of carpenter John Weeks Pepperell (1841-1914) and Almira (née Weymouth) (1840-1915), Sarah was born in Teignmouth in 1873. She was a self employed dressmaker working from her parents home in Teignmouth. Her sister Almira, wife of Walter Northam *[see p.25]*, was the school teacher living at The Villa, Hockworthy where Sarah died of heart disease aged 42.

PERRY   **B-15**

7 x children
Mary   d. 1860 (84 yrs)
William   d. 1834 (60 yrs)

Transcription

Sacred / to the memory of / William PERRY / of this Parish / who departed this life / April 22nd 1834 / Aged 60 years / Also Mary wife of the above / Who departed this life / April 16th 1860 Aged 84 years / Also 7 children of the above / Who lie near this stone / Watch therefore for ye know not / What hour your Lord doth come.

Description   Measurements
Stone peon top splayed sides to hipped lower section. Engraved lettering.   h-144cm w-81cm d-9cm

Mary, who was born in Hockworthy, outlived her husband by twenty-six years. The family lived at Hockford where Mary remained after her husband's death. William was a cooper *[a person skilled in making barrels, casks, etc.]*. There is possibly more than one Perry family in the area, but the Burial Register lists the following children, who are probably the seven mentioned on the headstone: 30 Oct 1802 James son of William & Mary Perry; 22 May 1803 Maria Perry; 29 Dec 1810 Thomas Perry; 2 Jan 1811 Mary Perry; 11 Nov 1811 Hannah Perry; 20 Nov 1814 John Perry aged 2 months and 10 Mar 1816 Elizabeth Perry aged 2 days. William & Mary are probably the parents of William Perry **A-4**.

PERRY   **A-4**

Mary   d. 1876 (64 yrs)
William

Transcription

In / memory of / Mary / wife of William PERRY / late of this parish / who died March the 16th 1876 / aged 64 years / Patient and meek beneath afflictions rod / and why her faith and hope were fixed on God / Also near the stone / lieth three children of the above.

Description   Measurements
Gothic stone. Engraved lettering.   h-136cm w-62cm d-8cm

William was a watch and clock maker born in Hockworthy. He could be the only surviving son of William and Mary Perry **B-15**. Mary was a dressmaker, born in Burlescombe. They lived at Hockford but after his wife's death, in 1881 he was with his married daughter Bridget North at Bathpool, near Taunton. The following have been identified in the Burial Registers as the children who are referred to on the headstone: James, buried 1834 "aged 1 fortnight"; Adra, buried 1839 aged 2 years and William buried 1848 aged 19 years.

PERRY   D-10
Joan Ada   *d. 1987 (67 yrs)*

Transcription

In / memory of / Joan Ada (Ann) / PERRY / 1920 – 1987 / Much loved by all her family / Her life a beautiful memory / her absence a silent grief.

Description	Measurements
Speckled grey polished granite. Engraved lettering.	Total: h-75cm w-53cm d-8cm Base: h-8cm w-61cm d-28cm

Mrs Perry lived in the bungalow built by Mrs Falls **C-12**. After her retirement from West Sussex County Council, she came to Staple Cross to be near her daughter from her second marriage, Sue Northam. She had met her two husbands, both pilots, when serving in the WAAF during the 1939-45 war. The family are not related to the other Perry family in the churchyard. Near the bungalow is the Staple well, from where the gypsies from Chimney Down would collect their water.

PRESCOTT		D-5
Amy	d. 2002 (74 yrs)	
Percy	d. 1999 (76 yrs)	

Transcription

In loving memory / of / a much loved husband / Percy PRESCOTT / died 15th July 1999 / aged 76 years / also his dear wife / Amy / died 1st June 2002 / Aged 74 years / Together again
[R Grant]

Description
Ogee light grey polished granite. Integral flower pot. Base on concrete plinth. Engraved black lettering.

Measurements
Total: h-72cm w-54cm d-8cm
Base: h-9cm w-62cm d-31cm

The son of James and Emily Prescott, Percy married Amy (daughter of Fred Curtis) in 1919. They farmed at Hurd's Farm. Percy's uncle Percy is commemorated on the war memorial [see p. 19] in the church, and several of his uncles are on the Roll of Honour in the porch [see pp. 25 and 27]

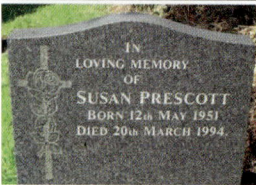

PRESCOTT		D-3
Susan	d. 1994 (42 yrs)	

Transcription

In / loving memory / of / Susan PRESCOTT / Born 12th May 1951 / died 20th March 1994

Description
Ogee, dark grey polished granite. Engraved cross and rose at the top. Integral flower pot in base. Base on concrete plinth. Engraved silver lettering.

Measurements
Total: h-73cm w-55cm d-8cm
Base: h-9cm w-62cm d-32cm

The daughter of Frank Kerslake and his wife Beatrice Watts (née Barnett) from Bristol who took over the running of the Staple Cross pub from Alice Redwood (who had continued holding the licence after the death of her husband John **A-3**). Frank ran the pub for c. 20 years. In 1972, Susan married Keith Prescott, a builder, who for many years has done an excellent job of maintaining Hockworthy church. Members of his family are commemorated on the two war memorials in the church.

PRESCOTT D-6
James *d. 1993 (75 yrs)*

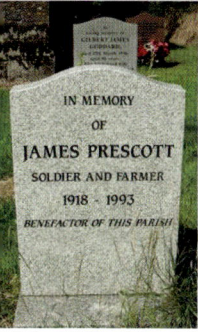

Transcription
In memory / of / James PRESCOTT / soldier and farmer / 1918 - 1993 / Benefactor of this parish

Description
Ogee, engraved black lettering. Light grey polished granite. Base on concrete plinth.
[R. Grant]

Measurements
Total: h-65cm w-44cm d-8cm
Base: h-9cm w-46cm d-26cm

The son of James and Alice Prescott, James (Jim) was born on 18 May 1918 in Hendon, Middlesex. His brother, a Royal Air Force pilot, was killed in 1940. Jim joined the London Scottish Regiment before the war and was serving with No.2 Commando when he took part in the raid on St Nazaire, "Operation Chariot", in March 1942. He left the army with the rank of Sergeant Major. After the war, his parents bought East Holelake, a privately owned farm in the middle of the Huntsham Estate, which Jim farmed until he moved to Honiton, where he died in 1993. His bequest to Hockworthy enabled the restoration of the village hall, which is now a centre for village activities. His family was not related to any of the other local Prescott families.

"This building was given / to the parish of Hockworthy / for use as a Village Hall / by the Trustees of the late / W F Wyndham Newman Esq. JP / of Hockworthy House / in memory of him and his family's / long association with the parish / AD 1953"

REDWOOD		A-3
Vera [Maud]	d. 1939 (30 yrs)	
Alice	d. 1950 (73 yrs)	
John	d. 1949 (76 yrs)	

Transcription

[east] In loving memory of / Vera / Daughter of John & Alice REDWOOD / fell asleep Aug. 12th 1939 / Aged 30 years.

[south] Also of / her father / John REDWOOD / who fell asleep / July 27th 1949 / Aged 76 years.

[north] Also of / her mother / Alice REDWOOD / who fell asleep / April 12th 1950 / aged 73 years.

Description	Measurements
Grey granite wheeled cross on tapered base on stone plinth. Square kerbs. Green glass chippings. Black lettering on polished surface.	Total: h-94cm
	Cross: h-61cm w-41cm d-10cm
	Base: h 31cm w 66cm d 32cm
	Kerbs: 200cm x 168cm

Although a carpenter and wheelwright, John (born in Hockworthy) and Alice (née Salisbury, born Huntsham) held the licence for the pub at Staple Cross for nearly 50 years. It was a Wiveliscombe Hancock brewery tied pub, only selling beer and cider, and no spirits, wine or food. After John's death, Alice continued to run the pub before going to live with her daughter. Engaged to be married to Mr W Newberry, Vera Maud, their youngest daughter, was living and working at the pub when she died of meningitis. Death certificate dates her death as 10 Aug 1940. The burial register records a date of 14th Aug 1940.

REDWOOD		D-4
Betty	d. 2006 (89 yrs)	
Lionel Jack	d. 1993 (80 yrs)	

Transcription

In / loving memory / of / Lionel / Jack / REDWOOD / a dear husband / and father / died 20th Nov. 1993 / aged 80 years. / Also / Betty REDWOOD / a beloved wife / and mother / Died 26th June 2006 / aged 89 years

Description	Measurements
Offset peon, light grey polished granite. Decorated with engraved church window and cross. Peon shaped base on concrete plinth. Engraved black lettering.	Total: h-87cm w-61cm d-8cm
	Base: h-8cm w-76cm d-26cm

The son of John and Alice **A-3**, who ran the Staple Cross pub, where Lionel was born. He took over his elder brother Herbert's butchery business in May 1944. He was well known hereabouts for his gift of healing, for which he never accepted payment. As well as curing warts and skin diseases in humans, he could walk amongst an infected herd of cattle and cure them of ring worm without even touching them. His wife, Hilda Betty (née Pearce) stayed at West View, Staple Cross after her husband's death. Their son Tony worked alongside his father delivering meat, and has kindly shared his encyclopaedic knowledge of the local area for this book.

ROBERTS	A-24
Elizabeth	d. 1850 (77 yrs)
NO NAME	**A-22 A-23**

Transcription
Elizabeth ROBERTS / Died / April 16th 1850 Aged / 77 years

Description	Measurements
Half round top. Stone. Half round foot stone. Engraved lettering. Elizabeth and John are flanked by 2 headstones with no lettering to the south (**A-22** and **A-23**) and another **A-26** to the north.	A-22: h-25cm w-34cm d-8cm A-23: h-25cm w-34cm d-8cm A-26: h-9cm w-30cm d-6cm A-24: h-50cm w-41cm d-10cm

Elizabeth was born c.1783, the wife of John Roberts **A-25**. It is unknown who lies under the similar shaped headstones alongside. With the exception of Henry Roberts, who was buried aged 18 months on 2 March 1817 who could be her son, there are no other likely children recorded in the Burial Registers. See **A-25** below.

ROBERTS	A-25 A-26
John	d. 1868 (97 yrs)

Transcription
John ROBERTS / died / December 10th 1868 / Aged 97 years

Description	Measurements
Half round top. Stone. Half round foot stone. Engraved lettering. Elizabeth and Robert are flanked by 2 headstones on their right and 1 on their left, no lettering. h-19cm w-34cm d-8cm [very small round topped headstone marker with unmarked footstone]	h-44cm w-41cm d-8cm

At 97, John is the oldest person recorded as being buried in the churchyard. He was from Lydeard St Lawrence in Somerset and lived at Queens Lodge, near The Villa, in Hockworthy. The 1851 census describes him as a "pauper, Ag. Lab". After his wife's death in 1850, a widow from Sampford Peverell, Elizabeth Harwood, became his housekeeper. She died six months after John, aged 84, and was buried at Hockworthy on 4 June 1869. Is it possible that she is buried alongside him in unmarked grave **A-26**?

SHATTOCK B-33

Robert White — d. 1893 (47 yrs)

HOW

Beatrice Elizabeth — d. 1897 (1 yr)
Gertrude Mary — d. 1897 (2 yrs)

Transcription

[west] In loving memory of / Robert White SHATTOCK / of Stallenge Thorn / who died April 27th 1893 / aged 47 years / "Lord remember me" Luke 23.42. *[south]* Beatrice Elizabeth HOW / died April 16th 1897 / Aged 1 year *[east]* Suffer little children / to come unto me *[north]* Gertrude Mary HOW / Died April 8th 1897 / Aged 2 years.

Description

Stone traditional wheeled cross on three tiered base with square kerb. Lead lettering.

Measurements

Total: h-154cm
Cross: h-89cm w-45cm d-11cm
1st base: h-22cm w-38cm d-36cm
2nd base: h-23cm w-49cm d-46cm
3rd base: h-20cm w-67cm d-64cm
Kerbs: 129cm x 248cm

Born in Ashbrittle, the son of Robert & Mary Jane (née White). In 1876 he married Charlotte Isabella (daughter of Charles & Charlotte How **B-30**) and they farmed at Stallenge Thorne. Robert was churchwarden 1888-93. They had two sons, Charles George b. 1890 and Robert William b. 1893. In 1894, after Robert's death, Charlotte married William J How, a school master, who later farmed near Reading. She died in Wallingford, Berks in 1946. Their two daughters are buried here with their grandfather.

SHOPLAND B-31

James — d. 1928 (80 yrs)
Mary Ann — d. 1911 (61 yrs)

Transcription

In / loving memory of / Mary Ann / the beloved wife of / James SHOPLAND / of Court Hall, / died Nov. 5th 1911, / aged 61 years. / "Thy will be done." / Also of the above named / James SHOPLAND / died March 11th 1928 / aged 80 years.

Description

Grey speckled polished granite cross on three bases. Surround square kerbs. Lead Lettering.

Measurements

Total: h-145cm
Cross: h-92cm w-46cm d-13cm
1st base: h-13cm w-26cm d-25cm
2nd base: h-18cm w-39cm d-38cm
3rd base: h-20cm w-51cm d-51cm
Kerbs: 214cm x 216cm

Two generations are buried side by side, James and Mary Ann being parents of Samuel **B-32**. James (born Burrington, Devon) and Mary Ann (born Kings Nympton) farmed at Denton Farm, Rose Ash, near South Molton, where five of their children were born. They began farming at Court Hall between 1891 and 1901. Mary Ann died at Court Hall, after which James moved to Uplowman. He was churchwarden of Hockworthy 1901-1905.

SHOPLAND B-32

| Rosina Charlotte | d. 1978 (83 yrs) |
| Samuel | d. 1965 (85 yrs) |

Transcription

In loving memory of / a dear husband / Samuel SHOPLAND / of The Villa / who fell asleep 4th October 1965 / aged 85 years. / Also his dear wife / Rosina Charlotte / who died 15th February 1978 / aged 83 years / Peace perfect peace

Description
Grey speckled granite square top with square shoulders and lead lettering. Kerbs extending from base of headstone with two square posts all set on concrete base.

Measurements
Headstone: h-77cm w-77cm d-10cm
Kerbs: 78cm x 190cm

Samuel and his wife Rosina lived at The Villa, his parents **B-31** having lived at Court Hall. Rosina (who married Samuel in 1924) was daughter of Samuel and Ellen Dart **B-18**. Samuel farmed with his father at Court Hall, and served in the Great War *[see p. 28]*. Of Samuel's sisters, Florence Emma, married James Cottrell in 1920; Mary Maria married Herbert Shattock in 1907, and Alice Jane married William Albert Stone **B-25**.

SMITH E-6

| Andrew J Bay | d. 1996 (86 yrs) |
| Barbara E G | d. 1995 (84 yrs) |

Transcription

Barbara E G SMITH / died 25 August 1995 / Aged 84. / Andrew J Bay SMITH / died 17 November 1996 / Aged 86. / "In thy presence / is fullness of joy" / Psalm 16. v. 11.

Description
Cremation stone. Grey slate. Engraved silver lettering.

Measurements
w-46cm d-30cm

Known as "Bay", Andrew John Smith was born in the Shetland Islands. He worked for a bank in Scotland before moving to London in 1933 where he met his wife, Barbara Evelyn Grosvenor Flower, who came from Surrey. He retired from the bank in 1970 and moved to Cornwall. In 1984 they bought Hole Lake No. 1 from the Huntsham Estate, and renamed it Briar Cottage.

SPRAGUE		B-40
Elizabeth	d. 1905 (80 yrs)	
Mary	d. 1865 (7 yrs)	
Robert	d. 1879 (66 yrs)	
Simon	d. 1899 (48 yrs)	

Transcription

In loving memory of / IHS / Robert SPRAGUE, / who died Sept 23rd 1879, / aged 66. / Also of Elizabeth, / his beloved wife / who died April 23rd 1905, / aged 80. / Simon, died July 25th 1899, / Aged 48. / And Mary, Jany 24th 1865, / aged 7 years. / Son and daughter of the above / "Not gone from memory, not gone from love / but gone to their father's home above"

Description	Measurements
Stone Gothic shape with ornate sides. Engraved lettering.	h-121cm w-71cm d-8cm
[under yew tree]	

Robert, an agricultural labourer born in Ashbrittle, married Elizabeth, daughter of Henry Broomfield in 1848. After Robert's death, in an accident in a quarry, Elizabeth remained at Hurford Cottage with her unmarried son Simon, a shoe maker, her daughter Mary Annie, a school teacher, and a lodger, Mrs Mary Moon **C-2**. Elizabeth was the sister of Henry Broomfield **B-39**. It has not been possible to identify who might be commemorated by the small cross beside the headstone **B-41**.

STEVENS		A-33
William Edward	d. 1858 (3 yrs)	

Transcription

In / memory / of William Edward STEVENS / of this Parish / who died Febry 17th 1858 / Aged 3 years. / The days of his youth hast thou shortened

Description	Measurements
Stone round top with square and scotia shoulders. Engraved line perimeter. Hole in the top. Engraved lettering.	h-104cm w-54cm d-7cm

Son of Sarah (née Mallett) and John Stevens, William Edward was born on 19 Jun 1854 at Hockworthy. A yeoman farmer, John worked 40 acres at Hurd's Farm, Hockworthy.

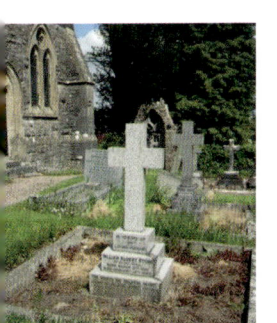

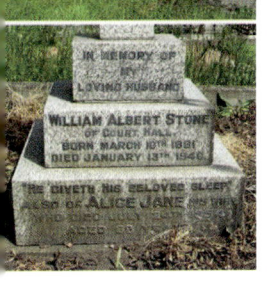

STONE		B-25
Alice Jane	d. 1954 (68 yrs)	
William Albert	d. 1946 (64 yrs)	

Transcription

In memory of / my / loving husband / William Albert STONE / of Court Hall, / born March 10th 1881 / died January 13th 1946. / "He giveth his beloved sleep." / Also of Alice Jane his wife / who died July 24th 1954 / aged 68 years

Description
Pale grey speckled polished granite cross on three tiered base and concrete plinth. Square Kerb surround. Pavement surround. Lead lettering.

Measurements
Total: h-137cm
Cross: h-87cm w-46cm d-10cm
1st base: h-16cm w-46cm d-41cm
2nd base: h-18cm w-46cm d-36cm
3rd base: h-18cm w-62cm d-57cm
Kerbs: 211cm x 199cm

Born in Morebath, in 1910 William married Alice, the daughter of James and Mary Shopland **B-31** who farmed Court Hall. He took over Court Hall when his father-in-law died in 1920. William was churchwarden 1921-1946, and manager of Hockworthy School. Alice was sister to Samuel Shopland **B-32**, and she moved to The Villa after William died.

STONE		E-3
Caroline Amy	d. 1989 (87 yrs)	

Transcription

In loving / memory of / Caroline / Amy / STONE / 1902 – 1989

Description
Light grey granite. Cremation stone. Engraved lettering.

Measurements
w-31cm d-31cm

Originally from Scarborough in Yorkshire, Caroline was the widow of a Sussex architect, George Henry Stone (1903-48). After his early death, she moved to Devon to be near her daughter, Delia Goodall. She lived at the Masonic Home in Exeter where she died.

TALBOT		A-15
John	d. 1861 (55 yrs)	
Mary	d. 1878 (75 yrs)	

Transcription

Sacred / to the memory of / John TALBOT / of this Parish / Who departed this life / July 28th 1861 Aged 55 years / In the midst of life / We are in death / Also of / Mary wife of the above / Who departed this life / On Christmas Day 1878 / Aged 75 years / Her end was peace.

Description
Gothic top with square shoulders. Leaning forwards. Engraved lettering.

Measurements
h-114cm w-56cm d-8cm

John and Mary (née Fowler) farmed at Holcombe Rogus and had seven children. The Talbots trace a long lineage to the beginning of the 18th century in Holcombe Rogus. By 1861 he had moved to Vicarage Farm, Hockworthy and was farm bailiff for Revd Newman **B-50**. Their third son, Jesse **A-14**, took over from his father as bailiff.

TALBOT		A-14
Albert Jesse		
Elizabeth	d. 1885 (41 yrs)	
Frederick Mark		
Jesse	d. 1902 (63 yrs)	
Lewis John		
Mabel Annie		

MELLEN
Katherine

EIVERS
Alice

Transcription

IHS / In loving memory of / Elizabeth TALBOT / who died May 9th 1885 / Aged 41 years / also Jesse husband of the above / who died March 1st 1902 / aged 63 years / We mourn the loss of those we loved / and did our best to save / beloved on earth regretted gone / remembered in the grave / Also in memory of / Mabel Annie TALBOT / Lewis John TALBOT / Albert Jesse TALBOT / Frederick Mark TALBOT / Katherine MELLEN / Alice EIVERS / who died in Australia.

Description
Tall Gothic upright stone. Front edges champhered of top 110cm. Flowerpot. Lead lettering.

Measurements
h-144cm w-74cm d-8cm

See following page for biographical information.

A-14 TALBOT
The son of John and Mary Talbot **A-15**, Jesse took over from his father as bailiff for the Newmans. He married Elizabeth Perry in 1864. Of their seven children, only their two eldest remained in England; Lewis John (b.1867 died in Bridgwater in 1913), and Edith (b.1866 and died in Taunton in 1917). The others emigrated to Australia: Albert Jesse (b. 1869 arrived in Queensland aged 17. He started work as a butcher, but moved around the country finally settling in Western Australia where he died a very successful farmer in 1952); Alice (b. 1872 married James Eivers. They had 3 children and she died in 1939); Frederick Mark (b. 1874, died Perth 27 Aug 1862); Mabel Annie (b. 1879 and died 19 June 1964) and Katherine (b. 1881. She married Sidney James Marshall who died in 1916. Her second husband was John Mellen and she died in Perth in 1946.)

TANNER B-16

Peter Treherne   *d. 2006 (73 yrs)*

Transcription

In loving memory of / Peter Treherne / TANNER / 7-5-1933 ~ 26-5-2006
[P.Hayman]

Description
White stone peon top framed by ivy, corn and floral engraving. Traditional wheeled cross design on the reverse.

Measurements
h-98cm w-56cm d-11cm

In 1989 Peter and his wife Sylvia moved from Cornwall to Thornlands, where Sylvia continues to live.

THOMAS C-8

Ruby Winifred   *d. 1995 (83 yrs)*
Walter Lionel   *d. 1965 (57 yrs)*

Transcription

In / loving memory of / a dear husband and father / Walter Lionel THOMAS / who fell asleep / 13th February 1965 / aged 57 years. / At Rest. / And his dear wife / Ruby Winifred / died 21st August 1995 / aged 83 years.

Description
Square top double rounded shoulders in light great polished granite. Oval fronted base on concrete plinth. Integral flower pot. Black lettering.

Measurements
Total: h-88cm w-61cm d-10cm
Base: h-11cm w-77cm d-21cm

The sixth of eight children of John and Nelly Thomas of Sparkhayne, Lionel married Ruby Winifred (née Reed from Oakford) in 1932. They farmed at Redwoods, as tenants of the Huntsham Estate, followed by their son Derek who bought the farm when outlying farms on the estate were sold in the 1960s. Of their two daughters, Enid married Paul Clark while Jean, the eldest, is married to Malcolm Goddard, son of Louis and Eveline Goddard **C-9**.

TOOZE A-29

| Mary | d. 1863 (75 yrs) |
| Samuel | d. 1862 (76 yrs) |

Transcription

In memory of Samuel TOOZE / of this parish who died / February 18th 1862 / Aged 76 years / Also Mary his wife / Who died July 29th 1863 / Aged 75 years.

Description

Stone half round with square and scotia shoulders. Engraved lettering.

Measurements

h-107cm w-53cm d-5cm

Both Samuel and Mary Tooze were born in Hockworthy. He was an agricultural labourer who lived at Bray's Cottage, which at that time was two separate dwellings. After Samuel and Mary died, one son William **A-28** continued living in their house with his sister Elizabeth, while their elder son Samuel, a shoemaker, and his family lived next door. The Burial Registers record Samuel and Mary's surname as Twoze, which contradicts the spelling on the headstone and census returns.

[Devon Heritage Service: 3083A/PR/1/8]

TWOSE A-28

| William | d. 1884 (61 yrs) |

Transcription

In / Memory of / William TWOSE / died August 25 1884. Aged 61 yrs / for 27 years a faithful servant / at Ashbrittle Rectory

Description

Stone. Square top with square and extended scotia shoulders. Hipped base. Bevelled edge. Engraved lettering. The inscription has recently been reengraved.

Measurements

h-77cm w-68cm d-8cm

Although the headstone reads Twose, William's death certificate and the Burial Register spell his name Tooze. The son of Samuel and Mary Tooze **A-29**, William and his unmarried sister Elizabeth continued living at Bray's Cottage after their parents died. Elizabeth was a seamstress who acted as his housekeeper. William was under-gardener at the Rectory, Ashbrittle. Their elder brother, Samuel, lived in the other half of Bray's Cottage, followed by his son Thomas, both of whom were shoemakers. The inscription has recently been re-engraved.

[Devon Heritage Service: 3083A/PR/1/8]

VICKERY		B-9
James	d. 1913 (73 yrs)	
Mary	d. 1915 (73 yrs)	

Transcription

IHS / In loving memory of / James VICKERY / who died July 30th 1913 / Aged 73 years / Also of Mary wife of the above / who died March 15th 1915 / aged 73 years / They rest in peace.
[Fewings, Tiverton]

Description
Round top with double ornate shoulders. Hipped lower section. Lead lettering.

Measurements
h-121cm w-68cm d-8cm

Born in 1840, James was the son of Benjamin and Frances (née Hobbs). A Hockworthy man, James married Mary Tarr from East Anstey. James was a dairyman at Holelake and he and Mary had ten children: Benjamin, Thomas, James, William, Alice, John, Mary, Lucy, Edward and Albert **A-5**.

VICKERY		A-5
Albert	d. 1958 (72 yrs)	
Maud	d. 1958 (70 yrs)	
Stella Frances	d. 2002 (81 yrs)	
Vera Florence	d. 2002 (77 yrs)	

Transcription

In loving memory of / Maud VICKERY / died / 24th March 1958 / aged 70 years / Albert VICKERY / died / 1st April 1958 / Aged 72 years. / *[Separate stone below]* and their daughters / Vera Florence / Died 3rd May 2002 / aged 77 years / Stella Frances / died 22nd Dec. 2002 / Aged 81 years

Description
Reclining open book of polished granite on plinth placed within champfered kerbs with square wing posts. Second stone flat on the ground in front of the book. Lead lettering.

Measurements
Book: h-45cm w-56cm d-11cm
Slate base: h-7cm w-61cm d-61cm
Tablet: h-30cm w-47cm d-5cm
Kerb:

The son of James and Mary **B-9**, Albert was born at Holelake. In 1913 he married Maud Baker from Cove and they had nine children. They took on the tenancy of a farm in Hampshire before settling at Kimmeridge Farm, near Wareham in Dorset. Their two unmarried daughters, Vera and Stella, whose ashes are buried here with their parents, bought a farm near Dorchester with one of their brothers. Both died in 2002 in Wareham.

WARE   B-44

| Elizabeth | d. 1909 (38 yrs) |
| Thomas | d. 1953 (86 yrs) |

Transcription

In loving memory of / Elizabeth WARE / who died Jan. 13th 1909 / Aged 38 years / Also of / Thomas WARE / husband of the above / who died Jan. 27th 1953 / Aged 86 years / "At Rest"

Description	Measurements
Round top with square and scotia shoulders. Engraved lettering.	h-100cm w-66cm d-8cm

Thomas was a carpenter and sub-postmaster in the Hockworthy Post Office, which was located in the western part of Hurfords Mead, at that time two dwellings. He was born in Holcombe Rogus, and Elizabeth his wife was born in Hockworthy. Their two sons Harold Edgar and David Alfred were also born in Hockworthy and their names are recorded on the tablet in the porch of the church *[see p.30]*. Thomas was a widower for 44 years.

WATKINSON   E-2

| Geoffrey | d. 2007 (88 yrs) |
| Greta | d. 1986 (67 yrs) |

Transcription

Greta WATKINSON / 24th Nov. 1919 / 15th Dec. 1986 / Geoffrey / WATKINSON / 5th May 1919 / 29th June 2007

Description	Measurements
Cremation stone. Slate beside south wall of church. Engraved lettering.	h-31cm w-46cm

Geoffrey and Greta (née Walker) married in Birmingham in 1943. They came from Uffculme to Copper Ridge (which had been built by Mary Ann Hussey **B-3** c. 1937 on Hole Farm land, which her son Maurice was farming). They had three daughters. Geoffrey was a farmer and latterly a postman at Uffculme. He is remembered for his flower arrangements in the church, a skill he taught after his retirement.

W.C.   B-19

see Cleeve, William

WENSLEY		A-17
Hannah	d. 1877 [76 yrs]	
William	d. 1868 (66 yrs)	

Transcription

In / memory of / William WENSLEY / who died Nov 4th 1868 / aged 66 years. / The day of the Lord / so cometh / as a thief in the night / also Hannah / wife of the above / who died March 16th 1877

Description	Measurements
Stone Norman shape with engraved lettering. *[Half buried behind the holly tree]*	h-70cm w-48cm d-8cm

Ashbrittle-born William, was a dairyman at Hendom, Hockworthy, a Huntsham estate farm. Hannah (née Winter) was born in Wellisford, Somerset. Their son James (a farmer at South Staple Downs) married Caroline, daughter of Robert and Jane Ash **A-31**. The holly tree is believed to mark the burial of a gypsy child who died on Chimney Down. Stories are told of how the open casket was carried round the caravans in the encampment with every family placing a posy of flowers in the coffin, before the child was brought down to the churchyard for burial.

WHITE		C-6
Harriett	d. 1892 (63 yrs)	

Transcription

Harriett WHITE / died Nov̲ 3rd 1892 aged 63 / "Whom the Lord loveth he chaseneth."

Description	Measurements
Small stone cross under yew tree. Engraved lettering.	h-68cm w-50cm d-14cm

Harriett was born in Upton, Somerset, c. 1830, and worked as a housemaid at Cowlings Farm on the Huntsham Estate before marrying Henry White from Wiveliscombe in 1854. He was a blacksmith and they lived at the smithy at Bone Gate (otherwise known as Borden Gate). Henry had earlier practiced his trade at Loxbeare, Devon. He was still at Borden Gate in 1906, but by 1911 the smithy had been taken on by Charles Carr and his wife Edith.

WHITE   B-47

Emma	d. 1876 (19 yrs)
Mary	d. 1865 (16 yrs)
Mary Ann	d. 1900 (82 yrs)
Thomas	d. 1887 (68 yrs)

Transcription

[west] In / loving / memory / of / Thomas WHITE / who died July 11th 1887 / Aged 68 years / "Thy will be done." / Also of Mary Ann / wife of the above / who died Nover 7th 1900 / Aged 82 years. *[J.Stemson]* *[north]* Also of his daughter / Emma / who died Seper 13th 1876 / aged 19 years *[south]* Also of his daughter / Mary / who died May 25th 1865 / aged 16 years.

Description
Stone cross on three tiered base with floral garland around the cross. Square kerbs with bevelled edge and pyramid corner and intermediate posts. Lead lettering.
[large unused space within the kerbs to the south, which may have a hidden inscription, now overgrown]

Measurements
Total: h-150cm
Cross: h-92cm w-57cm d-10cm
1st base: h-15cm w-34cm d-31cm
2nd base: h-23cm w-49cm d-47cm
3rd base: h-15cm w-67cm d-64cm
Kerbs: 216cm x 295cm

Born in Ottery St Mary, Thomas married Mary Ann Wheaton from Payhembury in 1847. They farmed 180 acres at Lea Barton, and Thomas served as churchwarden from 1868-1886. Of their known nine children, two daughters are buried here with their parents. After her husband's death, Mary Ann remained at Lea Barton until 1896 when the *Western Times* of 14 Feb 1896 reported a sale there of "live stock, implements, dairy goods and furniture", and moved to Bampton.

WOOD   B-1

| Fanny Ann | d. 1887 (21 yrs) |

Transcription

In loving remembrance of / Fanny Ann WOOD / who departed this life / 5th June 1887 / Aged 21 years / We loved her and no tongue can tell / how much we loved her and how well / God loved her too and thought it best / to take her home with him to rest

Description
Stone half round with small shoulders on small base. Carved lily and bevelled edge. Engraved lettering.
[fallen stone leaning on tree stump]

Measurements
h-75cm w-56cm d-8cm

The daughter of Mary and David Wood, a labourer from Rackenford, where Fanny was born, and where she had worked as a domestic servant at Wilson Farm. At the time of her death she was employed by Robert **B-33** and Charlotte Shattock at Stallenge Thorne farm as a domestic assistant.

FUNERAL ANNOUNCEMENT CARDS

[courtesy of Mrs Jean Goddard]

APPENDICES

Appendix A	Incumbents and Patrons	102
Appendix B	Church Rebuilding Faculty	104
Appendix C	Church Tablets	107
Appendix D	Churchwardens	109
Appendix E	Parish Farms and Houses	110
Appendix F	Monument Designs	112
Appendix G	Burial Registers 1578-2014	113
	Burial Registers Index	149

APPENDIX A

INCUMBENTS AND PATRONS
HOCKWORTHY CHURCH

When Christian worship started in Hockworthy is unknown. The earliest record is 1166. In 1184 the Patronage was given to the Canons of Leigh, to whom the Bishop of Exeter transferred the church in 1202.

INCUMBENTS		PATRONS
1166	Arnald	Henry de Berneville & Walter de Chevithorne
1184	Roger de Berneville (resigned)	Henry de Berneville & Walter de Chevithorne
1191	Ellis	The Prior of Canonsleigh
1274	Reginald de Molendinis	The Prior of Canonsleigh
1282	John de Kerdyf	The Prior of Canonsleigh
1309	John	Petronilla de Clare Abbess of Canonsleigh
1318	John de Menestoke	Petronilla de Clare Abbess of Canonsleigh
1325	William Chamberlayn	Margaret Aunger Abbess of Canonsleigh
1345	Thomas Sage	Juliana Lampre Abbess of Canonsleigh
1353	Simon Yem	Christina Edewis Abbess of Canonsleigh
1357	Roger Norman	Christina Edewis Abbess of Canonsleigh
1363	Walter Page	Christina Edewis Abbess of Canonsleigh
	Richard Covyntre	Christina Edewis Abbess of Canonsleigh
1399	William Redhode	Lucy Warre Abbess of Canonsleigh
1400	Thomas Whytyng	Lucy Warre Abbess of Canonsleigh
	William Cadyho	Lucy Warre Abbess of Canonsleigh
1427	John Penpaly	Mary Beauchamp Abbess of Canonsleigh
1454	John Westebeare	Joan Arundel Abbess of Canonsleigh
1464	Thomas Harry	Joan Arundel Abbess of Canonsleigh
1468	Walter at Wyll	Joan Arundel Abbess of Canonsleigh
1472	John Haselford	Alice Parker Abbess of Canonsleigh
1520	John Seccombe	Elizabeth Fowell Abbess of Canonsleigh

1575	Christopher Capron	John Blewette
1583	John Norris	John Blewette
1640	John Catford	John Bluett
1672	Thomas Bowring	John Bluett
1676	John Sharpe	Dorothea Wallop
1709	Thomas Thorne	Grace Sharpe
1732	Joseph Jones	John Jones
1750	Thomas Clarke	Robert Kerslake
1767	William Musgrave	John Withers
1779	The Hon. Francis Knollis	Thomas Sedgwick
1822	John Comins	Agnes Comins
1832	William Comins	John Lake
1860	William James Newman	William Newman
1880	William Frederick Newman	William Newman
1922	Edward Barton (with Holcombe Rogus)	F Wyndham Newman
1948	Noel Baron (with Holcombe Rogus)	Cuthbert Fleetwood-Hesketh
1952	John Adams (with Holcombe Rogus)	Helen Fleetwood-Hesketh
1956	John Davies (with Holcombe Rogus)	Helen Fleetwood-Hesketh
1964	Humphrey Peart (Sampford Peverell Team)	Helen Fleetwood-Hesketh
1976	Arthur Nelson (Sampford Peverell Team)	Helen Fleetwood-Hesketh
1981	Ivor March (Sampford Peverell Team)	Daphne Bruton
1986	Roy Perry (Sampford Peverell Team)	Daphne Bruton
1993	Brian Petty (Sampford Peverell Team)	Daphne Bruton
1999	Keith Gale (Sampford Peverell Team)	Daphne Bruton
2010	Susan Blade (Sampford Peverell Team)	John Doble

CURATES   (Vicars then often absent)

1714	Edward Locke			
1764	Josiah Wills	1833	Edmund Dicken
1769	Charles Vyvyan	1838	Lloyd Saunders
1788	George Lewis	1841	John Hayne
1801	Edmond Watts	1842	Epworth Luscombe
1807	Henry Hopkins	1845	Fred Trevor
1810	Henry Barker	1846	Thomas H Britton
1829	Charles Barne	1852	William J Newman
1831	Henry Ware	2002-10	Richard Cloete

APPENDIX B

CHURCH REBUILDING FACULTY

26 June 1863   FACULTY For taking down and Rebuilding the Parish Church of Hockworthy
Extracted by Frederick Sanders, Proctor – Exeter

To all to whom these Presents shall come

Henry by Divine permission Bishop of Exeter sends greeting. Whereas it has been represented unto us by Petition under the hands of The Reverend William James Newman Clerk Vicar of the Vicarage and Parish Church of Hockworthy, in the County of Devon and Diocese of Exeter and of the Churchwardens and other Inhabitants of the said Parish That the parish Church of Hockworthy aforesaid was and had been for some time past in a very dilapidated condition besides being too small and otherwise unfit for the accomodation of the Parishioners. That there were one hundred and twenty two sittings in the present Church all of which were inconvenient and uncomfortable and of these sittings twenty five were free and thirty (adapted for boys and adults) were in a Gallery at the West end of the Church and besides the proper sittings there were some moveable benches in the Chancel which accomodated about twenty persons.

That a Ground Plan of the then present Church shewing the arrangement of the sittings as was annexed to the said Petition marked 'A' - That in consequence of the dilapidated state of the said Church and to make better provision for the accomodations and requirements of the Parishioners it was proposed to take down the whole of the present Church except the Tower and to rebuild the church on an enlarged scale and seat the same according to certain plans prepared by Mr Greenway of Warwick Architect and a copy of one of the plans so prepared being a ground plan of the proposed new building was annexed to the said Petition marked 'B'.

That in the proposed new Church there would be no Gallery and instead of the then present high pews it was intended that the Church should be seated throughout in an uniform manner with open benches or sittings.

That the number of sittings in the new church would be one hundred and seventy four of which it was intended that one hundred and twenty three should be free and unappropriated.

That the estimated cost of taking down the said Church and rebuilding the same as aforesaid was nine hundred pounds of which six hundred and seventy pounds had been already raised by voluntary contributions and the residue was to be forthwith raised partly in like manner and partly by a Church rate and the said Petitioner the said William James Newman thereby undertook and guaranteed that such residue should be duly forthcoming when required.

That at a Vestry Meeting of the said parish of Hockworthy held on the eighth day of May one thousand eight hundred and sixty three and duly convened the said Plans were exhibited discussed and approved and it was resolved unanimously

"1. That the Parish Church was in a dilapidated state besides being too small and otherwise unfit for the accomodation of the Parishioners.
2. That the Vicar and Churchwardens be requested immediately "to Petition for a Faculty for taking down and rebuilding the Church.
3. That a Rate of sixpence in the pound which had been previously voted should be immediately collected and added to the other Funds already collected for the purpose of rebuilding the Church.
4. That Mr Ash be requested to keep an account of material drawn by the Parishioners for the Church (all the Farmers in the Parish having promised to double the value of their sixpenny rate by team labour).
5. That Mr Newman and Mr Darby be requested to forward the necessary plans and Statements to be inspected by the proper authorities previous to the obtaining a Faculty.
6. That all Mr Greenway's Plans and Specifications be accepted without any alterations and that measures be taken to increase the funds already collected. Mr Newman promised that he would guarantee to the Bishop and Chancellor the necessary sums.
7. That Mr Newman be requested to draw out a Petition for Faculty stating the above particulars ".

That in carrying out the said proposed works it would be necessary to remove certain Tablets and Monuments at present affixed against the Walls of the present church but the said Petitioners undertook that the greatest care should be observed in the removal of such Tablets and Monuments and that the same should be preserved and again affixed in some convenient part of the new Church when the same should have been built and completed.

That it would also be necessary to excavate and remove some portion of the earth surrounding the said Church or some parts thereof and in such excavation it might be necessary to remove certain graves monuments and headstones and to disinter any bodies that may be found there but the said Petitioners undertook to observe the greatest care and decency in such removals and to reinter any bodies and reinstate any monuments and headstones that it might be necessary to remove in a suitable and convenient part of the Churchyard of the said parish. That it was proposed immediately after the Faculty had been obtained for carrying out the matters aforesaid to commence the proposed works but previous to which an application would be made to the Lord Bishop of the Diocese for a Licence authorizing the due performance of Divine Service in the Schoolroom until the New Church should have been completed. The said Petitioners therefore humbly prayed that we would be pleased to grant our Licence or Faculty for the purposes aforesaid. And whereas an Intimation has been duly published in the said Church giving notice to all persons having anything to object to the premises that they should appear in the Cathedral Church of Saint Peter in Exeter in the Consistorial Court and place of Judicature there on the fifth day of June instant to propound their objicient And whereas upon the return of said Intimation all persons having anything to object to the Grant of the said License or Faculty were publically called in open court and no objection appeared And whereas the return of the said Intimation was continued until the twelfth day June instant on which last mentioned day all persons having anything to object to the Grant of the said Licence or Faculty were again publically called in open Court and no objicient appeared And whereas a copy of the said plan marked 'B' referred in the said Petition is hereto annexed

Now we the said Bishop do by these presents grant our License or Faculty for the several purposes mentioned in the said Petition according to the prayer thereof given under the seal of our Vicar General at Exeter this twenty sixth day June in the year of our Lord One thousand eight hundred and sixty three

Ralph Perkins

APPENDIX C

CHURCH TABLETS

Window 1
This window is erected by his / brothers and sisters in memory of / Charles Durnford GREENWAY Esquire / Born at Warwick July 7th 1837 Buried at Exeter / where he died on St John Baptist's day 1870
And to commemorate his gratuitous / services in the Restoration of this / Church which was carried out under his / designs and advice in the year of our / Lord 1864

Window 2
This window was erected in loving memory / of the Rev William James Newman / 26 years Vicar of this Parish during whose / incumbency and by whose efforts this Church was / rebuilt and the Vicarage much enlarged and improved / Born at Dartmouth Oct 6th 1819 Obit Jan 5th 1880

Also in loving memory of Caroline (neé Whitaker) wife of the above born at Bampton / Oxon April 23rd 1816 obit May 9th 1883. This woman / was full of good works and alms deeds which she did / by their two sons Rev W F and H R Newman Easter Day 1887

Chancel Wall
In loving Remembrance of / William Frederick Wyndham NEWMAN J P / of Hockworthy House in this Parish / who died on the 18th April 1947 in his 75 year / Grandson of William James NEWMAN and elder son / of William Frederick NEWMAN / Vicars of Hockworthy 1840 to 1920 / this tablet was erected by his wife Nora.
   [Revd William James Newman became curate of Hockworthy in 1852,
                      and was vicar from 1860 - 1880.
   His son Revd William Frederick Newman was vicar from 1880 - 1920]

Organ 1
This Organ was erected to the Glory of God / and in loving memory of Caroline Durnford, Alice Susanna and Frances Elizabeth Newman / by their brother Revd W Fred^{ck} Newman Jan 5th 1884.
Rebuilt by / Geo. Osmond / Organ Builder / Taunton

Organ 2
This organ was renovated and restored / by Wyndham Newman / In loving memory of his Father The Revd W F Newman / May 1929

Organ 3
Erected by grateful parishioners / In memory of / Phyllis Mary 'Molly' Heywood / 1918 – 2005 / who devoted her life to this Church / Organist for sixty five years

Near the Font
The Incorporated Society / for Building and Churches* / granted £60 towards rebuilding / this church, upon condition that / 123 seats numbered 1 to 13, and / 31 to 38 be reserved for the / use of the poorer inhabitants of / this parish.
[Wooden board]

*Incorporated Society for Promoting the Enlargement, Building and Repairing of Churches and Chapels

APPENDIX D

HOCKWORTHY CHURCHWARDENS

As no complete record of churchwardens has been located, this list is fragmentary.

YEAR	VICARS WARDEN	PEOPLES WARDEN
1721	Mr Jn Perry	
1723	Mr Richard Locke	
1726	Mr Thomas Locke	
1727	Mr Jonathan Bray	
1728	Mr Nicholas Stephens	
1729	Mr William Darby	
1730	Mr Jonathan Locke, jnr	
1754	Mr Robert Govier	
1808	Mr Edward Darby	
1843 –1851	Mr William Darby	
1852 - 1853	Mr Godfrey Webster	
1854 - 1858	Mr Henry Lucas	
1859 –1867	Mr Edward Darby	
1868 - 1884	Mr Thomas White	
1885 - 1886	Mr Thomas White	Mr Charles How
1887	Mr J White	Mr Charles How
1888 - 1893	Mr Robert W Shattock	Mr Charles How
1894 - 1895	Mr W H White	Mr Charles How
1896 - 1899	Mr Alfred White	Mr Charles How
1900	Mr Alfred White	Mr Obed I Hawkins
1901 - 1904	Mr Alfred White	Mr James Shopland
1905 - 1920	Mr Alfred Shattock	Mr James Shopland
1921	Mr Alfred Shattock	Mr William A Stone
1922 - 1946	Mr Wyndham Newman	Mr William A Stone
1947 - 1953	Mrs Wyndham Newman	Mr Merlin Heywood
1954 - 1964	Mr Lionel Thomas	Mr Merlin Heywood
1965 - 1978	Mr Gilbert J Goddard	Mr Merlin Heywood
1979 - 1986	Mr Merlin Heywood	Major Jack Daniell
1987 - 1992	Mr Merlin Heywood	Mrs Marjory Robins
1993 - 1999	Mrs Marjory Robins	Mrs Lavinia Elvy
2000 - 2002	Mrs Lavinia Elvy	Mr John Doble
2002 -	Mr John Doble	Mr David Goodall

APPENDIX E

PARISH FARMS AND HOUSES
[Numbers given are page numbers]

Beer Down Farm	Bucknell 42
Bences	Gamlin 59 Prescott 25
Borden/Bone* Gate	Carr 21 Prescott 19, 25, 27 White 98
Bray's Cottage	Butt 44 Tooze 95 Twose 95
Briar Cottage	Smith 89
Burnt House	Broomfield 41 Cockram 45 Cottrell 46 Tooze 29
Copper Ridge	Hussey 68 Watkinson 97
Court Hall	Browne 42 Cockram 45 Fellowes 56 How 67 Shopland 28, 88, 89 Stone 91 Tooze 29
Cowlings Farm	Darby 49 White 98
Crossways Cottage	Hocking 67
Cudmore	Kemp 69 Palfrey 78,79
Daggeridge	Hawkins 23 Moon 73
Dares Down	Goddard 60 Hilton 23, 66 Northam 18, 24
Doble Farm	Goddard 61
Durley	Bucknell 42
East Holelake	Prescott 85
Fenton Farm	Tooze 29
Glebe Cottage	Daniell 46 Hedgeland 23
Great Staple	Darby 47
Green House	Ash 38
Ham Mills	Ash 39 Moon 73
Hendom	Snow 78 Wensley 98
Hockford	Bowerman 40 Butt 44 Dart 50 Goffin 61 Hedgeland 63 Perry 82
Hockworthy House	Newman 75, 76 Parr 80
Hole Farm	Doble 53 Hussey 68 Lamphrey 69 Milton 72 Watkinson 97
Hole Lane Cottage	Hussey 68 Milton 72
Holelake	Prescott 85 Smith 89 Vickery 96
Home Farm	Newman 76
Huntsham Barton	Goddard 60, 61
Hurd's Farm	Northam 25 Prescott 84 Stevens 90
Hurford Cottage	Moon 73 Sprague 90
Hurford's Mead	Fellowes 56 Ware 97
Kerswell	Darby 22, 47, 48, 49
Lake Cottage	Redwood 28

Lea (Barton and Cottages)	Cockram 17 Crook 22 Dinham 53 Dunn 54 Farley 56 Hawkins 23 Heywood 64, 65 Lewis 16, 24 Moon 73 White 99 Yarde 56
Little Hockford	Dart 50
Locks Cottage	Lock 70
Loudwells Cottage	Dinham 53
Lucklies (leys)	Cockram 22 Redwood 28, 78
Meadow View	Goddard 61
Morles/Morrells	Redwood 27 Darby 47
New Buildings	Milton 72
Poor House	Milton 72
Quarry Hockford	Greedy 62 Vickery 29
Queen's Lodge	Roberts 87
Redwoods	Bucknell 42 Goddard 60 Thomas 94
Rose Cottage	Ash 38
Roundmoor Cott.	Hobbs 23 Thomas 19
Slantycombe	Dinham 53 Goddard 60 Hill 66
South Staple	Forgan 20 Wensley 98
Sparkhayne	Thomas 94
Stallenge Thorne	Hussey 68 Shattock 88 Wood 99
Staple Court	Dester 23, 51 Falls 55
Staple Cross	Brewer 40 Broomfield 41 Burston 16 Dunn 55 Ferris 57 Filmer 59 Goddard 60 Hocking 67 Kidley 20 Pavey 81 Perry 83 Prescott 27 Tooze 29
Staple Cross pub	Kerslake 27, 84 Prescott 84 Redwood 27, 28, 86
Staplemere	Filmer 59
Staple Well	Falls 55 Perry 83
Steels Farm	Heywood 64
Stuckleys	Burnett 44 Dunn 54
The Lodge	Hawkins 63
The Villa	Cottrell 46 Longman 70 Pepperell 81 Shopland 28, 89 Stone 91
Thornlands	Goddard 60, 61 Hussey 68 Lucas 71 Pavey 81 Tanner 94
Turnham Farm	Chidgey 22 Newman 76 Parr 80
Vicarage	Hawkins 63 Newman 75, 76 Parr 80
Vicarage Farm	Talbot 92
Waterslade	Hamilton 62 Lamprey 69 Morrish 73 Newman 76
West View	Hedgeland 63 Redwood 86
West End	Hedgeland 23

*Over the years place names were written differently, as they may have sounded to map-makers or other officials.   Thus Borden Gate, as an example, has been variously recorded as Bongate, Boarding Gate or Bone Gate *[see maps on p.x]*

APPENDIX F

MONUMENT DESIGNS

- ROUNDED TOP WITH ROUNDED SHOULDERS
- GOTHIC
- PEON
- OVAL WITH SCOTIA SHOULDERS
- CROSS ON THREE BASES
- OGEE
- OVAL WITH SHOULDERS
- OGEE WITH CHECKS
- LEDGER
- TWO BASES
- SQUARE KERBS WITH WING POSTS
- MALTESE CROSS

STONE MASONS

Fewings, Tiverton *pp.49, 50, 81, 96*
Fudge, Paul *p.44*
Grant, R *pp.84, 85*
Manning & Knight *p.65*

Burial Registers

APPENDIX G

BURIAL REGISTERS
1578 – 2014

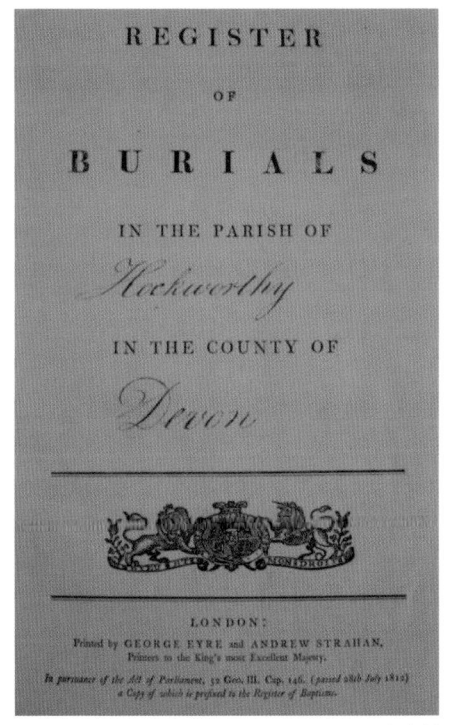

REGISTER

OF

BURIALS

IN THE PARISH OF

Hockworthy

IN THE COUNTY OF

Devon

LONDON:
Printed by GEORGE EYRE and ANDREW STRAHAN,
Printers to the King's most Excellent Majesty.

*In pursuance of the Act of Parliament, 52 Geo. III. Cap. 146. (passed 28th July 1812)
a Copy of which is prefixed to the Register of Baptisms.*

[Devon Heritage Service: 3083A/PR/1/8]

1663

[3083A/PR/1/1]

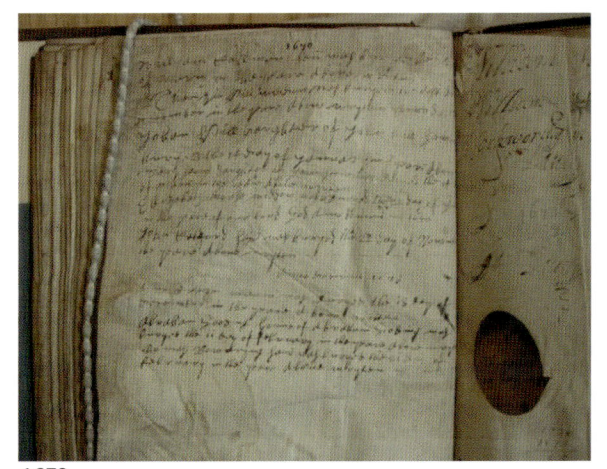

1670

[3083A/PR/1/1]

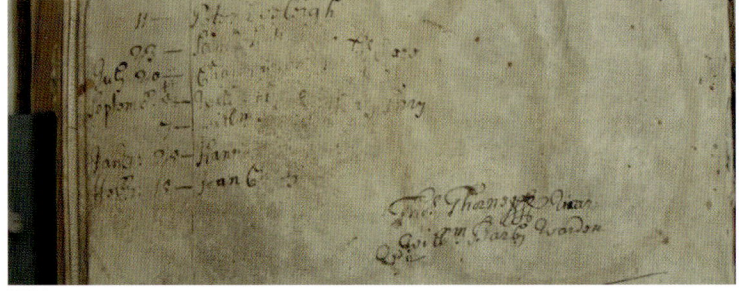

1729

[3083A/PR/1/1]

Hockworthy Burial Registers

[reproduced with the kind permission of the Devon Heritage Service]

BURIAL REGISTERS 1578 – 2014

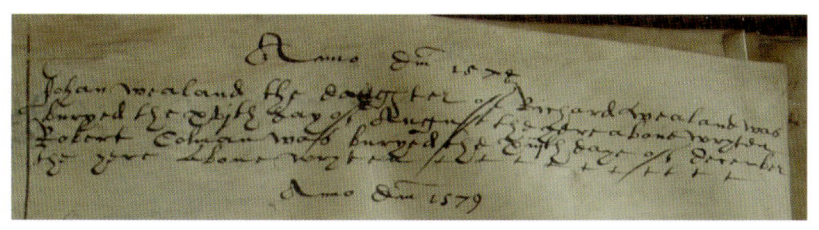

[Devon Heritage Service: 3083A/PR/1/1]
The first entry in the registers, 1578

With the re-building of the church in the 1860s and the resulting lack of earlier memorials, the Burial Registers crucially fill in the missing centuries. With just under five hundred and forty years to transcribe, it has been a challenge; not only interpreting the handwriting, but parts had decayed and the ink faded. Happily, registers are now lodged for safe-keeping at the Devon Heritage Centre in Exeter, where they are kept in controlled conditions, safely protected from damp vestries.

The early registers are leather bound and written on parchment. The hole in the page *[see central illustration on p.114]* is a flaw caused by earlier injuries (bites or disease) to the skin of the sheep.

The spelling of names changes from year to year, or incumbent to incumbent, and they have been listed as written. The alphabetical index which follows the registers *[p.149]* is therefore only a guide, and alternative spellings of family names should be checked. For simplification, words such as wyddow, wyfe, buryed and ye have been spelt as a 21st century reader will recognise them, and dates have been standardised to day/month/year, with months shortened to three letters. Where there is doubt over a name, ***italics*** have been used. Any entries marked with an asterix * are those with headstones still surviving in the churchyard.

1738 [3083A/PR/1/1]

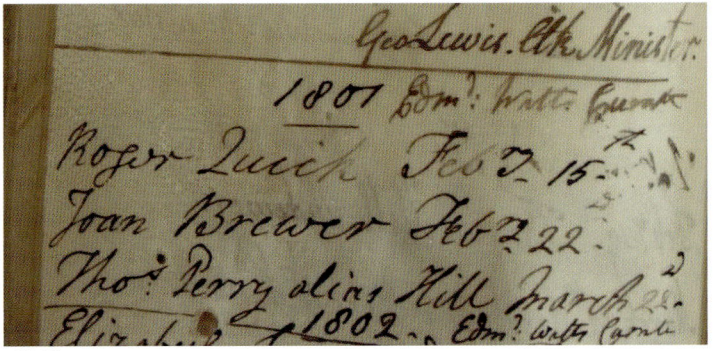

1801 [3083A/PR/1/2]

1917 [3083A/PR/1/8]

Hockworthy Burial Registers

[reproduced with the kind permission of the Devon Heritage Service]

Burial Registers

Between 1649 and 1655 there are no entries; in 1655 there is an authorisation, still extant in the Registers and reproduced below, for the parish clerk to resume making entries. In 1649 King Charles I had been executed; Presbyterian and other radical puritan sects took control of religious affairs, banning the Book of Common Prayer, even celebrations at Christmas. This fundamentalism may have affected even our (then) remote village with the people, especially the parish clerk, fearful of getting into trouble, if they continued the normal procedures of the Church of England.

> 'Having rec^d a Certificate under the hands of John Catford, Nicholas Stephens, Peter Shorland, Richard Stone and Wm Colman Inhabitants of the parish of Hockworthy in the said County that they have chosen Edward Mylles of the said parish to be their parish Register of all Marriages, Births & Buryall, according an Act of Parlyment in that Case made & provided; I do hereby approve the said Edward Milles (sic) to be their parish Register and accordingly have Sworn him this present 24th of Sept: 1655'
>
> *[Devon Heritage Service: 3083A/PR/1/1]*

Sad stories emerge. Who, for example, was the 'Stranger whose name was unknown' in 1697? And what must the vicar, Revd Thomas Thorne, have felt having lost his wife and four daughters between 1722 and 1730? But delight, too, in the entry for John Locke, in 1738, 'As honest a man as could live' or George Webber, two years later, described as 'A very honest virtuous poor man'. The first regular entries giving an age at death were in 1813. The number of children, sometimes infants of a mere few hours of life, as well as tragic accidents and unpleasant fatalities, such as burning to death in a lime kiln, all demonstrate the fragility of life. The longest living recorded age was 97 years *[see p.87]*.

Following the inscriptions is an alphabetical index of the names *[p.149]*.

BURIAL REGISTERS 1578 – 2014

* = surviving headstone in churchyard
***Italics** = uncertain transcription*

Surname	Forenames	Burial date	Age	Notes
WEALAND	Johan	16 Aug 1578		Dau of Richard Wealand
COLMAN	Robert	13 Dec 1578		
STONE	Henry	25 Aug 1579		
SHORLAND	Johan	6 Sep 1579		Widow
SHORLAND	Robert	14 Feb 1580		
WEALAND	Johan	25 Nov 1581		Widow
DAWE	Johan	30 Nov 1582		Dau of Raphe Dawe
COODEN	Elizabeth	6 Sep 1583		
COLMAN	Agnes	21 Oct 1583		Wife of Richard Colman
NORRIS	John	13 Nov 1584		Son of John Norris
BRAYE	Suzanna	28 Jun 1585		Dau of Robert Braye
CHAMBERLINE	Johan	7 Nov 1585		Widow
SHORLAND	Henry	3 Feb 1585		Son of Henry Shorland
SHORLAND	Elizabeth	14 Mar 1585		Wife of John Shorland
SHORLAND	Nicholas	20 Apr 1586		Son of John Shorland
GOODDING	Johan	14 Jan 1586		Wife of John Gooding
SANDER	Thomas	7 May 1587		
WEALAND	Elizabeth	31 Jan 1587		Dau of John Wealand
WENE	Nicholas	21 Feb 1587		
GOODDING	John	28 Apr 1588		
CLEEKE	Thomas	29 May 1588		
COLMAN	John	22 Apr 1589		Als Staleings
GOODDING	Robert	26 Jul 1589		
SHORLAND	John	3 Aug 1589		
COLMAN	Richard	31 Aug 1589		
COLMAN	Johan	5 Nov 1589		Wife of John Colman
STONE	Henry	2 Aug 1590		
STEVEN	Nicholas	3 Aug 1590		
WEBBER	Thomas	3 Aug 1590		Son of William Webber
CLEEKE	John	3 Nov 1590		
CLEEKE	Anne	7 Nov 1590		
CLEEKE	Peter	3 Nov 1590		Son of Thomas *Cleeke*
LAB	Johan	25 Nov 1590		Wife of Xxofer Lab
STEPHEN	Robert	14 Nov 1591		
MORRELL	Rychard	9 Apr 1592		Son of Vincent Morrell
SHORLAND	**Peter**	21 Nov 1592		
SHORLAND	Robert	14 Jan 1592		Son of Thomas Shorland
CHAMBERLIN	Elianor	30 Jan 1592		Dau of Thomas Chamberlin
SHEPPARD	Walter	9 Jul 1593		Son of Walter Sheppard
STONE	Jullon	4 Jan 1593		WIdow
COLMAN	Alice	20 May 1594		Dau of Alice Colman
COLMAN	Agnes	24 Jun 1594		Dau of Nicholas Colman
COLMAN	Ellen	29 Jan 1594		Wife of Matthew Colman
COLMAN	Nicholas	20May 1595		
WEBBER	William	27 May 1595		

Burial Registers

SANDER	Marrian	13 Jul 1596	
STEPHEN	Edmond	17 Feb 1596	
STEPHEN	Johan	3 Apr 1596	Widow
GOULD	Julion	19 Aug 1597	Dau of Henry Gould
WEALAND	Edmond	20 Aug 1597	Son of John Wealand
COLMAN	Agnes	9 Sep 1597	Wife of Mathew Colman
COLMAN	William	12 Sep 1597	
COLMAN	Nicholas	10 Nov 1597	Son of Edyth Colman
SHORT	John	24 Jan 1597	
COLMAN	Mathew	13 Jun 1598	
CHAMBERLINE	John	22 Jun 1598	
COLMAN	John	1 Jul 1598	
GRAUNT	Robert	10 Aug 1598	
SHORLAND	Johan	7 Nov 1598	Wife of Edmond Shorland
GOODDINGE	William	7 Jun 1599	Son of John Gooddinge
SHACKELL	Alice	24 Jul 1599	Wife of Thomas Shackell
ALLEY	Susan	13 Nov 1599	Als *Lawrence*
NORRIS	John	5 Dec 1599	
BERNER	Clemente	20 Jan 1599	
STEPHEN	Alice	20 Jan 1599	Wife of Richard Stephen
GOODDINGE	John	28 Feb 1599	
THORNE	William	28 Jun 1600	
HARRIS	Agnes	14 Jan 1600	
STEPHEN	John	6 Feb 1600	Son of Richard Stephen
WENE	Elizabeth	19 Sep 1601	
CAPRON	John	18 Jan 1601	
CLEAKE	Agnes	24 Apr 1602	
SANDER	Agnes	29 May 1602	
CHAMBERLINE	Christian	11 Jul 1602	Dau of Johan Chamberline
GOULD	Elizabeth	21 Jun 1603	Dau of Henry Gould
SHORLAND	Agnes	10 Jan 1604	Dau of Edmond Shorland
GRAUNT	Grace	26 Apr 1605	Widow
SHORLAND	Edmond	18 Jun 1605	
SHORLAND	**Christian**	21 Dec 1605	Widow
GOULD	Edmond	11 May 1606	Son of Henry Gould
COLMAN	Edith	17 Jun 1606	
CLEEKE	Thomazine	9 Dec 1608	Dau of John Cleeke
CURTON	Henry	26 Mar 1609	Als Sully
STONE	Ellinnor	30 Aug 1609	Widow
CLEEKE	Robert	2 Nov 1609	Son of John Cleeke
STONE	Elinnor	26 Nov 1609	Widow
CURTON	Humfry	20 Feb 1609	
WEALAND	John	21 Oct 1610	
SHARLAND	Robert	20 Nov 1610	Son of Henry Sharland
WEALAND	Elizabeth	20 May 1611	Widow
THOMAS	Roger	2 Jun 1611	"Welchman servant of Thos Chamberlyne"
GOWER	Agnes	1 Jul 1611	Wife of Henry *Gover*
WEARE	Agnes	7 Jan 1611	Wife George Weare
WATERMAN	William	1 Feb 1611	Son of Edmond Waterman
CLEAKE	Thomas	7 Apr 1612	Son of Thomas Cleake
SHARLAND	George	13 May 1612	

BOWDEN		23 Dec 1612	Dau of George Bowden
CLEAK	John	May 1613	Son of John Cleak
WEBBER	Johan	15 Dec 1613	Widow
HILL	Christopher	2 Jan 1613	
BOWDEN	Avis	12 Feb 1613	Widow
CHAMBERLINE	Johan	3 Jul 1614	Widow
SANDER	Thomas	8 Oct 1614	
GOULD	Christian	22 Mar 1615	Wife of Henry Gould
SHORLAND	Christopher	7 Oct 1616	Son of Nicholas Shorland
CHAMBERLINE	John	10 Oct 1616	Son of John Chamberline
FARTHINGE	Agnes	9 Nov 1616	Dau of Raph Farthinge
CHAMBERLINE	Thomas	29 Mar 1617	
STONE	Dorothy	29 Oct 1617	Dau of A.... Stone
COLMAN	Alice	6 Apr 1618	Widow
STEPHEN	Richard	19 May 1618	
GOULD	Johan	30 Jul 1618	
BOWDEN	William	21 Jan 1618	
COLMAN	Johan	21 Aug 1619	Dau of Richard Colman
CAPRON	Alice	16 Nov 1619	Widow
COLMAN	Elinor	21 Jan 1619	Wife of George Colman
GOODDINGE	Thomas	24 Sep 1620	
COLMAN	Johan	28 Jan 1620	Widow
CLARKE	Thomas	4 Sep 1621	
THOMAS	John	10 Dec 1621	
BOLLMAN	John	17 Mar 1621	
FARTHING	Agnis	10 Sep 1622	Dau of Raph Farthing
CHAMBERLIN	Alice	5 May 1623	Widow
SHORLAND	Elizabeth	1 May 1623	Wife of Henry Shorland
BOWDEN	John	14 Jun 1623	
SHORLAND	Henry	22 Jun 1623	
GOODDING	Agnes	12 Aug 1623	Widow
SANDER	John	14 Aug 1623	Son of Ellen Sander, widow
SANDER	Thamzin	14 Aug 1623	Dau of Ellen Sander, widow
MORRIS	Margaret	26 Aug 1623	Wife of John Morris
COLMAN	Edith	5 Sep 1623	Widow
SANDER	Grace	8 Sep 1623	
COLMAN	Amy	4 Oct 1623	
CHAMBERLINE	Elnor	4 Feb 1623	
CATFORD	Jone	19 Jun 1624	Wife of William Catford
WINE	Agnis	18 Apr 1624	
WATERMAN	Edmund	29 May 1625	Son of Edmund Waterman
WEBBER	Martine	3 Jun 1625	
GOULDE	Henry	21 Oct 1626	
CATFORD	William	31 Jan 1626	The elder
GOULD	William	19 Feb 1626	
BOWDEN	Grace	18 Apr 1627	Dau of Henry Bowden
LOWMAN	George	21 May 1627	
CATTFORD	Agnis	29 Mar *1628*	Widow
GOODDINGE	Elinor	5 Apr *1627*	
BRAYE	William	5 Aug 1628	
HILL	Susanna	12 Nov 1628	
SHORLAND	Jone	9 Feb 1629	Wife of Nicholas Shorland
HYNDHAM	Edward	7 Jul 1630	

Burial Registers

HYNDHAM	John	16 Jul 1630		
HYNDHAM	Du...ens	15 Aug 1630		Widow
SHORLAND	Thamzin	25 Sep 1630		Wife of Nicholas Shorland
INGERIME	Willmet	9 Jan 1630		[Ingram?]
HYNDHAM	John	6 Apr 1631		Junior
HYNDHAM	Jonn	10 Apr 1631		Senior
WYETT	Jone	7 Apr 1633		Dau of Stuckly Wyett
TWOZE	John	11 Jan 1634		
LOCKE	Jone	17 Feb 1634		Dau of Richard Locke
CLEACKE	John	27 Aug 1635		
BRAYE	Thomas	28 Sep 1635		Son of Richard Braye
STONE	Richard	12 Jan 1635		Son of Richard Stone
CHRAZE	William	12 Apr 1636		Son of Thomas Chraze
LOCKE	Jone	7 Sep 1636		Wife of Richard Locke
WYETT	Alles	28 Sep 1636		Dau of John Wyett
DAVIE	Samuell	22 Oct 1636		Son of William Davie
GRAUNTE	Jone	8 Dec 1636		
BRAYE	Marie	9 May 1637		
WYETT	Stucklye	28 Oct 1637		
CAPRON	Jane	20 Nov 1637		Dau of John
GOOLD	William	9 May 1638		
CHAMBERLINE	William	15 Jan 1638		
CHAMBERLINE	Margot	17 Jan 1638		Dau of John Chamberline
SANDER	Grace	15 May 1639		
WYETT	Suzanna	5 Jul 1639		
SAYER	Grace	7 Aug 1639		
HILL	James	20 Dec 1639		Son of John Hill
NORRIS	John	21 Mar 1639	41	Vicar
BRAY	Dorothie	20 Oct 1640		Dau of Richard Bray
CHURLY	Maud	2 Feb 1640		
DAVIE	William	10 Mar 1640		Son of William Davie
BOWDEN	Henry	30 Apr 1641		
COLLMAN	Johan	8 May 1641		
BOWDEN	Jane	6 Dec 1642		Widow
OSEMOND	Hellen	15 Dec 1642		Wife of John Osemond
STONE	Augustine	12 Feb 1642		
ENGERUM	Mariery [Marjery]	12 Mar 1642		Wife of William Engerum
CHURLEY	William	13 Apr 1642		Son of John Churley
CHRAZE	Richard	15 Jun 1643		
WILMOTON	Francis	2 Jul 1643		Wife of Richard Wilmoton
FFARTHINGE	Ralph	9 Sep 1643		
SAUNDER	William	11 Jan 1643		
GOODINGE	Katherine	4 Apr 1643		
STEPHEN	Thamzine	20 Apr 1643		Wife of Henry Stephen
OSEMOND	John	16 May 1643		
WEBBER	Alice	25 Jun 1644		Widow
CHAMBERLINE	Thomas	18 Sep 1644		
CHAMBERLINE	George	21 Sep 1644		Son of widow Chamberline
COLLMAN	George	22 Sep 1644		Son of William Collman
CHAMBERLINE	Jane	3 Oct 1644		Widow
GOVIER	Dorothie	13 Nov 1644		Wife of Nicholas Govier
COLLMAN	Mary	19 Nov 1644		Wife of Robert Collman

CHAMBERLYNE	Johan	29 Nov 1644	Widow
HYLL	William	3 Jan 1644	
STEPHEN	Thomazine	27 Mar 1645	Wife of Nicholas Stephen
MORLE	Laurence	9 Feb 1645	
GRANT	Richard	18 Mar 1645	
SHORLAND	Nicholas	9 Aug 1647	
BRAY	Richard	10 Sep 1647	Senior
STONE	Alice	15 Jun 1648	Wife of Richard Stone
BOWDEN	Thomazine	15 Jul 1649	
GOVIER	Nicholas	29 Jul 1649	
FLERE	Thomas	29 Jul 1649	
GOVIER	Francis	2 Sep 1649	Son of Nicholas Govier
WOLTERMAN	Edith	20 Oct 1649	Wife of Edmund Wolterman
STONE	Edith	Nov 1649	Widow
COLLMAN	Humfrey	6 Jan 1649	
NO ENTRIES FOR SIX YEARS			
GOVER	Agnis	16 Dec 1655	Dau of Nicholas Gover
STONE	*Philip*	21 Feb 1655	
STONE	Johan	13 Mar 1655	
AMMARYE	John	20 Apr 1656	
STONE	Agnes	17 Jun 1656	Wife of Rich Stone
GOODING	Ansilla	27 Nov 1656	Wife of John Gooding
STEVEN	Ellen	21 May 1659	Wife of Nicholas Steven
AUGUSTINE	Pearce	31 Jul 1659	Son of Richard Pearce
BRAYE	Richard	5 Sep 1659	Son of Richard Braye
LOCKE	Elizabeth	14 Jan 1659	Dau of John Locke
COLLMAN	Thomas	8 Feb 1659	Son of William Collman
CAFENDEN	Anne	29 Oct 1659	Wife of William Cafenden
LOCKE	Allce	10 Nov 1659	Wife of Richard Locke
CAPRON	Ellinor	17 Jul 1661	Wife of John Capron
STEEPFIN	Nicholas	17 Aug 1661	
HILL	Mary	5 Jun 1662	Dau of John Hill senior
STONE	Susan	14 Jun 1662	Dau of Humphrey Stone
ROW	John	28 Nov 1662	
GOLD	Margaret	1 Mar 1662	
WATERMAN	Thomazine	16 Jan 1662	Dau of Edmond
HILL	John	1 Mar 1662	Senior
STEEPHIN	Henrye	14 Sep 1663	Senior
FARTHING	Sullinger	30 Oct 1663	Widow
LOCKE	Rich	3 Nov 1663	
SHORLAND	Thomzin	21 Mar 1663	Wife of Will Shorland
BARBYE	Andrew	14 Apr 1664	
WEBER	Grace	8 May 1664	Wife Ellice Weber
COLLMAN	Ellinor	15 Apr 1664	Dau of Robert Collman
SHORLAND	Will	17 Nov 1664	
GOVIER	Nicholas	18 Nov 1664	
GOVIER	Stephen	18 Nov 1664	Son of Nicholas Govier
PERCE	Johan	25 Nov 1664	Wife of Richard Peace*[Pearce]*
HEARD	Johan	1 Dec 1664	
MORSE	Richard	21 Jan 1664	Senior
PROUT	Robert	23 Dec 1664	
CRAZE	Thomas	16 Nov 1665	
BRAYE	Johan	20 Jul 1665	Widow

Burial Registers

WYETT	Johan	8 Oct 1665	Wife of Frances Wyett
STONE	Humphrey	17 Jan 1665	
SHORLAND	Nicholas	26 Jan 1665	
SCOTT	Samuel	13 Feb 1666	
SCOTT	John	13 Feb 1666	Son of Samuell Scott
CRAZE	Thomas	6 Jun 1667	Son of Francis Craze
BROOKE	John	21 Jun 1667	
GOODING	John	24 Jun 1667	[Good, Junior?]
STONE	Charley	22 Sep 1667	Son of Rich. Stone
STONE	Richard	5 Nov 1668	Son of John Stone
DAW	Alice	7 Nov 1668	Widow
CRAZE	Elizabeth	28 Feb 1668	Dau of Francis Craze
GOVER	Richard	16 Feb 1669	
CRAZE	Mary	6 May 1670	Dau of Francis Craze
HILL	Luke	2 Aug 1670	
GOODING	Thomas	22 Oct 1670	
BARBYE	Agnes	23 Oct 1670	Wife of Andrew
WYLBROKE	Johan	19 Feb 1670	Wife of John Wylbroke
STONE	Thomazine	5 Mar 1670	Dau of Hugh Stone
COLLMAN	William	21 Mar 1670	Senior
HILL	Thamzin	31 Dec 1670	Widow
HILL	Johan	14 Jan 1671	Dau of John Hill
STONE	Mary	14 Mar 1671	Dau of Jonas Stone
MORSE	Elizabeth	22 Jun 1672	Widow
CATFORD	John	22 Nov 1672	
CRAZE	Anne	13 Dec 1673	Widow
GOODING	Abraham	2 Feb 1673	Son of Abraham Gooding
BOWERING	Thomas	22 Feb 1673	*Senior*
MARSHELL	William	6 Aug 1674	
COWLING	Grace	25 Feb 1674	
COWLING	Thamzine	9 Jun 1674	Wife of Tho Cowling
BOWERING	Tho:	6 Oct 1675	
SHARLAND	Elizabeth	20 Jan 1675	Wife of Peter Sharland
STONE	Grace	30 Apr 1676	
NORMAN	Johan	1 Oct 1676	Dau of Hugh
MORSE	Richard	1 Dec 1676	
STONE	Richard	20 Feb 1676	
COLLMAN	Mary	22 Mar 1676	Dau of Nicholas
STONE	Allice	25 Jul 1677	Widow
CHURLYE	Mary	10 Feb 1677	Dau of Robert Churlye
SHARLAND	John	17 Feb 1677	
COLLMAN	George	19 Jul 1678	Son of William Collman
STONE	John	16 Sep 1678	
WILLCOKE	John	17 Sep 1678	
ALLIN	Elizabeth	17 Nov 1678	Dau of John Allin
NORMAN	John	27 Dec 1678	Son of Hugh Norman
ALLIN	John	1 Jan 1678	
PAINE	John	15 Feb 1678	
HILL	John	16 Feb 1678	*Junior*
HILL	John	9 Mar 1678	*Senior*
COWLING	Thomas	31 Mar 1679	
HARKE	Ellynor	25 Oct 1679	Widow [Hawke?]

COLLMAN	Robert	12 Dec 1679	
CRAZE	Willmott	18 Jan 1679	Dau of Franciss Craze
SHARLAND	Agnis	20 Oct 1680	Widow
RIDWOOD	Richard	6 Feb 1680	
STONE	Christopher	20 Aug 1681	
RIDWOOD	John	1 May 1681	Son of Richard Ridwood
ENGGRUM	Elizabeth	15 Jul 1681	Wife of Will Enggrum
STONE	Hugh	17 Jul 1681	
JAMES	Richard	24 Dec 1682	Son of William James
REDWOOD	Suzana	16 Dec 1683	Dau of John Redwood
WEBBER	Grace	9 Mar 1683	
DAVYE	George	20 Mar 1683	Son of John Davye
TALLBUT	Dorythy	2 May 1684	
MORSE	Ellizabeth	5 Jun 1684	Widow
PEACE	Mary	18 Jul 1684	Wife of Richard Peace
MORSE	Suzanah	7 Sep 1684	Dau of John Morse
MORSE	Nicholas	4 Oct 1684	
CARIE	William	27 Mar 1685	
HARBER	Mary	19 Jun 1685	
PEARCE	Richard	20 Jul 1685	Senior
COLLMAN	Ellyzabeth	16 Aug 1685	
STONE	Henry	12 Sep 1685	
STONE	Elizabeth	12 Sep 1685	
HILL	Mary	12 Nov 1685	Widow
MILLTON	Mary	28 Nov 1685	Widow
STONE	Richard	27 Jan 1685	
WIEAT	Henry	29 Jan 1685	
MORSE	Hannah	25 Feb 1685	
COLLMAN	Johan	1 Jun 1686	Widow
MORSE	John	6 Jun 1686	
INGGRUM	William	21 Jun 1686	[see ENGGRUM above]
BATTIN	Mary	17 Jul 1686	
MORSE	Suzannah	25 Jul 1686	Dau of John Morse
BIDGOOD	Dorothy	22 Aug 1686	
MORSE	Ffrancis	29 Dec 1686	
CAPRON	John	20 Feb 1686	
WATERMAN	Edward	13 Mar 1686	
GOODING	Grace	5 Apr 1687	Wife of Robert Gooding
RIDWOOD	Thomas	4 Jun 1687	
MILLS	Anne	17 Nov 1687	
SHARLAND	Robert	1 Dec 1687	
PULLIN	Francis	2 Apr 1688	
CAPRON	George	8 May 1688	
SHARLAND	Richard	15 Dec 1688	Son of Richard Sharland
COLLMAN	David	22 Dec 1689	Son of William Collman
GOODING	*Sullingar*	19 Jan 1689	Dau of Abraham Gooding
NORMAN	Ellinor	30 Mar 1690	Dau of Hugh Norman
STONE	Agnes	25 May 1690	Wife of Augustine Stone
BIDGOOD	Thomas	6 Jul 1690	
COLLMAN	William	15 Nov 1690	
PEARCE	Augustin	19 Jan 1690	
STONE	Chrystyan	23 Feb 1690	
COLLMAN	Thamzin	8 Mar 1690	Dau of William Collman

Burial Registers

Surname	Given	Date	Notes
JAMES	Johan	15 Mar 1690	Dau of William James
STONE	Robert	22 Mar 1690	
WYATT	John	25 Mar 1691	
COLLING	Elizabeth	3 Apr 1691	Wife of Tristram Cowling
GLASS	Anne	26 Apr 1691	
RIDWOOD	Emanuel	2 Aug 1691	
QUICKE	Mary	27 Jan 1691	"Was buryed in linniy""
MORSE	William	1 May 1692	
JAMES	Agnes	28 Aug 1692	Dau of William James
COSIN	John	4 Dec 1692	Son of John Cosin
MILLS	Edmon	5 Feb 1692	Clarke of this parish
CRAZE	Joan	16 Apr 1693	Dau of Ffrancis Craze
STONE	John	20 May 1693	
STONE	Richard	27 Aug 1693	Son of Chrestover Stone
COLLMAN	Ann	9 Sep 1693	Widow
CHAMBERLLERN	William	19 Nov 1693	
INGGARMAN	Agnice	9 Mar 1693	Widow
GOODING	Robert	22 Apr 1694	
CRAZE	Isaac [sic]	6 Jul 1694	Wife of John Craze
LOCKE	John	28 Nov 1694	
DAVEY	Elizabeth	5 Feb 1694	Wife of John Davey
COLLMAN	Richard	10 Feb 1694	Son of Will Collman
HOCKESTON	Ann	31 Mar 1695	Dau of Ja: Hockeston
GOODING	Abraham	12 Apr 1695	
WIETT	Johan	12 May 1695	Widow
PEARSE	Augustine	7 Jul 1695	Son of Richard Pearse
LOCK	Elizabeth	28 Jul 1695	Dau of Richard Lock
MORLE	Hugh	20 Sep 1695	Son of Thomas Morle
KAMPE	Alice	8 Nov 1695	
DAVY	Mary	12 Dec 1695	Dau of John & Christian
DAVY	Elizabeth	22 Dec 1695	Wife of Edmond Davy
STONE	Humphry	15 Mar 1695	Son of Susanna Stone
STEPHENS	Nicholas	24 Jul 1696	Son of Henry & Christian
PEARSE	Jone	16 Aug 1696	Dau of Richard & Sarah
DAVY	Edmund	13 Sep 1696	
CHAMBERLEINE	Martha	20 Oct 1696	
LOCK	Mary	29 Oct 1696	Dau of Richard Lock
JAMES	Nicholas	11 Dec 1697	Of Ashbrittle
UNKNOWN		8 Dec 1697	"A stranger whose name was unknown"
SHARPE	John	7 Nov 1698	Son of John & Grace
COWLINGE	Bridget	28 Nov 1698	Wife of Thomas Cowlinge
COWLING	John	23 Feb 1698	Senior
PATCH	**Emmon**	2 Mar 1698	
COLLMAN	Robert	29 Feb 1698	Son of William Colman
STUCKLY	Joan	14 May 1699	Als Wyatt
STONE	Joan	4 Jun 1699	Wife of Christopher Stone
BIDGOOD	Thomas	2 Jul 1699	Son of Thomas Bidgood
HOXLINE	Susannah	30 Jul 1699	Dau of John & Margaret
STUCKLY	Robert	10 Aug 1699	Als Wyatt. Senior
JAMES	Elizabeth	13 Aug 1699	Wife of William James
CHAMBERLINE	Elinor	15 Oct 1699	*Widow*

LOCK	Walter	29 Oct 1699	Son of Richard Lock
LOCK	Anne	13 Apr 1700	Widow
JETSON	Susannah	25 Apr 1700	
MORLE	Elinor	27 Apr 1700	Dau of Thomas Morle
MORLE	Elizabeth	9 Jun 1700	Wife of Tho Morle
REDWOOD	Thamzine	25 May 1700	Widow
MORLE	John	26 Jun 1700	Son of Richard
MORLE	Elizabeth	1 Jul 1700	Dau of Thomas Morle
COLMAN	Elinor	7 Jul 1700	Dau of Robert Colman
WYATT	Agnis	20 Oct 1700	Widow
CHURLY	Jane	3 Nov 1700	Wife of Robert Churly
DAVY	Jo	26 Jan 1700	A Welchman
REDWOOD	Joan	9 Mar 1700	Wife of Tho Redwood
FOURAKER	Andrew	13 Mar 1700	
COLMAN	Thomas	25 May 1701	Son of John Colman
CAMPE	John	20 Feb 1701	Son of Philip Campe
COLMAN	Joan	29 Mar 1702	Dau of Humphry Colman
GOODING	Catherine	12 Apr 1702	Widow
SHARPE	Elizabeth	19 Jun 1702	"Dau of John Sharpe, Vicar, and Grace his wife was buried in the chancell of Dulverton"
HURFORD	Elizabeth	27 Aug 1702	Dau of Hugh Hurford
STONE	Grace	27 Sep 1702	Of Huntsham
PALMER	Joan	20 Jan 1702	Wife of Ffrancis Palmer
REDWOOD	Mary	30 Jan 1702	Wife of John Redwood
WYATT	Robert	13 Mar 1702	
CHURLY	Robert	5 Dec 1703	Son of John Churly
CHURLY	John	12 Mar 1703	Son of John Churly
HURFORD	Ann	30 Mar 1704	Wife of Hugh Hurford
KERSLAKE	Robert	24 Oct 1705	
WYATT	Henry	18 Jun 1705	
GOODING	Thomas	3 Feb 1705	
STONE	Lydia	3 Mar 1705	
BONNY	Elizabeth	31 Mar 1706	Dau of Jo: Bonny
COLMAN	Jane	28 Apr 1706	Widow
REDWOOD	Mary	4 May 1706	Wife of Jo: Redwood
WYAT	Thomas	29 May 1706	
STONE	Susan	8 Sep 1706	Widow
PERRY	Jane	17 Nov 1706	Dau of William Perry
LOCKE	Agnis	12 Mar 1706	Wife of John Locke
HERD	Elizabeth	19 Apr 1707	
CAMPE	Joane	5 Oct 1707	Wife of Phillip Campe
CHURLY	Jane	14 Jan 1707	Dau of John Churly
PAYNE	Mary	17 Mar 1707	Dau of John Payne
COLLMAN	William	21 Mar 1707	Son of William & Mary Collman of Ashbrittle
WILLKINS	Joane	12 Dec 1708	Dau of Richard Willkins
SHARPE	John	24 Jan 1708	Vicar of this parish
SCOTT	John	30 Jan 1708	Son of Samuel Scott
MORSE	Richard	1 May 1709	
PEARSE	Thomas	8 May 1709	Son of Richard Pearse
GOODING	Ann	15 May 1709	Dau of Anstis Gooding
HILL	Sarah	12 Jun 1709	Dau of William Hill
CRACE	John	19 Jun 1709	Sen

Burial Registers

BRAY	Joan	14 Aug 1709	Widow
COLMAN	Jane	5 Feb 1710	Dau of William Colman
CAMP	Ann	19 Mar 1710	Dau of Phil: Camp
COLMAN	Joan	27 Mar 1710	Wife of *Robert* Colman
CRAZE	Sicily	23 Jul 1710	Widow
BANFIELD	Grace	20 Aug 1710	Widow
CRAZE	Joan	1 Oct 1710	Wife of Theo Craze
CHURLY	Robert	25 Feb 1711	
COLMAN	Robert	17 Mar 1711	
PERRY	William	25 Mar 1711	Als Hill
JOHNSHING	Susanna	1 Apr 1711	"Wife of James Johnshing of Sampford Pevrul"
HILL	Katharan	12 Jul 1711	Widow
CRAZE	James	15 Apr 1711	Son of Thomas Craze
SHARPE	David	26 Oct 1711	Son of Mrs Grace Sharpe, Widow
GOODING	Anstice	9 Nov 1711	Widow
HAWKLING	William	9 Dec 1711	Son of Mary Hawkling
PERRY	Thomas	25 Dec 1711	Als Hill
BRAY	Jno:	18 Apr 1712	
HILL	Grace	27 Jul 1712	Wife of William Hill als Perry
GOODING	Joan	27 Jul 1712	Dau of Francis Gooding
CROCKHAM	Elizabeth	31 Aug 1712	Dau of Will: Crockham
GOODING	Jno:	28 Sep 1712	Son of Francis Gooding
FFARNAM	Mary	21 Oct 1712	Wife of Jno: Ffarnam of Orchard, Somerset
GLASS	Rd:	1 Nov 1712	
COWLIN	Tristram	7 Apr 1713	
REDWOOD	Elizabeth	24 May 1713	
BIDGOOD	Mary	31 May 1713	Dau of Nich: Bidgood
CAMP	Phillip	5 Sep 1714	
HILL	William	14 Nov 1714	Als Perry
PEASE	Richard	4 Mar 1715	Of this parish
MANLY	Joan	31 Mar 1715	Wife of John Manly
STEPHENS	Thomazin	23 Apr 1715	Dau of Mr Henry Stephens
CRAZE	Joane	1 May 1715	Dau of Thomas Craze
BELLEM	Mary	18 May 1715	Wife of Joshua Bellem, Willand
COLLMAN	Mary	21 Mar 1715	Wife of Humphrey Collman
CHAPPEL	Elizabeth	22 Apr 1716	Wife of Jasper Chappel
STONE	Susannah	6 May 1716	
DAVEY	Susannah	21 Jul 1716	Wife of Jon: Davey junior
CHANTER	Jon:	10 Aug 1716	Son of John Chanter
BIDGOOD	Martin	24 Aug 1716	
LOCK	Ann	12 Apr 1717	Dau of Roger Lock of Ashford
PERRY	Jane	14 Jul 1717	Als Hill. Widow
WATERMAN	Margaret	11 Aug 1717	Widow
COLLMAN	Robert	22 Dec 1717	Son of William Collman of Ashbrittle
DUCKAM	Thomas	23 Feb 1717	

BROOME	Martha	23 Feb 1718	Dau of William & Jane
COLLMAN	Joane	20 Apr 1718	*Dau of Amos …*
WATTERMAN	Thomas	27 Apr 1718	
BIDGOOD	Tempance	18 May 1718	Dau of William & Joan
CRAZE	Mary	27 Jul 1718	Wife of Thomas Craze
WELLAND	Mary	17 Aug 1718	Dau of Jon: Welland
CROKHAM	Jon:	5 Oct 1718	Son of William & Mary
BUCKNELL	Betty	12 Apr 1719	Dau of John & Frances
STONE	William	19 Apr 1719	
SHARPE	Grace	27 Nov 1719	Widow of John Sharpe, Vicar
COLLMAN	Joan	31 Jan 1720	Dau of William & Joan Collman of Greenham
BRYANT	Mary	7 Oct 1720	Wife of John Bryant of Bampton
HURFORD	Joan	16 Nov 1720	Wife of Hugh Hurford
COLLMAN	Amy	20 Nov 1720	Wife of Robert Collman
BRYANT	Mary	26 Feb 1721	Dau of John Bryant
PALLMAN	Frances	21 May 1721	
SHORLLAND	Alice	28 May 1721	Wife of Richard Shorlland
DAVEY	Christian	9 Jul 1721	Widow
REDWOOD	Mary	16 Jul 1721	Wife of John Redwood
COLLMAN	Susanah	30 Nov 1721	Dau of William & Margaret
CHAMBERLLEN	William	14 Jan 1722	Als Lockly
COLLMAN	Nichollas	11 Feb 1722	
MORSE	Dennis	18 Apr 1722	
HEARD	Nicholas	29 Apr 1722	
REDWOOD	Thomas	20 May 1722	Of Huntsham
HEARD	Amos	20 May 1722	
REDWOOD	Mary	24 Jun 1722	Dau of Thos Redwood, jnr
REDWOOD	John	18 Aug 1722	
THORNE	Betty	29 Oct 1722	Dau of Thomas Thorne, vicar of this parish
GOVIERE	Thomas	11 May 1723	Of this parish *Bachiller*
STEPHENS	Henry	17 May 1723	Mr, of this parish
CROKAM	William	26 May 1723	Son of William Crokam
LOCKE	Rogger	30 Jun 1723	Son of Rogger Locke
STONE	Ellenor	18 Jul 1723	Wife of Charles Stone of Clayhanger
LOCK	Richard	14 Aug 1723	Junior
DAVEY	Richard	22 Sep 1723	Son of Jon: Davey Clerke of this parish
CROKHAM	Joane	29 Sep 1723	Dau of William Crokham
THORNE	Dorothy	11 Dec 1723	Dau of Mr Thomas Thorne
CROKHAM	Elizabeth	15 Dec 1723	Dau of William Crokham
COLLMAN	William	19 Jan 1724	Son of William Collman
GOODING	Ffrances	23 Feb 1724	
COLLMAN	Sarah	17 Mar 1724	Dau of William Collman of Ashbrittle
WOLLAND	Ellenor	23 Apr 1724	Wife of Jon: Wolland
REDWOOD	Grace	5 Jul 1724	Wife of Thomas Redwood of Huntsham
HILL	Ann	24 Sep 1724	Wife of Thomas Hill

Burial Registers

LOCKE	Betty	21 Dec 1724	Dau of Mr Jon: Locke
CHORLY	Mary	23 Dec 1724	Dau of John Chorly
JAMES	William	31 Jan 1725	
COWLIN	Jno:	16 Jul 1725	
CHORLY	Jno:	5 Sep 1725	
BUCKNEL*	Sarah	12 Nov 1725	Dau of Art: Bucknel
MARTYN	Jno:	14 Nov 1725	Son of Jno: Martyn
DAVEY	Jno:	23 Jan 1726	Son of Jno: Davey
COWLIN	Thomas	31 Mar 1726	
COLEMAN	Mary	3 Apr 1726	Dau of Henry Coleman
WOOLLAND	Mary	14 May 1726	Dau of Jno: Woolland
BIDGOOD	Nich:	12 Jun 1726	
COLEMAN	Henry	17 Jun 1726	
COLEMAN	Henry	1 Jul 1726	Son of Henry Coleman
LANGE	Allse	30 Oct 1726	Wife of Edward Lange
BUCKNAL	Art:	18 Nov 1726	
COWLIN	Mary	18 Dec 1726	
FOURACRE	Mary	15 Jan 1726	
BREWER	William	19 Feb 1726	Son of Hum: Brewer
SHORLAND	Richard	26 Feb 1726	
THORNE	Betty	17 Mar 1726	Dau of Mr Tho: Thorne vicar
HURFORD	Hugh	7 Apr 1727	Senior
COLEMAN	Jno:	17 Nov 1727	
MORLE	Thomas	12 May 1728	
BRYANT	Thomas	12 May 1728	Son of Isaac Bryant
THORNE	Mary	27 Jan 1729	Dau of Tho Thorne vicar
REDWOOD	Thamasin	27 Apr 1729	
LUTLY	Mary	4 May 1729	Als Chamberlin
HERD	Dorothy	6 May 1729	
EVELEIGH	Peter	11 May 1729	
SCOT	Samuel	23 May 1729	
CRAZE	Charles	20 Jul 1729	Son Of Thomas
H...WOOD	William	5 Sep 1729	
PERRY	William	7 Sep 1729	Son of Henry
[ILLEGIBLE]	Hannah	25 Jan 1729	
CHOOLY	Joan	15 Feb 1729	[Chorly?]
THORNE	Mrs ...	10 Apr 1730	Wife of Tho Thorne vicar
WEBBER	Mary	21 Jun 1730	Wife of George Webber
BRAY	S...	25 Jun 1730	
MARTYN	Mary	26 Jul 1730	Dau of Jno: Martyn
DAGERY	Jno:	4 Oct 1730	
HEARD	Ann	18 Apr 1731	Widow
COLMAN	Mary	30 Apr 1731	Dau of Will Colman
WYAT	Henry	4 Jul 1731	Als Stuekly
COLMAN	Joan	29 Jul 1731	Wife of William Colman
COLMAN	John	29 Jul 1731	Son of William Colman
REDWOOD	John	11 Aug 1731	Son of Hugh Redwood
LOCKE	Joanna	16 Feb 1731	Widow
SUTTON	Mary	12 Mar 1731	Widow
MARTIN	Mary	11 Jun 1732	Dau of John Martin
STONE	Richard	30 Aug 1732	
CROSHAM	Mary	17 Sep 1732	Wife of William Crosham

Surname	Given	Date	Notes
WYETT	Thomisin	18 Oct 1732	Dau of Thomas Wyett
COLEMAN	Humpherey	21 Feb 1733	
THORNE	Richard	19 Mar 1733	
PERCY	Thomas	4 Apr 1733	Als Hill
CRAZE	Thomas	8 Apr 1733	
HEARD	Robartt	20 Oct 1733	
DAVY	Dorrathy	18 Nov 1733	
DAVY	John	27 Jan 1734	"Ye Auld Clark"
QUICK	Joan	31 Mar 1734	Dau of Hugh Quick
CRAZE	Elinor	23 Jun 1734	Dau of Joan Craze
COLMAN	Joane	10 Nov 1734	Dau of Henry Colman
STONE	Mary	26 Dec 1734	Dau of William Stone at Towerhill
HEARD	Ann	20 Apr 1735	Dau of William Heard
MORAL	Ann	25 May 1735	Widow
HOPSLAND	John	18 Dec 1736	
STONE	William	2 Apr 1736	Carpenter
STONE	Thoz ..zne	30 May 1736	Widow
PASCHE	John	24 Apr 1737	"Son of John Pasche & Mary Perry alias Hill. Base born"
COLEMAN	Margaret	31 Jul 1737	Wife of William Coleman
BIDGOOD	Joan	7 Aug 1737	Wife of William Bidgood
STEPHENS	Mrs	16 Sep 1737	Widow
BRAY	Susannah	2 Oct 1737	
WATERMAN	Elinor	9 Oct 1737	
WIATE	Joan	16 Nov 1737	Dau of Tho & Mary Wiate
ALLIN	Margery	22 Jan 1738	
BONEY	Ann	7 May 1738	Als Chanter
EWENS	Mary	25 Jun 1738	Dau of George & Ann Ewens
EWENS	Elizabeth	25 Jun 1738	Dau of George & Ann Ewens
LOCKE	John	18 Nov 1738	Senior. "As honest a Man as Could Live"
DAVEY	Hannah	27 Feb 1739	
BIDGOOD	William	6 May 1739	Als Crowder
SCOT	Elizabeth	5 Aug 1739	
BREWER	William	30 Sep 1739	Son of Humphry & Mary of Uplowman
COLEMAN	William	16 *Oct* 1739	Senior
CHAPEL	Elizabeth	27 Jan 1740	"No affidavit brought within eight days gave notice of it to churchwarden & officers by a paper dated February 10th"
WEBBER	George	17 Feb 1740	"A very honest virtuous poor man"
FOURACRES	Elizabeth	25 Mar 1740	
CHAPPEL	John	6 Apr 1740	
CHANTER	John	4 May 1740	
QUICK	Joseph	6 Jul 1740	Son of Hugh & Elizabeth
LOCKE	Richard	21 Sep 1740	
BUCKNAL	Joseph	28 Dec 1740	
BROWN	William	11 Jan 1741	Son of Nicholas & Joan
WELCH	George	31 Jan 1741	"No affidavit brought within eight days after his internment. Gave notice thereof to ye Churchwarden and Overseer ye 8th of Feby"

Burial Registers

COLEMAN	Nicholas	16 Feb 1741	Of Sampford Peveral
WELCH	Dorothy	21 Feb 1741	
DAVY	Elizabeth	27 Feb 1741	Wife of Augustine Davy
SHARLAND	Thomas	6 Mar 1741	
COSENS	Ann	20 Mar 1741	
GOVIER	Robert	26 May 1741	"The elder"
BIDGOOD	Elinor	2 Jun 1741	Wife of Abram Bidgood, junior
BIDGOOD	Abram	7 Jun 1741	Husband to the above Elinor
BIDGOOD	Abram	18 Jun 1741	Son of the above Abram Bidgood
COLEMAN	Isaac	6 Sep 1741	
BIDGOOD	Mary	29 Nov 1741	Wife of Nicholas Bidgood
REDWOOD	Thomas	25 Nov 1741	"Son of Thomas Redwood & Mary Farthing. base born"
STET	William	19 Dec 1742	"Apprentice to Stephen Coleman brought in Man Slaughter against ye said Stephen by ye Coroners Inquest"
CHORLY	**Dunce**	25 Dec 1742	
CROCUM	William	24 Jun 1743	
SANDERS	Susannah	7 Jul 1743	
HOCKSLIN	Margaret	4 Sep 1743	
COLEMAN	Thomazin	8 Apr 1744	
MORSE	Eliner	27 May 1744	
COLEMAN	Robert	19 Aug 1744	
BRAY	John	7 Oct 1744	"Ye Younger"
DAVEY	John	16 Dec 1744	
DAVY	Martha	10 Feb 1745	"Wife of ye above John"
DAVY	Elizabeth	11 May 1746	Wife of Edward Davy
YEOENS	Elizabeth	6 Jul 1746	Dau of George [Ewens?]
BRAY	Susannah	3 Aug 1746	
STONE	William	23 Nov 1746	Of Old Close
HURFORD	Nich:	1749	
QUICK	Ann	2 Apr 1749	
QUICK	Elizabeth	30 Apr 1749	
STONE	Christopher	2 May 1749	
SHORLAND	Thomas	6 Aug 1749	
JONES	Elizabeth	3 Dec 1749	Dau of Thomas & Jane
QUICK	Sarah	12 Aug 1750	Dau of Margaret Quick
COLMAN	Sarah	23 Sep 1750	
FARTHING	Thomas	25 Nov 1750	
QUICK	Hugh	13 Jan 1751	The younger
TAYLOR	Elizabeth	27 Jan 1751	Inf
HEARD	Ann	31 Mar 1751	
HURFORD	Grace	11 Sep 1751	Widow
COLMAN	Ann	15 Jul 1752	Wife of Stephen Colman
CHORLY	Thomasine	3 Dec 1752	
FARTHING	Thomas	7 Jan 1753	
PERRY	Dennis	6 Jul 1753	Son of Henry Perry als Hill
ALLEN	Thomasine	20 Sep 1753	
D'ASSIGNY	Sarah	2 Dec 1753	Dau of John D'Assigny

SHORLAND	Elizabeth	23 Dec 1753	
MORSE	Nicholas	4 Jan 1754	
GOODING	John	6 Jan 1754	Son of Thomas Gooding
DAVY	Elizabeth	27 Jan 1754	Wife of Edward Davy
SULLY	Mary	16 Jun 1754	Dau of --- Sully
COLMAN	Susanna	1 Sep 1754	
DAGWORTHY	Joan	19 Jan 1755	
KNOWLES	Susanna	23 Feb 1755	
HILL	Ann	25 May 1755	Dau of Thomas Hill
LOCK	John	15 Jun 1755	
OLAND	John	29 Jun 1755	
SULLY	Mary	11 Oct 1755	
BRAY	John	26 Oct 1755	Sexton
VOWLER	Joan	11 Jan 1756	Dau of Hugh Vowler
PERRY	John	20 Mar 1756	Son of John Perry als Hill
PEARCE	Sarah	4 Apr 1756	
HILL	Thomas	2 May 1756	Son of Thomas Hill
QUICK	Jane	2 May 1756	Dau of Roger Quick
HILL	Elizabeth	2 Jan 1757	Dau of John Hill
TAYLOR	Elizabeth	16 Jan 1757	Dau of Edward Taylor
HOSEGOOD	Elizabeth	10 Apr 1757	Dau of John Hosegood
WOOD	Anne	21 Aug 1757	
MORSE	William	21 Apr 1758	
PERRY	Thomasin	30 Apr 1758	
DAVEY	Richard	24 Nov 1758	
COLMAN	William	4 Feb 1759	
KNIGHT	Joan	26 May 1759	
TUCKFIELD	Anne	24 Jun 1759	
SHORLAND	Alice	22 Jul 1759	
TUCKFIELD	Sarah	7 Oct 1759	
PERRY	John	21 Jan 1760	
OLAND	Mary	25 May 1760	
QUICK	Hugh	8 Aug 1760	
LOCKE	John	7 Jun 1761	
PERRY	Sarah	14 Jun 1761	
BREWER	Nicholas	6 Dec 1761	
SHAPTON	John	25 Dec 1761	
COLMAN	Matthew	27 Dec 1761	
LOCKE	John	27 Jan 1763	Of Kerswell
HALL	Thomas	6 Feb 1763	
STEPHENS	Nicholas	10 May 1763	
DAVEY	Betty	10 Apr 1763	
COLMAN	Stephen	6 Jan 1764	
BUCKNELL	Jacob	2 Mar 1764	
COLMAN	Sarah	14 Sep 1764	
PERRY	Henry	5 May 1765	
REDWOOD	Anne	19 May 1765	
TAYLOR	Mary	6 Oct 1765	
WARD	Thomasin	16 Oct 1765	
REDWOOD	Mary	4 Dec 1765	
REDWOOD	Richard	4 Dec 1765	
BONNEY	William	8 Dec 1765	
HALL	Joan	21 Dec 1765	

Burial Registers

BUCKNELL	Robert	22 Dec 1765	
MORSE	John	2 Apr 1766	
PERRY	Henry	23 Aug 1766	
DAVEY	Peter	7 Sep 1766	
STUTE	Jno: & William	15 Feb 1767	
COLMAN	Sarah	6 Apr 1767	
LUCKFELL	Jno:	24 May 1767	
BUCKNELL	Elizabeth	12 Jun 1767	
COLMAN	Robert	2 Aug 1767	
COLMAN	Joan	9 Aug 1767	
BUCKNELL	Jacob	28 Aug 1767	
BIDGOOD	Henry	1 Nov 1767	
BIDGOOD	Susanne	8 Nov 1767	
WAYETT	Mary	3 Jan 1768	
SAIER	Mary	12 Jun 1768	
FOULER	Mary	31 Jul 1768	
HURD	William	14 Aug 1768	
LOCKE	Mary	20 Nov 1768	
LOCKE	Grace	18 Dec 1768	
DAVEY	John	16 Jul 1769	
PEARSE	Ann	10 Sep 1769	
BIDGOOD	Mary	15 Oct 1769	
DAVEY	Sarah	10 Dec 1769	
WOOD	William	31 Dec 1769	
HATTING	Ann	29 Jan 1770	
LOCKE	Thomas	18 Feb 1770	
PEARSE	Sarah	18 Feb 1770	
MORSE	Elizabeth	14 Apr 1770	
WOOD	Susanna	15 Sep 1770	
BOWERMAN	Samuel	16 Sep 1770	
DAGGERY	Jane	24 Mar 1771	
HOSEGOOD	John	9 Jun 1771	And Mary his wife
HOSEGOOD	Mary	9 Jun 1771	Wife of John Hosegood
PEARSE	John	7 Jul 1771	
DOWDNEY	John	1 Dec 1771	Of Burlescombe
COLLMAN	Henry	6 Jan 1772	
STONE	Thomas	1 Mar 1772	
LOCKE	Susanna	10 Jun 1772	Mrs
HERD	Ann	27 Dec 1772	
BONEY	Sarah	27 Dec 1772	
GOODING	Mary	23 May 1773	
PEARSE	Mary	3 Oct 1773	
COLLMAN	John	3 Apr 1774	
BATTEN	Mary	28 Aug 1774	
LOCKE	Thomas	13 Nov 1774	Senior
STILL	John	6 Aug 1775	Senior
TAYLOR	Richard	29 Nov 1775	Of Holcombe Rogus
COLLMAN	Thomazin	29 Nov 1775	Of Sampford Arrondal
MORSE	Elizabeth	29 Dec 1775	
DAVY	Jane	18 Feb 1776	
PHILIPS	Robert	3 Mar 1776	
EWINGS	Ann	28 Jul 1776	

BUCKNELL	Arthur	20 Aug 1776	Junior
REDWOOD	Hugh	12 Sep 1776	
DAVY	Arthur	17 Nov 1776	Junior
GOVIER	Mary	14 Mar 1777	
PERRY	Mary	1 Jun 1777	
STONE	Robert	18 Jan 1778	
FOWLER	Mary	17 Jan 1779	
SANDERS	Sarah	24 Jan 1779	
DAVY	Arthur	31 Jan 1779	Junior
REDWOOD	Mary	21 Mar 1779	
COLLMAN	William	13 Jun 1779	
EWINGS	Thomas	27 Jun 1779	
STONE	Matthew	16 Jul 1779	
WOOD	Mary	17 Oct 1779	
MORSE	Jane	31 Oct 1779	
SHAPTON	Christopher	7 Nov 1779	
STILL	Joan	13 Feb 1780	The elder
GOODING	Thomas	26 Jun 1780	The elder
BIDGOOD	Henry	23 Jul 1780	
BUCKNELL	Mary	4 Sep 1780	Wife of Arthur Bucknell
GOODING	Sarah	6 May 1781	
GALE	Anne	2 Jun 1781	Of Tiverton
LUCAS	William	26 Aug 1781	
LOCKE	Sarah	11 Nov 1781	Widow
GOVIER	Robert	15 Mar 1782	
SHARLAND	William	12 May 1782	
HERD	Elinor	1 Oct 1782	
DAVEY	Susanna	27 Oct 1782	The Younger
WEBBER	William	3 Nov 1782	
GREENWAY	James	23 Feb 1783	
STITT	Joan	11 Mar 1783	
BATTING	John	30 Mar 1783	
HARRISS	William	6 Apr 1783	A child
WARD	Thomas	21 Sep 1783	A child
PHILIPS	Susanna	28 Sep 1783	
STONE	Elizabeth	21 Dec 1783	A pauper
EWINGS	George	16 Feb 1784	A pauper
STEPHENS	Henry	23 May 1784	
WOOD	Richard	6 Nov 1785	
BRAY	Elizabeth	28 Dec 1785	
DAVEY	Mary	14 Jan 1786	Pauper
GOODING	Thomas	6 Aug 1786	Pauper
SHAPTON	Jane	8 Oct 1786	Pauper
STEPHENS	John	12 Nov 1786	
DAVEY	Susanna	12 Nov 1786	Pauper
FERRISS	William	8 Apr 1787	A child
LOCKE	Mary	10 Jun 1787	Wife of Thomas Locke
CROAKHAM	Elizabeth	1 Jul 1787	Pauper
DAVEY	Anne	9 Mar 1788	Dau of Arthur Davey
BIDGOOD	Sarah	11 May 1788	Dau of Abrm: Bidgood pauper
CRAZE	Francis	8 Jun 1788	Of Bathelton Somerset
CROAKHAM	Mary	3 May 1789	Spinster Pauper

Burial Registers

EWINGS	Mary	25 May 1789	Pauper
REDWOOD	John	19 Jun 1789	Pauper
STUKELEY	Thomas	12 Jul 1789	Als Wyeat
BREWER	Joan	13 Sep 1789	Spinster
BIDGOOD	Thomazin	11 Jan 1790	Wife of Abraham Bidgood
KERSLAKE	Thomas	14 Mar 1790	Pauper
WARD	Grace	11 Apr 1790	Wife of John Ward pauper
TAYLOR	Ann	16 May 1790	Spinster. Pauper
DAVEY	Arthur	16 Nov 1790	Pauper
GOODING	Francis	17 Jan 1791	Batchelor
NOTT	Joan	4 Feb 1791	Wife of James Nott
GOODING	Anne	6 Mar 1791	Dau of Thomas & Joan
WEBSTER	Charles Esq	18 Mar 1791	Widower
NORMAN	Nicholas	24 Apr 1791	Son of Nicholas and Sarah
SAYER	George	15 May 1791	"Parish Clark"
SULLEY	James	20 Nov 1791	
LUCAS	Richard	17 Dec 1791	
WYATT	Elizabeth	29 Jan 1792	Spinster
MAY	Sarah	10 Jun 1792	Wife of James May
HOLCOMBE	Mary	22 Sep 1793	Dau of William & Mary
COLMAN	Anne	6 Apr 1794	Widow
SULLEY	Susannah	13 Jul 1794	Widow
TAYLOR	Mary	13 Jul 1794	Spinster
FERRIS	George	7 Dec 1794	
HILL	Elizabeth	18 Jan 1795	Wife of Thomas Hill
DAVEY	Joseph	2 Aug 1795	Widower
KERSLAKE	William	16 Aug 1795	Son of John & Jane Kerslake
SULLEY	Eleanor	1 Nov 1795	Spinster
GOODING	Betty	19 Feb 1796	Dau of John & Betty
TAYLOR	Edward	26 Jun 1796	Widower
MAY	James	11 Sep 1796	Widower
WYATT	Mary	16 Oct 1796	Widow
HILL	Thomas	19 Feb 1797	Widower
MAY	Sarah	19 Mar 1797	Dau of Harry & Anne May
REDWOOD	Thomas	2 Apr 1797	
HAWKINGS	James	2 Apr 1797	Son of William & Mary
FERRIS	Mary	11 Feb 1798	Widow
NORMAN	Nicholas	10 Jun 1798	Son of Nicholas & Sarah
LOCK	Rich	29 Mar 1798	
SHARLAND	Susannah	10 Feb 1799	Widow
BUCKNELL	Arthur	30 Mar 1799	Yeoman
FERRIS	Elizabeth	31 Mar 1799	Dau of John & Mary Ferris
DARBY	Henry	1 Apr 1799	Son of John & Mary Darby
WEBSTER	Edward	13 Aug 1799	Esq
BROOKS	Mary	29 Jan 1800	Dau of Thomas & Sarah
LUCAS	Susannah	6 Apr 1800	Widow
BUSSEL	James	3 Jun 1800	Batchelor
BRYANT	James	17 Nov 1800	Widower
BUCKNELL	Sarah	23 Nov 1800	Spinster
QUICK	Roger	15 Feb 1801	
BREWER	Joan	22 Feb 1801	
PERRY	Thomas	22 Mar 1801	Als Hill

SAYER	Elizabeth	21 Feb 1802		Widow
LOCK	Joan	22 May 1802		Widow
PERRY	James	30 Oct 1802		Son of William & Mary
COTTRELL	Jane	1 May 1803		
PERRY	Maria	22 May 1803		
HATTEN	William	30 Oct 1803		
GOODWIN	Maria	11 Mar 1804		
QUICK	Elizabeth	18 Mar 1804		
GELL	Thomasin	6 Jun 1804		Of Tiverton
KERSLAKE	Mary	22 Jul 1804		
DAVY	Henry	27 Jan 1805		
LUCAS	John	21 Apr 1805		
GREENSLADE	Mary	6 Mar 1807		
QUICK	Mary	15 Mar 1807		
LARANCE	Henry	22 Jan 1808		
REDWOOD	Mary	17 Apr 1808		
WATTS	Margaret	22 Apr 1808		~~Dau of William & Susanna~~
DIN	Mark	17 Nov 1809		[?Dinham]
STUTT	John	8 Jul 1810		
LAURENCE	James	5 Aug 1810		
LUCAS	Betty	7 Oct 1810		
PERRY	Thomas	29 Dec 1810		
PERRY	Mary	2 Jan 1811		
PERRY	Hannah	11 Nov 1811		
HATTING	James	29 Mar 1812		
FERRIS	Mary	10 May 1812		
COTTREL	William	17 May 1812		
MORSE	Dorothy	6 Jun 1812		
WEBSTER	Adria West	17 Oct 1812		
LUCAS	Susannah	28 Feb 1813	6 w	Uplowman
WOOD	Elizabeth	25 Apr 1813	1 m	
MAY	Sarah	30 May 1813	20	
NORMAN	Sarah	26 Sep 1813	59	
WOOD	John	27 Mar 1814	2 w	
HILL	Sarah	4 Sep 1814	53	
PERRY	John	20 Nov 1814	2 m	
BUCKNELL	Sarah	14 Dec 1814	21	
WEBBER	Mary	9 Jul 1815	63	
HAWKINS	Charles	24 Sep 1815	9 m	
MAY	Mary	15 Oct 1815	14	
PERRY	Elizabeth	10 Mar 1816	2 d	
MAY	Ann	22 Sep 1816	49	
ROBERTS	Henry	2 Mar 1817	18 m	
BRAY	Mary	6 Apr 1817	82	
GREENSLADE	Horatio	13 Jun 1817	7	
DARBY	John	19 Jul 1818	6 m	
BREWER	Mary	23 Aug 1818	75	
FARTHING	Ann	25 Oct 1818	74	
LUCAS	Susannah	3 Jan 1819	14 m	
PERRY	Sarah	14 Mar 1819	70	
WEBSTER	James	11 Apr 1819	2 d	
SAYER	Nicholas	6 Jun 1819	74	
QUICK	John	24 Oct 1819	2	

Burial Registers

REDWOOD	Mary	25 Dec 1819	12	
BARNETT	Thomas	13 Feb 1820	2 w	
NEEDS	Mary	14 May 1820	68	
SHAPLAND	William	4 Jun 1820	36	
ASH*	Betty	6 Aug 1820	45	
HALL	James	8 Oct 1820	74	
DIBBLE	William	24 Dec 1820	2 w	
ARTHURS	Jane	3 Jun 1821	14	
BROWN	Roberts	21 Oct 1821	28	
LUCAS	John	30 Dec 1821	19 m	
PAVEY	Henry	1 Jan 1822	10 d	
GREENSLADE	Thomas	24 Feb 1822	63	
PERRY	Henry	25 Aug 1822	28	
PARR	Emma	17 Nov 1822	2 m	
TOZE	Sarah	9 Nov 1823	61	
NEEDS	Thomas	4 Jan 1824	81	
GREENWOOD	Mary	25 Jul 1824	35	
DAVY	Mary	21 Nov 1824	42	
DAVY	Ann	20 Nov 1825	77	
TAYLOR	V	18 Dec 1825	72	
THORN	John	4 Feb 1827	55	
PERRY	Eliza	25 Feb 1827	17	
WYNN	Christopher	15 Jul 1827	27	
HILL	Thomas	9 Sep 1827	66	Formerly parish clerk
MORRIS	William	23 Sep 1827	17	"Died in the smallpox"
WYNN	Christopher	23 Sep 1827	3	"Died in the small pox"
NORMAN	Nicholas	11Nov 1827	76	Holcombe Rogus
RADFORD	Mary Ann	2 Dec 1827	24	
COOD	Robert	6 Jan 1828	78	
MAY	Harriet	9 Mar 1828	3	Holcombe Rogus
LOCK	John	5 Jul 1828	65	Yeoman of Sandford. Late of Holelake.
JEWELL	Mary	20 Apr 1829	19	
PERRY	Iohn	26 Apr 1829	79	
DISNEY	Mary	13 Oct 1829	85	
TOOZE	Ann	14 Mar 1830	1	
WEBSTER	Charles	5 Apr 1830	50	
NEEEDS	John	14 Apr 1830	50	
LUCAS	Mary Ann	25 Apr 1830	3 w	
REDWOOD	John	17 Oct 1830	67	
SQUIRE	Mary	12 Nov 1830	4	
SQUIRE	Edwin	25 Jan 1831	1 m	
SAYER	Nicholas	1 Apr 1831	50	
PAINE	William	9 Apr 1831	33	Sandford Peverell
PAVEY*	Mary	14 Jun1831	73	
PERRY	Elizabeth	21 Jan 1832	28	
FERRIS	Mary	9 Jun 1832	12	
PERRY	Maria	3 Nov 1832	25	
HALL	Sarah	18 Nov 1832	87	
PALMER	William	8 Dec 1832	44	
PERRY	William	30 Mar 1833	81	Clayhanger
ASH*	Jane	8 Sep 1833	34 m	

Surname	Given	Date	Age	Notes
SLOMAN	Richard	12 Jan 1834	89	
WEBSTER	Adria	18 Jan 1834	44	
ASH*	James	10 Mar 1834	10 m	
PAVEY	Joseph	22 Mar 1834	9 m	
DARBY	Mary Ann	5 Apr 1834	14	
WEBSTER	Adria	5 Apr 1834	20	Shepton Mallet. Dau of above Adria Webster
PERRY*	William	1 May 1834	60	
HOBBS	John	3 Jun 1834	8	
DARBY	Henry	16 Jun 1834	8 d	
PERRY	James	22 Jun 1834	14 d	
MAY	John	26 Oct 1834	18	Holcombe Rogus
SHAPCOTT	Elizabeth	26 Oct 1834	56	
HOBBS	Samuel	7 Dec 1834	69	"Late Sexton"
MAY	Elizabeth	8 Mar 1835	4	
PERRY	William	20 Sep 1835	57	
SCOTT	William	15 Nov 1835	55	
CLARKE	Ann	3 Jan 1836	81	
LUCKIS	Henry	5 Feb 1836	16 h	
MAY	Henry	22 Aug 1836	73	
GREENSLADE	Elizabeth	11 Jan 1837	55	
GREENSLADE	Grace	5 Feb 1837	73	
HILL*	Betty	11 Feb 1837	72	
WADDLETON	Elizabeth	19 Feb 1837	83	
DARBY*	Edward	23 Mar 1837	61	
CLEEVE*	William	20 Apr 1837	48	
DAVY	James	21 Jan 1838	57	
MOORE	Thomas	3 Mar 1838	28	"Killed by the quarry falling in on him"
NEEDS	Keziah	4 Mar 1838	49	
MILTON	Charlotte	3 Apr 1838	6 m	
NEEDS	Elizabeth	13 Apr 1838	23	
HUNT	May Ann	1 Jul 1838	1	
HOLMES	James	29 Jul 1838	40	
TURNER	Robert	25 Aug 1838	4 d	
GILLARD	Thomas	2 Dec 1838	23	
NEEDS	Harriett	9 Dec 1838	6	
LUCAS	Mary Ann	11 May 1839	11 m	
NEEDS	Thomas	28 May 1839	19	Hemyock
PERRY	Adra	28 Jul 1839	2	
COCKRAM	Elizabeth	8 Sep 1839	1y	
MILTON	Robert	22 Sep 1839	23	
TURNER	Elizabeth	1 Jan 1840	38	
GILLARD	Elizabeth	12 Apr 1840	15	Ashbrittle, Somerset
BAKER	Sarah	11 Apr 1841	33	
TURNER	Robert	5 Jun 1841	18 m	Trebarrow, Somerset
GAMLIN	John	6 Nov 1841	8	
JEWELL	William	22 Nov 1841	Inf	
HILL	John	21 Apr 1842	77	
ASH*	James	23 Jul 1842	2 d	
HOLMES	Henry	4 Sep 1842	16	Borden Gate
BABBAGE	Jane	27 Oct 1842	10	
BABBAGE	Charlotte	27 Oct 1842	7	

Burial Registers

GAMLIN	James	11 Nov 1842	1 y	
TOTTLE	Samuel	20 Nov 1842	4	
GAMLIN	Selina	30 Nov 1842	4	
KERSLAKE	Elizabeth	7 Dec 1842	7	
ASH*	Elizabeth	18 Feb 1843	18	
ASH*	Abel	2 Mar 1843	7 m	
HOBBS	Mary	3 Sep 1843	79	
HURFORD	William	15 Apr 1844	57	
HILL	Sarah	28 Apr 1844	32	
DUNN	John	16 Jun 1844	72	
LOVELL	Maria	19 Jun 1844	11m	
STANLEY	Phoebe	6 Nov 1844	5 w	Bedminster nr Bristol
GILLARD	James	10 Nov 1844	22	Bampton
LUCAS	Ann	28 Jun 1845	12	Burlescombe
WYNN	John	17 Oct 1845	58	
OSMOND	George	22 Nov 1845	30	
GAMLIN	Mary	11 Apr 1846	37	Benstice Farm
COYNN	Samuel	1 Aug 1846	18	Lea
WYNN	Christopher	8 Aug 1846	14	Lea
GILLARD	Elizabeth	25 Oct 1846	63	Stucklies
FOLLETT	Jane Lyddon	3 Jan 1847	Inf	Cottage on Redwoods
DUNN	James	2 Jan 1848	12	Stucklies
MILTON	Thomas	13 Feb 1848	28	Waterslade
BERE	Mary Ann	26 Feb 1848	16	Herds Farm
GILLARD	John	26 Mar 1848	42	Chimney Down
MILTON	Robert	1 Apr 1848	2 m	Poor House
PERRY	William	15 Jun 1848	19	Huntsham Mills
LUCKIS/LUCAS	Martha	4 Aug 1848	-	"Thorne Land"
DUNN*	Harriet	6 Aug 1848	36	Staple Cross
ASH*	William	25 Nov 1848	22	
BOND	Mary	30 Jan 1849	75	Poor House
MOON	John	12 Aug 1849	6	Holelake
ASH*	Emma	7 Nov 1849	15	
SHORLAND	Jane	23 Dec 1849	83	Cottage on Daggeridge
MILTON*	Charles	14 Apr 1850	25	Waterslade
ROBERTS*	Elizabeth	25 Apr 1850	77	
GARDINER	Eli	25 Apr 1850	Inf	Lucklies Lane
ROSSITER	William	8 Sep 1850	61	Holelake
MILTON	John	17 Aug 1851	79	Hole Lane
DARBY*	Loveday	18 Sep 1851	80	Morebath
FROST	Henry	30 Sep 1851	64	Daggeridge Cottage
PAVEY*	Henry Allen	18 Oct 1851	87	Staple
DUNN	Susan	14 Dec 1851	77	Staple Cross
HILL	John	25 Apr 1852	78	Staple Cross
LONGMAN*	William Courtenay	15 May 1852	5	Hockworthy Town
ENDICOTT	Maria	9 Jan 1853	Inf	
MOGFORD	Ann	13 Feb 1853	35	
ASH*	William	9 Mar 1853	80	
FORDS	John	10 Apr 1853	80	Lea
HALL	Henry	Apr 1853	84	Hockford
DUNN	Mark	15 May 1853	13 m	
WEST	John Townsend	22 Jun 1853	44	

LOVELL	Mark	2 Jul 1853	2	
FISHER	John	25 Sep 1853	61	
MAY	Henry	2 Nov 1853	48	
PERRY	James	13 Jan 1854	19	Hockford
HOWE	Thomas	14 May 1854	61	
LITTLEJOHN	John	24 Jul 1854	Inf	Died on day of birth.
MOON	Ellen	17 Dec 1854	67	Lea
LAMPREY*	Susan	17 Jun 1855	11 m	Waterslade
RESTORICK	Elizabeth	21 Aug 1855	38	
GAMLIN	Robert	15 Mar 1856	41	
PARR	George	11 May 1856	86	
WEBSTER	Charles	19 Jun 1856	40	Wenvoe in Wales
BERRY	Jane	7 Aug 1856	34	
LUCAS	John	20 Aug 1856	16	Thornlands
STEPHENS	Thomas	24 Aug 1856	13	Ridge in Sampford
BROOMFIELD	Sarah	14 Sep 1856	19	
BROOMFIELD	Henry	12 Oct 1856	64	
BUCKNELL*	John	3 Jan 1857	53	Durley Farm
STEPHENS	Mathew	8 Feb 1857	8	Ridge in S/Peverell
LOVEL	Eliza	22 Feb 1857	2	Waterslade
MILTON	Ann	4 Oct 1857	80	Chimney Down
RUSSELL	Frances	19 Oct 1857	18	Lea
WEBBER	Harriet	10 Jan 1858	4	Lea
ASH*	Jane	20 Feb 1858	56	
MAY	Caroline	21 Feb 1858	27	
STEPHENS*	William Edward	25 Feb 1858	4	
MAY	Mary Anna	28 Feb 1858	14 m	
FERRIS*	Edmund Tom	29 Apr 1858	4 m	Staple Cross
MAY	Walter	3 May 1858	3	
MAY	James	6 Jun 1858	37	
ASH*	Jane	12 Jun 1858	17	
OSMOND	Susan	20 Jun 1858	Inf	
GRIDLEY	Emma	19 Nov 1858	Inf	
LAMPREY	Amelia Elizabeth	10 Apr 1859	11 m	Hole
GAMLIN*	John	23 Jul 1859	53	Bentice
WOOD	Ann	16 Oct 1859	76	Hockford Water
BAWDEN	Sarah	23 Oct 1859	2	Hendom
DARBY*	William	29 Oct 1859	72	Lamb Inn, Uffculme
STRONG	John	9 Nov 1859	65	
HAWKINS	Mary	8 Jan 1860	77	
ASH*	Joan	30 Mar 1860	75	Bishop's Hull
LUCAS	William	12 Apr 1860	44	
PERRY*	Mary	27 Apr 1860	84	
FERRIS*	Mark	10 May 1860	1	
GARDENER	Elizabeth	18 Jun 1860	85	
FISHER	Francis	Aug 1860	12	"Found drowned"
LONGMAN*	Elizabeth R	31 Oct 1860	21	
TALBOT*	John	28 Jul 1861	55	"Suddenly"
FERRIS	John	1 Dec 1861	67	Died at the Union, Tiverton
TOTTLE	Elizabeth	15 Dec 1861	19	Chimney Down
FERRIS*	Martha Sarah	19 Dec 1861	1	Staple Cross
DART	Maria	9 Feb 1862	1	
TWOZE*	Samuel	23 Feb 1862	76	

Burial Registers

FROAKE	Eliza	1 Jun 1862	Inf	
LOCK*	John	29 Nov 1862	3	
FROST*	Mary	29 Jan 1863	77	
TWOOZE	Samuel	28 Mar 1863	Inf	
DUNN	Robert	10 Jun 1863	48	
MILTON	John	13 Jun 1863	57	"John Milton was burnt to death in a lime kiln"
TWOZE*	Mary	2 Aug 1863	75	
BROMFIELD	Sarah Ann	3 Sep 1863	4	
COTTRELL*	William Walter	20 Sep 1863	4	
FERRIS*	Sarah	6 Jan 1864	71	Staple Cross
ASH*	Robert	20 Jan 1864	65	
FERRIS*	Tom	20 Apr 1864	1	
FERRIS*	Mark	26 Jun 1864	2	
MARKS*	John	22 Oct 1864	3 m	
STEPHENS	Elizabeth	5 Nov 1864	6	
NEWMAN*	Alice Susanna	28 Dec 1864	14	
ASH*	Robert	28 Dec 1864	27	
SPRAGUE*	Mary	29 Jan 1865	7	
WHITE*	Mary	31 May 1865	16	
DINHAM*	Albert	15 Jun 1865	11 m	
DUNN	Harriet	9 Jul 1865	4	
BROOMFIELD	May Jane	15 Oct 1865	2	
FROAKE	William	11 Mar 1866	8 m	
LAMPREY*	Samuel	29 Apr 1866	25	
WOODBERRY	Edward	10 May 1866	7	"Drowned"
PARR	Harriet	12 May 1866	53	Hockford
NEEDS	Richard	27 May 1866	87	
LOCK*	Bessie	3 Jun 1866	1 y	Ridge in Sampford Parish
MOON	William	17 Jun 1866	52	
FERRIS*	Elizabeth	28 Jul 1866	36	
GILLARD	Robert	23 Sep 1866	86	
MILTON	John	23 Sep 1866	17	
PAUL	Lucy Hannah	23 Sep 1866	11 m	
REDWOOD	Elizabeth	June 1867	Few d	
BAKER	Mary	7 Sep 1867	69	Sampford Peverell
HAWKINS	Robert	5 Apr 1868	52	
HOLLAND	John	12 Apr 1868	77	
LOCK*	Maria	26 Aug 1868	44	Uplowman
WENSLEY*	William	10 Nov 1868	66	
HAWKINS	Anne	28 Nov 1868	80	Tiverton
ROBERTS*	John	19 Dec 1868	97	
GOFFIN*	William	23 May 1869	31	
GUNNINGHAM	Samuel	23 May 1869	60	Sampford Peverell Commonly called Gunny
HARWOOD	Elizabeth	2 Jun 1869	84	
GUNNINGHAM	Mary	12 Jun 1869	50	Ridge in Sampford Peverell Commonly called Gunny
RIDGEWAY	Robert	26 Dec 1869	21 m	
GAMLIN	Martha	19 Feb 1870	69	
DISNEY	Edith	1 Sep 1870	Inf	
MOON	John	26 Mar 1871	71	

BUCKNELL	Charles Henry	30 May 1871	5	Burlescombe
BROMFIELD	Johanna	18 Jun 1871	77	
WENSLEY	Caroline	1 Jul 1871	26	
BUCKNELL*	Eliza	26 Jul 1871	2	Uplowman
GARDINER	Mary	6 Aug 1871	57	
DARBY	Susannah	2 Sep 1871	75	Burlescombe
GOFFIN*	Mary	26 Nov 1871	68	
JONES	James	17 Mar 1872	6	
WENSLEY	William Robert	10 May 1872	Inf	
HAGLEY	Sarah	6 Aug 1872	23 m	
VENN	William	2 Nov 1872	23	
STEPHENS	William	2 Dec 1872	73	Bowdens
WENSLEY	Caroline Emma	5 Jan 1873	Int	
RIDGEWAY	Mary	24 Jul 1873	12	
DUNN	John	12 Oct 1873	70	
LOVELL	Edward	22 Oct 1873	11 m	
NOTT	Frederick	16 Nov 1873	10 m	Bowden Gate
REDWOOD	Jane	17 Jan 1874	68	
MOON	James	25 Jan 1874	68	
WENSLEY	William James	25 Apr 1874	Inf	
LUCAS*	Henry	17 Oct 1874	70	
HOWE	Mary Elizabeth	20 Dec 1874	74	
FISHER	Sarah	7 Mar 1875	86	
HALLETT	William	17 Apr 1875	40	Sampford Peverell
MOON*	Samuel	18 Apr 1875	66	
DARBY*	William Edward	6 Aug 1875	65	Kerswell
TOTTLE	Mary Ann	22 Aug 1875	23	
HAGLEY	Elizabeth	29 Dec 1875	60	
BRYANT	Daniel	26 Jan 1876	Inf	
PERRY*	Mary	23 Mar 1876	64	Burlescombe
FROST	Mary	16 Apr 1876	84	
FISHER	Henry	18 May 1876	52	"Husband and wife were buried together"
FISHER	Hannah	18 May 1876	61	
WHITE*	Emma	20 Sep 1876	19	Lea
SULLY	Richard	25 Jan 1877	10 m	
TWOZE	Samuel	15 Feb 1877	59	
WENSLEY*	Hannah	24 Mar 1877	76	
CORNISH	Harry	3 Jan 1878	7 m	
BROOMFIELD	Henry John	30 Jun 1878	4 m	
GAMLIN	Lena	7 Jul 1878	1	
BROOMFIELD	Caroline	29 Sep 1878	44	
FERRIS	Albert Jesse	10 Nov 1878	5	Staple Cross
TALBOT*	Mary	31 Dec 1878	75	
FOWLER*	Mary Ann	18 Jan 1879	42	Cove, Tiverton
ELLACOTT	Thomas	31 Jan 1879	68	Bowdens
LONGMAN*	Ann Elizabeth	11 Apr 1879	67	Wiveliscombe
DUNN*	Mary	27 Apr 1879	71	
REDWOOD	John	5 May 1879	77	
HALLETT	Elizabeth	7 Jun 1879	21	
SPRAGUE*	Robert	28 Sep 1879	66	"NB was killed in a quarry"
WOODBURY	Jane	7 Dec 1879	39	
GAMLIN	William	8 Jan 1880	85	Washfield

Burial Registers

NEWMAN*	William James	13 Jan 1880	60	"N.B. Vicar of the parish for 26 years and curate 2 years"
CORNISH	Lucy	16 May 1880	15 m	Ridge, Sampford Peverell
STEPHENS	Maria	8 Sep 1880	36	Holelake
MOON	Jessie Florence	16 Oct 1880	7 w	Stucklies
COTTRELL*	James	25 Jun 1881	50	
CRISP	Amy Ann	4 Sep 1881	15	
LONGMAN*	Samuel	15 Dec 1881	76	Wiveliscombe
REDWOOD	Jesse	12 Mar 1882	2	Lucklies
JENNINGS	Jane	10 Jun 1882	7	
SNOW	Lily Laura	2 Jul 1882		Hendom
NEWMAN*	Frances Elizabeth	12 Jul 1882	26	South Town Hse Dartmouth
STEVENS	Elizabeth	13 Nov 1882	77	Bowdens
COTTRELL	Louis John	10 Feb 1883	1	
TARR	Elizabeth	1 Apr 1883	70	
NEWMAN*	Caroline Durnford	3 Apr 1883	39	
NEWMAN*	Caroline	16 Jul 1883	67	Dartmouth
GAMLIN	Sarah	6 Oct 1883	82	
DINHAM*	Charles	5 Apr 1884	78	
MARKS	William James	19 Apr 1884	46	
PERRY	William	2 May 1884	79	West Monkton
NOTT	James	5 Jun 1884	69	
TOOZE*	William	30 Aug 1884	61	
BUCKNELL	Robert Richard	8 Oct 1884	3 m	
HAGLEY	John	28 Jan 1885	77	Uplowman
MAY	Charity	7 Mar 1885	82	Uplowman
TOOTLE	Jim	7 Mar 1885	10	
WENSLEY	William Henry	11 Mar 1885	1	
TALBOT*	Elizabeth	15 May 1885	41	
WENSLEY	James	15 Aug 1885	45	
MARKS	Elizabeth	27 Aug 1885	53	
STEVENS	Robert Timewell	11 Sep 1885	35	
PARR	John	12 Sep 1885	71	Stawley, Somerset
MOON*	Mary	31 Oct 1885	84	
HAWKINS	James	7 Nov 1885	59	
GARD	Frances Elizabeth	5 Jan 1886	59	
SNOW	Henry Charles	10 Jan 1886	10 m	
REDWOOD	Alfred	6 Feb 1886	5 m	
WEBBER	Eliza	15 Apr 1886	69	
DART	Charlotte	17 Apr 1886	65	
BROOMFIELD*	Henry	12 Mar 1887	46	Huntsham
WOOD*	Fanny Ann	8 Jun 1887	21	Stallenge Thorne
BURTON	Sydney	20 Jun 1887	15 m	
WHITE*	Thomas	15 Jul 1887	68	Lea Barton. "For 20 years Churchwarden"
REDWOOD	Hugh	1 Jan 1888	3	
DART	Charlotte Ann	24 Apr 1888	1 m	
GOFFIN*	William	23 Jun 1888	76	Parish Sexton for 37 yrs
SMITH	William Sydney	11 May 1889	11	
HAWKINS	Ann	1 Dec 1889	1 d	
FERRIS*	John	10 Mar 1890	67	Chipstable, Somerset
STEPHENS	Thomas	4 Nov 1890	55	Uplowman

WESTCOTT	John Clapp	23 Dec 1890	7	Speedlands, S/Peverell	
WESTCOTT	Caroline	18 May 1891	42	Speedlands, S/Peverell	
HAWKINS	Laura	16 Aug 1891	5 m		
NEWMAN*	Herbert Roope	2 Dec 1891	43	Heavitree, Devon	
HOW*	Charles	17 Dec 1891	76	Court Hall. Churchwarden	
CORNISH	Mary	22 Dec 1891	42	Sampford Peverell	
CORNISH	Charles	22 Dec 1891	5 d	Sampford Peverell	
WESTCOTT	William	15 Mar 1892	76	Speedlands, Sampford Peverell	
DART	John	17 Sep 1892	76		
WHITE*	Harriett	10 Nov 1892	63		
MOORE	Mary	6 Jan 1893	86		
WOODBURY	Mary	10 Mar 1893	27		
LYDDON	William	23 Mar 1893	82		
SHATTOCK*	Robert White	3 May 1893	47	Stallenge Thorne. "Vicars churchwarden for Hockworthy"	
FOURACRE	Emily	20 May 1893	21		
FORGAN	Dorothy Kate	5 Jun 1893	10 w		
STEVENS	Elizabeth	8 Jun 1893	28		
FORGAN	David	7 Jul 1893	69		
KEMP*	Frank	2 Aug 1893	41	Cudmoor, Bampton	
HALL	James	14 Aug 1893	11		
REDWOOD	Frederick George	12 Sep 1893	16		
HAWKINS*	Frederick William	25 Nov 1893	4		
BUCKNELL	Frederick John	31 Jul 1894	68		
DARBY*	Jane	18 Aug 1894	82	Kerswell	
HAWKINS	William	27 Feb 1895	70		
DUNN*	William	4 Apr 1895	89	"Parish clerk for nearly 50 years"	
TOTTLE	Thomas	5 Oct 1895	77		
HAWKINS*	Ellen Lucy	28 Nov 1895	3		
MOON	John	28 Dec 1895	50		
TOTTLE	Elizabeth	27 Jan 1896	71		
GODDARD*	Sarah	6 Mar 1896	76		
TROAKE	Harry William C	2 Mar 1897	3		
HURFORD	Annie Susan	6 Apr 1897	2 m		
HOW*	Gertrude Mary	14 Apr 1897	2	Bolham in Tiverton	
HOW*	Beatrice Elizabeth	21 Apr 1897	16 m	Bolham in Tiverton	
DUNN*	William	15 Oct 1897	64	Stuckleys	
HAWKINS	Florence	11 Oct 1898	1 m		
VICKERY	John	1 Nov 1898	78		
HOW*	Frances Catherine	3 Dec 1898	5		
DUNN*	Jesse	21 Jan 1899	25		
CARNELL	Eliza	1 May 1899	33	Sampford Peverell	
GOFF	William	17 May 1899	70		
SPRAGUE*	Simon	30 Jul 1899	48		
HANOVER	Andrew	15 Mar 1900	65		
DART	Thomas	21 Apr 1900	43		
WHITE*	Mary Ann	12 Nov 1900	82	"Coombehead, Bampton, Late of Lea Barton, Hockworthy"	
TROAKE	Henry	26 Mar 1901	76		
FOLLET*	Charles	3 Jul 1901	53		
MARKS	Samuel	26 Jul 1901	62	Herds	

Burial Registers

TALBOT*	Jesse	6 Mar 1902	63	Hemyock
WARREN	Laura May	19 May 1902	12 d	
TARR	Henry	7 Sep 1902	85	
HAGLEY	Eliza	6 Dec 1902	69	Holcombe Rogus
BRICE	Alice Emma	21 May 1903	6	Little Ridge, Sampford Peverell
HAWKINS	Elizabeth	9 Jan 1904	81	
MOON	Eliza	30 Apr 1904	26	
MORRELL	Cecil James	7 May 1904	13 m	
ALDRIDGE	Ann	7 Jan 1905	61	
STENNER	Maud	18 Jan 1905	5 d	
SPRAGUE*	Elizabeth	29 Apr 1905	80	
PALFREY*	Herbert Charles	9 Dec 1905	6	Cudmoor in Bampton
BROOMFIELD	Caroline Joanna	22 Mar 1906	32	Tiverton
MOON	Henry	26 Mar 1906	72	Holcombe Rogus
SPRAGUE	Henry	1 May 1906	69	
COTTEY	Richard	5 Sep 1906	64	Bampton Devon
HOW*	Charlotte	17 Apr 1907	85	"Cudmoor, Bampton. Widow of Charles How"
MOON	Gilbert W S	22 Jun 1907	19 m	[Gilbert William Stephens]
MORRELL	William	23 Jul 1907	83	
TOOZE	Jane	10 Jul 1908	71	
TOOZE	William	26 Jul 1908	18 m	
WARE*	Elizabeth	19 Jan 1909	38	
FERRIS*	Emma	1 May 1909	70	Chipstable
HAGLEY	John	21 Sep 1909	70	Holcombe Rogus
WOODBURY	William	3 Jan 1911	69	Parish sexton for 22 years
STEPHENS	Jane	4 Mar 1911	72	Ashbrittle
HUSSEY*	William Robert	8 May 1911	24	Thornlands
HANOVER	Harriet	21 Jul 1911	67	Berry Farm, Clayhanger
MORRELL	Ann	10 Sep 1911	75	
LYNHAM	Percy Arthur Lewis	13 Oct 1911	2 d	Burnt House
STEPHENS	John	8 Nov 1911	70	Ashbrittle
SHOPLAND*	Mary Ann	11 Nov 1911	61	Court Hall
MAY	John	21 Mar 1912	77	Staple Cross
SPACKMAN	John	25 Oct 1912	42	
PRESCOTT	William Thomas	5 Jun 1913	24	
VICKERY*	James	5 Aug 1913	73	Hole Lake
VICKERY*	Mary	18 Mar 1915	73	Bampton. Widow of James
BROOMFIELD	Thomas	7 Apr 1915	89	
BROOMFIELD*	Emma	8 May 1915	71	Huntsham
TRUDE	Archibald	1 Nov 1915	29	Lake Farm
GODDARD*	Edwin	13 Nov 1915	85	Staple Cross
PEPPERELL*	Sarah Mary	5 Jan 1916	42	
MOON	Edith Mary	3 Feb 1916	2	Ashbrittle
DART	James	14 Jul 1916	65	"Died in the Devon and Exeter Hospital"
REDWOOD*	Bessie Mary	2 Dec 1916	57	Sampford Peverell
BREWER	Francis John	13 Apr 1917	2	
BROOMFIELD	Elizabeth	26 Apr 1917	77	West Buckland
DESTER*	William	3 May 1917	89	Staple Court. JP. Chairman of Tiverton Rural District Council for 16 years.

GARDINER	Mary Ann	20 Aug 1917	69	Lea Cottage
VICKERY	John	3 Aug 1918	72	
FORGAN	Maria	22 Nov 1918	88	Wick Farm, Bampton
PALFREY*	Francis James How	12 Mar 1919	16	Cudmore Farm
NORTHAM	John Walters	9 Apr 1919	69	Herds Farm
DARBY*	Edward	22 Jul 1919	39	Kerswell
DART*	Samuel	9 Mar 1920	66	
HUSSEY*	William White	1 May 1920	58	Thornlands
NEWMAN*	William Frederick	23 Jun 1920	74	The Vicarage
BREWER*	Francis	10 Mar 1921	36	
MEARS	Francis Ann	29 Oct 1921	59	
COURT	Elizabeth	27 Feb 1922	80	
HAWKINS	Mary	1 Jul 1922	55	
DART	Sarah	22 Aug 1922	74	Ham, West Buckland
DARBY*	Mildred	9 Oct 1922	66	
MEERS	William John	23 Oct 1922	56	Turnham Cottage
DARBY*	Louis	23 Jan 1923	76	Kerswell
MOON	Mary	19 Oct 1923	73	Lea
HILTON*	James	19 Apr 1924	62	Dares Down
PALFREY*	Catherine	13 May 1925	65	Cudmoor
DESTER*	Anne	10 Feb 1926	76	Staple Court
THOMAS	William	13 Feb 1926	74	Burnt House
COLLEY	Mary Ann	12 Apr 1927	78	Moor Cottage, Huntsham
THOMAS	Louisa	3 Sep 1927	77	South Street, Holcombe Rogus
TAYLOR	William	23 Dec 1927	61	Staple Cross
SHOPLAND*	James	15 Mar 1928	80	Court Hall
CROOK	Eli	10 Apr 1928	49	Waterslade
CROOK	Lydia Mary	22 Jun 1928	54	Booberry, Sampford Peverell
HILTON*	Geoffrey	9 Apr 1929	28	
GOFF	Charles Henry	11 Apr 1931	71	Staple Cross
DESTER*	Maude Blanche	25 Jun 1931	56	9 High Street, Taunton. "Otherwise Hall."
COCKRAM	Alice	12 Aug 1931	57	
HAWKINS*	William Thomas	17 Feb 1932	66	
BOWERMAN*	William	10 Sep 1932	76	Quarry Hockford
HUSSEY*	Frank	2 Mar 1933	40	Thornlands
NEWMAN*	Frances Emma	9 Jul 1933	86	South Town Hse Dartmouth
MATTHEWS	Bertha Louise	8 Feb 1934	54	Hurfords
PALFREY*	George	3 Mar 1934	63	Venn Lake, Huntsham
BOWERMAN*	Sarah	16 Feb 1935	78	Quarry Hockford
TOOZE	Thomas	8 Jun 1935	83	Bray's Cottage
HAWKINS	John	5 Oct 1935	75	Fore Street, Holcombe Rogus
LOVERIDGE	Edwin	4 Feb 1936	7	Chimney Down
HUSSEY*	Mary Ann	1 May 1937	77	The Bungalow, Staple Cross
PHILLIPS	Emily Mary	17 Oct 1938	68	Holcombe Rogus
BUTT*	Hannah	24 Oct 1938	87	Bray's Cottage
HAMILTON*	Kathleen Munro	23 Feb 1939	60	Nicholashayne, Som.
REDWOOD*	Vera Maud	14 Aug 1940	30	Staple Cross
CHIGEY	Charlotte	13 Feb 1941	80	Cottage Court, Uffculme
COOK	George Joseph	27 Feb 1941	84	Hurfords
BUTT*	George	9 Jan 1942	78	Brays Cottage

Burial Registers

HEDGELAND*	Fanny Mabel	23 Jul 1942	69	West View *
DESTER*	William Staple	13 Jan 1943	65	9 High Street, Taunton. "Otherwise Hall"
TRUDE	Mary Jane	17 Feb 1943	86	Hole Lake Farm
GREEDY*	William James	29 Sep 1944	64	Hockford Cottage
HEYWOOD*	Albert Tom	15 Nov 1944	60	Lea Barton
NORTHAM	Jessie	28 Dec 1944	85	2 Hurfords
MORRELL	Lucy	24 Feb 1945	70	
BROOM	George	14 Nov 1945	82	Herds Farm
STONE*	William Albert	16 Jan 1946	64	Court Hall
BURNETT*	Henry	14 Jun 1946	66	Stuckly's Cottage
PONSFORD	Alec Albert	22 Apr 1947	9	Daggeridge Cottage
NEWMAN*	William Frederick W	22 Apr 1947	74	Hockworthy House
HAWKINS*	Elizabeth Ann	18 Feb 1948	86	192 Rockwell Green
MCCANCE*	Joseph Bill	27 Jan 1949	49	Yew Tree House, Nicholashayne
DART*	Ellen	25 Apr 1949	80	Morebath
REDWOOD*	John	31 Jul 1949	76	Staple Cross
REDWOOD*	Alice Annie	15 Apr 1950	73	Cove, Tiverton
BROOM	Charlotte	10 Jun 1950	82	
HILL	Walter	2 Feb 1952	62	
WARE*	Thomas	30 Jan 1953	86	Halmoor Hospital, Taunton
FELLOWES	Margaret	13 Jun 1953	84	Court Hall
COCKRAM	Frederick William	19 Aug 1953	82	Petton
STONE*	Alice Jane	30 Jul 1954	68	
CURTIS	Sidney Thomas	23 Dec 1954	48	Baggeridge Cottage
HEDGELAND*	Frederick Charles	1 Feb 1955	80	Tiverton
WENSLEY	Lucy	18 Apr 1955	76	
DESTER*	Cecil Bates	5 Oct 1955	70	
TOTTERDELL	Frederick John	10 Feb 1956	74	
VICKERY*	Maud	24 Mar 1958	70	Kimmeridge Farm, Wareham Dorset
VICKERY*	Albert	3 Apr 1958	72	Kimmeridge Farm, Wareham Dorset
WENSLEY	William John	26 Feb 1959	82	
YARDE	Andrew Joseph	24 Aug 1962	66	Lea Cottage.
THOMAS*	Walter Lionel	18 Feb 1965	57	Redwoods Farm
SHOPLAND*	Samuel	8 Oct 1965	85	The Villa
NORTHAM	Almira Weymouth	9 May 1966	81	South View
NORTHAM	Walter	28 Mar 1968	79	South View
FALLS*	Janet Margaret G	1 Jun 1968	72	Staplewell
BRAY	Thomas Henry	1968	84	Home Farm. "Service Before cremation, Taunton"
COCKRAM*	Margaret	22 Jan 1969	62	Middle Pit Uplowman
HILL	Emily	13 Aug 1969	86	5 Culm Haven Uffculme
GODDARD*	Louis	14 Nov 1969	68	Dares Down House
SHATTOCK	Frank Heard	24 Feb 1970	77	Slade Hill
NORTH	Annie	2 Jul 1970	72	Crossways Staple Cross
PRESTON	Ruby Almira	10 Apr 1971	80	South View
YARDE	Minnie Hannah	23 Aug 1972	69	Lea Cottages
DESTER*	Lillian Ann	5 Oct 1972	87	Silver Arrow, Mount Nebo, Taunton

HEYWOOD*	Louisa	24 Jan 1973	90	Lea Barton
IBBETSON	Peter William	18 Mar 1975	66	Old Smithy, Staple Cross
GODDARD*	Eveline	4 Sep 1975	80	Slantycombe Farm
SHOPLAND*	Rosina Charlotte	25 Feb 1978	83	The Villa
TOTTERDELL	Alice	4 Oct 1985	96	The Lodge
PARR*	Frederick John	12 Mar 1986	67	4 Marina Way Tiverton
WATKINSON*	Greta	20 Dec 1986	67	Copper Ridge
MORRISH*	Derek John	7 Oct 1984	-	Waterslade (Ashes only)
HEYWOOD*	Edith Louise	20 Jan 1987	79	14 Drakes Park Wellington
PERRY*	Joan Ada Ann	10 Dec 1987	67	South Staple Farm
DANIELL*	John Ninian Averell	15 May 1988	73	Glebe Cottage
HOCKING*	Winifred Alice	19 May 1989	82	Crossways Cott Staple Cross
FILMER*	George Henry	21 Oct 1992	79	Staple Mere, Staple Cross
HEYWOOD*	Merlin John	28 Mar 1993	79	Lea Barton
PRESCOTT*	James Anthony	3 Sep 1993	75	Honiton Hospital
COCKRAM*	Alfred	24 Sep 1993	89	Longforth Nursing Home, Wellington
REDWOOD*	Lionel Jack	25 Nov 1993	80	Westleigh, Staple Cross
PRESCOTT*	Susan	25 Mar 1994	42	
SMITH*	Barbara Evelyn G	30 Aug 1995		
THOMAS*	Ruby Winifred	1 Sep 1995	83	Redwoods Farm, Uplowman
HEYWOOD*	Laura Mary	22 Jan 1995	75	Lea Barton (Ashes only)
GODDARD*	Gilbert James	22 Mar 1996	86	Lower Town, Sampford Peverell
PARR*	Mary	25 Jun 1996	75	4 Marina Way Tiverton
SMITH*	Andrew John	19 Jan 1997	86	Briar Cottage (Ashes only)
KIDLEY	Walter Dennis	4 Jan 1999	77	Paddock Cottages, Staple Cross
PRESCOTT*	Percy	21 Jul 1999	76	Herds Farm
GODDARD*	Mildred Ruth	26 Sep 2000	93	Larches Res. Home Tiverton
PRESCOTT*	Amy	12 Jun 2002	74	Herd Farm
VICKERY*	Vera Florence	d. 3 Apr 2002	77	Wareham Dorset
HEYWOOD*	Christine May	22 Dec 2004	93	14 Drakes Park Wellington
VICKERY*	Stella Frances	d. 22 Dec 2002	81	Wareham Dorset
AUTON*	Herbert James	d. 15 Mar 1992	82	Lantern Cottage Bampton
AUTON*	Nora Mary	d. 5 May 2003	89	Pinnesmoor House Tiverton
HEYWOOD*	Phyllis Mary	10 May 2005	87	Lea Barton "Molly"
TANNER*	Peter Treherne	7 Jun 2006	73	Thorn Lands Staplecross
REDWOOD*	Hilda Betty	30 Jun 2006	89	West View Staplecross
WATKINSON*	Geoffrey Oates	d. 29 Jun 2007	88	Copper Ridge.
HEYWOOD*	Nina Mildred	17 Jun 2009	87	Park Road Tiverton
BROWNE*	Peter Finlay	27 Feb 2014	83	
KIDLEY	Freda May	6 Aug 2014	86	

The Burial Registers are reproduced by kind permission of the Devon Heritage Service.

Burial Registers Index

BURIAL REGISTERS 1578 – 2014

INDEX

The Registers give variable spellings for surnames and they are listed as read.
Where transcription is in doubt, the name is shown in italics.

ALDRIDGE	7 Jan 1905	BIDGOOD	6 Jul 1690
ALLEN	20 Sep 1753	BIDGOOD	2 Jul 1699
ALLEY	13 Nov 1599	BIDGOOD	31 May 1713
ALLIN	17 Nov 1678	BIDGOOD	24 Aug 1716
ALLIN	1 Jan 1678	BIDGOOD	18 May 1718
ALLIN	22 Jan 1738	BIDGOOD	12 Jun 1726
AMMARYE	20 Apr 1656	BIDGOOD	7 Aug 1737
ARTHURS	3 Jun 1821	BIDGOOD	6 May 1739
ASH	6 Aug 1820	BIDGOOD	2 Jun 1741
ASH	8 Sep 1833	BIDGOOD	7 Jun 1741
ASH	10 Mar 1834	BIDGOOD	18 Jun 1741
ASH	23 Jul 1842	BIDGOOD	29 Nov 1741
ASH	18 Feb 1843	BIDGOOD	1 Nov 1767
ASH	2 Mar 1843	BIDGOOD	8 Nov 1767
ASH	25 Nov 1848	BIDGOOD	15 Oct 1769
ASH	7 Nov 1849	BIDGOOD	23 Jul 1780
ASH	9 Mar 1853	BIDGOOD	11 May 1788
ASH	20 Feb 1858	BIDGOOD	11 Jan 1790
ASH	12 Jun 1858	BOLLMAN	17 Mar 1621
ASH	30 Mar 1860	BOND	30 Jan 1849
ASH	20 Jan 1864	BONEY	7 May 1738
ASH	28 Dec 1864	BONEY	27 Dec 1772
AUGUSTINE	31 Jul 1659	BONNEY	8 Dec 1765
AUTON	d. 15 Mar 1992	BONNY	31 Mar 1706
AUTON	*d. 5 May 2003*	*BOWDEN*	*23 Dec 1612*
BABBAGE	27 Oct 1842	BOWDEN	12 Feb 1613
BABBAGE	27 Oct 1842	BOWDEN	21 Jan 1618
BAKER	11 Apr 1841	BOWDEN	14 Jun 1623
BAKER	7 Sep 1867	BOWDEN	18 Apr 1627
BANFIELD	20 Aug 1710	BOWDEN	30 Apr 1641
BARBYE	14 Apr 1664	BOWDEN	6 Dec 1642
BARBYE	23 Oct 1670	BOWDEN	15 Jul 1649
BARNETT	13 Feb 1820	BOWERING	22 Feb 1673
BATTEN	28 Aug 1774	BOWERING	6 Oct 1675
BATTIN	17 Jul 1686	BOWERMAN	16 Sep 1770
BATTING	30 Mar 1783	BOWERMAN	10 Sep 1932
BAWDEN	23 Oct 1859	BOWERMAN	16 Feb 1935
BELLEM	18 May 1715	BRAY	20 Oct 1640
BERE	26 Feb 1848	BRAY	10 Sep 1647
BERNER	20 Jan 1599	BRAY	14 Aug 1709
BERRY	7 Aug 1856	BRAY	18 Apr 1712
BIDGOOD	22 Aug 1686	BRAY	25 Jun 1730

BRAY	2 Oct 1737	BUCKNELL	12 Jun 1767
BRAY	7 Oct 1744	BUCKNELL	28 Aug 1767
BRAY	3 Aug 1746	BUCKNELL	20 Aug 1776
BRAY	26 Oct 1755	BUCKNELL	4 Sep 1780
BRAY	28 Dec 1785	BUCKNELL	30 Mar 1799
BRAY	6 Apr 1817	BUCKNELL	23 Nov 1800
BRAY	1968	BUCKNELL	14 Dec 1814
BRAYE	28 Jun 1585	BUCKNELL	3 Jan 1857
BRAYE	5 Aug 1628	BUCKNELL	30 May 1871
BRAYE	28 Sep 1635	BUCKNELL	26 Jul 1871
BRAYE	9 May 1637	BUCKNELL	8 Oct 1884
BRAYE	5 Sep 1659	BUCKNELL	31 Jul 1894
BRAYE	20 Jul 1665	BURNETT	14 Jun 1946
BREWER	19 Feb 1726	BURTON	20 Jun 1887
BREWER	30 Sep 1739	BUSSEL	3 Jun 1800
BREWER	6 Dec 1761	BUTT	24 Oct 1938
BREWER	13 Sep 1789	BUTT	9 Jan 1942
BREWER	22 Feb 1801	CAFENDEN	29 Oct 1659
BREWER	23 Aug 1818	CAMP	19 Mar 1710
BREWER	13 Apr 1917	CAMP	5 Sep 1714
BREWER	10 Mar 1921	CAMPE	20 Feb 1701
BRICE	21 May 1903	CAMPE	5 Oct 1707
BROMFIELD	3 Sep 1863	CAPRON	18 Jan 1601
BROMFIELD	18 Jun 1871	CAPRON	16 Nov 1619
BROOKE	21 Jun 1667	CAPRON	20 Nov 1637
BROOKS	29 Jan 1800	CAPRON	17 Jul 1661
BROOM	14 Nov 1945	CAPRON	20 Feb 1686
BROOM	10 Jun 1950	CAPRON	8 May 1688
BROOME	23 Feb 1718	CARIE	27 Mar 1685
BROOMFIELD	14 Sep 1856	CARNELL	1 May 1899
BROOMFIELD	12 Oct 1856	CATFORD	19 Jun 1624
BROOMFIELD	15 Oct 1865	CATFORD	31 Jan 1626
BROOMFIELD	30 Jun 1878	CATFORD	22 Nov 1672
BROOMFIELD	29 Sep 1878	CATTFORD	29 Mar *1628*
BROOMFIELD	12 Mar 1887	CHAMBERLEINE	20 Oct 1696
BROOMFIELD	22 Mar 1906	CHAMBERLIN	30 Jan 1592
BROOMFIELD	7 Apr 1915	CHAMBERLIN	5 May 1623
BROOMFIELD	8 May 1915	CHAMBERLIN	4 May 1729
BROOMFIELD	26 Apr 1917	CHAMBERLINE	7 Nov 1585
BROWN	11 Jan 1741	CHAMBERLINE	22 Jun 1598
BROWN	21 Oct 1821	CHAMBERLINE	11 Jul 1602
BROWNE	27 Feb 2014	CHAMBERLINE	3 Jul 1614
BRYANT	7 Oct 1720	CHAMBERLINE	10 Oct 1616
BRYANT	26 Feb 1721	CHAMBERLINE	29 Mar 1617
BRYANT	12 May 1728	CHAMBERLINE	4 Feb 1623
BRYANT	17 Nov 1800	CHAMBERLINE	15 Jan 1638
BRYANT	26 Jan 1876	CHAMBERLINE	17 Jan 1638
BUCKNAL	18 Nov 1726	CHAMBERLINE	18 Sep 1644
BUCKNAL	28 Dec 1740	CHAMBERLINE	21 Sep 1644
BUCKNEL	12 Nov 1725	CHAMBERLINE	3 Oct 1644
BUCKNELL	12 Apr 1719	CHAMBERLINE	15 Oct 1699
BUCKNELL	2 Mar 1764	CHAMBERLLEN	14 Jan 1722
BUCKNELL	22 Dec 1765	CHAMBERLLERN	19 Nov 1693

Burial Registers Index

CHAMBERLYNE	29 Nov 1644	COLEMAN	19 Aug 1744
CHANTER	10 Aug 1716	COLLEY	12 Apr 1927
CHANTER	7 May 1738	COLLING	3 Apr 1691
CHANTER	4 May 1740	COLLMAN	8 May 1641
CHAPEL	27 Jan 1740	COLLMAN	22 Sep 1644
CHAPPEL	22 Apr 1716	COLLMAN	19 Nov 1644
CHAPPEL	6 Apr 1740	COLLMAN	6 Jan 1649
CHIGEY	13 Feb 1941	COLLMAN	8 Feb 1659
CHORLY	23 Dec 1724	COLLMAN	15 Apr 1664
CHORLY	5 Sep 1725	COLLMAN	21 Mar 1670
CHORLY	15 Feb 1729	COLLMAN	22 Mar 1676
CHORLY	25 Dec 1742	COLLMAN	19 Jul 1678
CHORLY	3 Dec 1752	COLLMAN	12 Dec 1679
CHRAZE	12 Apr 1636	COLLMAN	16 Aug 1685
CHRAZE	15 Jun 1643	COLLMAN	1 Jun 1686
CHURLEY	13 Apr 1642	COLLMAN	22 Dec 1689
CHURLY	2 Feb 1640	COLLMAN	15 Nov 1690
CHURLY	3 Nov 1700	COLLMAN	8 Mar 1690
CHURLY	5 Dec 1703	COLLMAN	9 Sep 1693
CHURLY	12 Mar 1703	COLLMAN	10 Feb 1694
CHURLY	14 Jan 1707	COLLMAN	29 Feb 1698
CHURLY	25 Feb 1711	COLLMAN	21 Mar 1707
CHURLYE	10 Feb 1677	COLLMAN	21 Mar 1715
CLARKE	4 Sep 1621	COLLMAN	22 Dec 1717
CLARKE	3 Jan 1836	COLLMAN	20 Apr 1718
CLEACKE	27 Aug 1635	COLLMAN	31 Jan 1720
CLEAK	May 1613	COLLMAN	20 Nov 1720
CLEAKE	24 Apr 1602	COLLMAN	30 Nov 1721
CLEAKE	7 Apr 1612	COLLMAN	11 Feb 1722
CLEEKE	29 May 1588	COLLMAN	19 Jan 1724
CLEEKE	3 Nov 1590	COLLMAN	17 Mar 1724
CLEEKE	7 Nov 1590	COLLMAN	6 Jan 1772
CLEEKE	3 Nov 1590	COLLMAN	3 Apr 1774
CLEEKE	9 Dec 1608	COLLMAN	29 Nov 1775
CLEEKE	2 Nov 1609	COLLMAN	13 Jun 1779
CLEEVE	20 Apr 1837	COLMAN	13 Dec 1578
COCKRAM	8 Sep 1839	COLMAN	21 Oct 1583
COCKRAM	19 Aug 1953	COLMAN	22 Apr 1589
COCKRAM	22 Jan 1969	COLMAN	31 Aug 1589
COCKRAM	24 Sep 1993	COLMAN	5 Nov 1589
COLEMAN	3 Apr 1726	COLMAN	20 May 1594
COLEMAN	17 Jun 1726	COLMAN	24 Jun 1594
COLEMAN	1 Jul 1726	COLMAN	29 Jan 1594
COLEMAN	17 Nov 1727	COLMAN	20 May 1595
COLEMAN	21 Feb 1733	COLMAN	9 Sep 1597
COLEMAN	31 Jul 1737	COLMAN	12 Sep 1597
COLEMAN	16 *Oct* 1739	COLMAN	10 Nov 1597
COLEMAN	16 Feb 1741	COLMAN	13 Jun 1598
COLEMAN	6 Sep 1741	COLMAN	1 Jul 1598
COLEMAN	8 Apr 1744	COLMAN	17 Jun 1606

COLMAN	6 Apr 1618	COYNN	1 Aug 1846
COLMAN	21 Aug 1619	CRACE	19 Jun 1709
COLMAN	21 Jan 1619	CRAZE	16 Nov 1665
COLMAN	28 Jan 1620	CRAZE	6 Jun 1667
COLMAN	5 Sep 1623	CRAZE	28 Feb 1668
COLMAN	4 Oct 1623	CRAZE	6 May 1670
COLMAN	7 Jul 1700	CRAZE	13 Dec 1673
COLMAN	25 May 1701	CRAZE	18 Jan 1679
COLMAN	29 Mar 1702	CRAZE	16 Apr 1693
COLMAN	28 Apr 1706	CRAZE	6 Jul 1694
COLMAN	5 Feb 1710	CRAZE	23 Jul 1710
COLMAN	27 Mar 1710	CRAZE	1 Oct 1710
COLMAN	17 Mar 1711	CRAZE	15 Apr 1711
COLMAN	30 Apr 1731	CRAZE	1 May 1715
COLMAN	29 Jul 1731	CRAZE	27 Jul 1718
COLMAN	29 Jul 1731	CRAZE	20 Jul 1729
COLMAN	10 Nov 1734	CRAZE	8 Apr 1733
COLMAN	23 Sep 1750	CRAZE	23 Jun 1734
COLMAN	15 Jul 1752	CRAZE	8 Jun 1788
COLMAN	1 Sep 1754	CRISP	4 Sep 1881
COLMAN	4 Feb 1759	CROAKHAM	1 Jul 1787
COLMAN	27 Dec 1761	CROAKHAM	3 May 1789
COLMAN	6 Jan 1764	CROCKHAM	31 Aug 1712
COLMAN	14 Sep 1764	CROCUM	24 Jun 1743
COLMAN	6 Apr 1767	CROKAM	26 May 1723
COLMAN	2 Aug 1767	CROKHAM	5 Oct 1718
COLMAN	9 Aug 1767	CROKHAM	29 Sep 1723
COLMAN	6 Apr 1794	CROKHAM	15 Dec 1723
COOD	6 Jan 1828	CROOK	10 Apr 1928
COODEN	6 Sep 1583	CROOK	22 Jun 1928
COOK	27 Feb 1941	CROSHAM	17 Sep 1732
CORNISH	3 Jan 1878	CROWDER	6 May 1739
CORNISH	16 May 1880	CURTIS	23 Dec 1954
CORNISH	22 Dec 1891	CURTON	26 Mar 1609
CORNISH	22 Dec 1891	CURTON	20 Feb 1609
COSENS	20 Mar 1741	D'ASSIGNY	2 Dec 1753
COSIN	4 Dec 1692	DAGERY	4 Oct 1730
COTTRELL	20 Sep 1863	DAGGERY	24 Mar 1771
COTTEY	5 Sep 1906	DAGWORTHY	19 Jan 1755
COTTREL	17 May 1812	DANIELL	15 May 1988
COTTRELL	1 May 1803	DARBY	1 Apr 1799
COTTRELL	25 Jun 1881	DARBY	19 Jul 1818
COTTRELL	10 Feb 1883	DARBY	5 Apr 1834
COURT	27 Feb 1922	DARBY	16 Jun 1834
COWLIN	7 Apr 1713	DARBY	23 Mar 1837
COWLIN	16 Jul 1725	DARBY	18 Sep 1851
COWLIN	31 Mar 1726	DARBY	29 Oct 1859
COWLIN	18 Dec 1726	DARBY	2 Sep 1871
COWLING	25 Feb 1674	DARBY	6 Aug 1875
COWLING	9 Jun 1674	DARBY	18 Aug 1894
COWLING	31 Mar 1679	DARBY	22 Jul 1919
COWLING	23 Feb 1698	DARBY	9 Oct 1922
COWLINGE	28 Nov 1698	DARBY	23 Jan 1923

Burial Registers Index

DART	9 Feb 1862	DESTER	10 Feb 1926
DART	17 Apr 1886	DESTER	25 Jun 1931
DART	24 Apr 1888	DESTER	13 Jan 1943
DART	17 Sep 1892	DESTER	5 Oct 1955
DART	21 Apr 1900	DESTER	5 Oct 1972
DART	14 Jul 1916	DIBBLE	24 Dec 1820
DART	9 Mar 1920	DIN	17 Nov 1809
DART	22 Aug 1922	DINHAM	15 Jun 1865
DART	25 Apr 1949	DINHAM	5 Apr 1884
DAVEY	5 Feb 1694	DISNEY	13 Oct 1829
DAVEY	21 Jul 1716	DISNEY	1 Sep 1870
DAVEY	9 Jul 1721	DOWDNEY	1 Dec 1771
DAVEY	22 Sep 1723	DUCKAM	23 Feb 1717
DAVEY	23 Jan 1726	DUNN	16 Jun 1844
DAVEY	27 Feb 1739	DUNN	2 Jan 1848
DAVEY	16 Dec 1744	DUNN	6 Aug 1848
DAVEY	24 Nov 1758	DUNN	14 Dec 1851
DAVEY	10 Apr 1763	DUNN	15 May 1853
DAVEY	7 Sep 1766	DUNN	10 Jun 1863
DAVEY	16 Jul 1769	DUNN	9 Jul 1865
DAVEY	10 Dec 1769	DUNN	12 Oct 1873
DAVEY	27 Oct 1782	DUNN	27 Apr 1879
DAVEY	14 Jan 1786	DUNN	4 Apr 1895
DAVEY	12 Nov 1786	DUNN	15 Oct 1897
DAVEY	9 Mar 1788	DUNN	21 Jan 1899
DAVEY	16 Nov 1790	ELLACOTT	31 Jan 1879
DAVEY	2 Aug 1795	ENDICOTT	9 Jan 1853
DAVIE	22 Oct 1636	ENGERUM	12 Mar 1642
DAVIE	10 Mar 1640	ENGGRUM	15 Jul 1681
DAVY	12 Dec 1695	EVELEIGH	11 May 1729
DAVY	22 Dec 1695	EWENS	25 Jun 1738
DAVY	13 Sep 1696	EWENS	25 Jun 1738
DAVY	26 Jan 1700	EWINGS	28 Jul 1776
DAVY	18 Nov 1733	EWINGS	27 Jun 1779
DAVY	27 Jan 1734	EWINGS	16 Feb 1784
DAVY	27 Feb 1741	EWINGS	25 May 1789
DAVY	10 Feb 1745	FALLS	1 Jun 1968
DAVY	11 May 1746	FARTHING	10 Sep 1622
DAVY	27 Jan 1754	FARTHING	30 Oct 1663
DAVY	18 Feb 1776	FARTHING	25 Nov 1750
DAVY	17 Nov 1776	FARTHING	7 Jan 1753
DAVY	31 Jan 1779	FARTHING	25 Oct 1818
DAVY	27 Jan 1805	FARTHINGE	9 Nov 1616
DAVY	21 Nov 1824	FELLOWES	13 Jun 1953
DAVY	20 Nov 1825	FERRIS	7 Dec 1794
DAVY	21 Jan 1838	FERRIS	11 Feb 1798
DAVYE	20 Mar 1683	FERRIS	31 Mar 1799
DAW	7 Nov 1668	FERRIS	10 May 1812
DAWE	30 Nov 1582	FERRIS	9 Jun 1832
DESTER	3 May 1917	FERRIS	29 Apr 1858

FERRIS	10 May 1860	GARDINER	20 Aug 1917
FERRIS	1 Dec 1861	GELL	6 Jun 1804
FERRIS	19 Dec 1861	GILLARD	2 Dec 1838
FERRIS	6 Jan 1864	GILLARD	12 Apr 1840
FERRIS	20 Apr 1864	GILLARD	10 Nov 1844
FERRIS	26 Jun 1864	GILLARD	25 Oct 1846
FERRIS	28 Jul 1866	GILLARD	26 Mar 1848
FERRIS	10 Nov 1878	GILLARD	23 Sep 1866
FERRIS	10 Mar 1890	GLASS	26 Apr 1691
FERRIS	1 May 1909	GLASS	1 Nov 1712
FERRISS	8 Apr 1787	GODDARD	6 Mar 1896
FFARNAM	21 Oct 1712	GODDARD	13 Nov 1915
FFARTHINGE	9 Sep 1643	GODDARD	14 Nov 1969
FILMER	21 Oct 1992	GODDARD	4 Sep 1975
FISHER	25 Sep 1853	GODDARD	22 Mar 1996
FISHER	Aug 1860	GODDARD	26 Sep 2000
FISHER	7 Mar 1875	GOFF	17 May 1899
FISHER	18 May 1876	GOFF	11 Apr 1931
FISHER	18 May 1876	GOFFIN	23 May 1869
FLERE	29 Jul 1649	GOFFIN	26 Nov 1871
FOLLET	3 Jul 1901	GOFFIN	23 Jun 1888
FOLLETT	3 Jan 1847	GOLD	1 Mar 1662
FORDS	10 Apr 1853	GOODDING	14 Jan 1586
FORGAN	5 Jun 1893	GOODDING	28 Apr 1588
FORGAN	7 Jul 1893	GOODDING	26 Jul 1589
FORGAN	22 Nov 1918	GOODDING	12 Aug 1623
FOULER	31 Jul 1768	GOODDINGE	7 Jun 1599
FOURACRE	15 Jan 1726	GOODDINGE	28 Feb 1599
FOURACRE	May 20 1893	GOODDINGE	24 Sep 1620
FOURACRES	25 Mar 1740	GOODDINGE	5 Apr *1627*
FOURAKER	13 Mar 1700	GOODING	27 Nov 1656
FOWLER	17 Jan 1779	GOODING	24 Jun 1667
FOWLER	18 Jan 1879	GOODING	22 Oct 1670
FROAKE	1 Jun 1862	GOODING	2 Feb 1673
FROAKE	11 Mar 1866	GOODING	5 Apr 1687
FROST	30 Sep 1851	GOODING	19 Jan 1689
FROST	29 Jan 1863	GOODING	22 Apr 1694
FROST	16 Apr 1876	GOODING	12 Apr 1695
GALE	2 Jun 1781	GOODING	12 Apr 1702
GAMLIN	6 Nov 1841	GOODING	3 Feb 1705
GAMLIN	11 Nov 1842	GOODING	15 May 1709
GAMLIN	30 Nov 1842	GOODING	9 Nov 1711
GAMLIN	11 Apr 1846	GOODING	27 Jul 1712
GAMLIN	15 Mar 1856	GOODING	28 Sep 1712
GAMLIN	23 Jul 1859	GOODING	23 Feb 1724
GAMLIN	19 Feb 1870	GOODING	6 Jan 1754
GAMLIN	7 Jul 1878	GOODING	23 May 1773
GAMLIN	8 Jan 1880	GOODING	26 Jun 1780
GAMLIN	6 Oct 1883	GOODING	6 May 1781
GARD	5 Jan 1886	GOODING	6 Aug 1786
GARDENER	18 Jun 1860	GOODING	17 Jan 1791
GARDINER	25 Apr 1850	GOODING	6 Mar 1791
GARDINER	6 Aug 1871	GOODING	19 Feb 1796

GOODINGE	4 Apr 1643	HAMILTON	23 Feb 1939
GOODWIN	11 Mar 1804	HANOVER	15 Mar 1900
GOOLD	9 May 1638	HANOVER	21 Jul 1911
GOULD	19 Aug 1597	HARBER	19 Jun 1685
GOULD	21 Jun 1603	HARKE	25 Oct 1679
GOULD	11 May 1606	HARRIS	14 Jan 1600
GOULD	22 Mar 1615	HARRISS	6 Apr 1783
GOULD	30 Jul 1618	HARWOOD	2 Jun 1869
GOULD	19 Feb 1626	HATTEN	30 Oct 1803
GOULDE	21 Oct 1626	HATTING	29 Jan 1770
GOVER	16 Dec 1655	HATTING	29 Mar 1812
GOVER	16 Feb 1669	HAWKINGS	2 Apr 1797
GOVIER	13 Nov 1644	HAWKINS	24 Sep 1815
GOVIER	29 Jul 1649	HAWKINS	8 Jan 1860
GOVIER	2 Sep 1649	HAWKINS	5 Apr 1868
GOVIER	18 Nov 1664	HAWKINS	28 Nov 1868
GOVIER	18 Nov 1664	HAWKINS	7 Nov 1885
GOVIER	26 May 1741	HAWKINS	1 Dec 1889
GOVIER	14 Mar 1777	HAWKINS	16 Aug 1891
GOVIER	15 Mar 1782	HAWKINS	25 Nov 1893
GOVIERE	11 May 1723	HAWKINS	27 Feb 1895
GOWER	1 Jul 1611	HAWKINS	28 Nov 1895
GRANT	18 Mar 1645	HAWKINS	11 Oct 1898
GRAUNT	10 Aug 1598	HAWKINS	9 Jan 1904
GRAUNT	26 Apr 1605	HAWKINS	1 Jul 1922
GRAUNTE	8 Dec 1636	HAWKINS	17 Feb 1932
GREEDY	29 Sep 1944	HAWKINS	5 Oct 1935
GREENSLADE	6 Mar 1807	HAWKINS	18 Feb 1948
GREENSLADE	13 Jun 1817	HAWKLING	9 Dec 1711
GREENSLADE	24 Feb 1822	HEARD	1 Dec 1664
GREENSLADE	11 Jan 1837	HEARD	29 Apr 1722
GREENSLADE	5 Feb 1837	HEARD	20 May 1722
GREENWAY	23 Feb 1783	HEARD	18 Apr 1731
GREENWOOD	25 Jul 1824	HEARD	20 Oct 1733
GRIDLEY	19 Nov 1858	HEARD	20 Apr 1735
GUNNINGHAM	23 May 1869	HEARD	31 Mar 1751
GUNNINGHAM	12 Jun 1869	HEDGELAND	23 Jul 1942
HAGLEY	6 Aug 1872	HEDGELAND	1 Feb 1955
HAGLEY	29 Dec 1875	HERD	19 Apr 1707
HAGLEY	28 Jan 1885	HERD	6 May 1729
HAGLEY	6 Dec 1902	HERD	27 Dec 1772
HAGLEY	21 Sep 1909	HERD	1 Oct 1782
HALL	6 Feb 1763	HEYWOOD	15 Nov 1944
HALL	21 Dec 1765	HEYWOOD	24 Jan 1973
HALL	8 Oct 1820	HEYWOOD	20 Jan 1987
HALL	18 Nov 1832	HEYWOOD	28 Mar 1993
HALL	Apr 1853	HEYWOOD	22 Jan 1995
HALL	14 Aug 1893	HEYWOOD	22 Dec 2004
HALLETT	17 Apr 1875	HEYWOOD	10 May 2005
HALLETT	7 Jun 1879	HEYWOOD	17 Jun 2009

HILL	2 Jan 1613	HOW	14 Apr 1897
HILL	12 Nov 1628	HOW	21 Apr 1897
HILL	20 Dec 1639	HOW	3 Dec 1898
HILL	5 Jun 1662	HOW	17 Apr 1907
HILL	1 Mar 1662	HOWE	14 May 1854
HILL	2 Aug 1670	HOWE	20 Dec 1874
HILL	31 Dec 1670	HOXLINE	30 Jul 1699
HILL	14 Jan 1671	HUNT	1 Jul 1838
HILL	16 Feb 1678	HURD	14 Aug 1768
HILL	9 Mar 1678	HURFORD	27 Aug 1702
HILL	12 Nov 1685	HURFORD	30 Mar 1704
HILL	12 Jun 1709	HURFORD	16 Nov 1720
HILL	25 Mar 1711	HURFORD	7 Apr 1727
HILL	12 Jul 1711	HURFORD	*1749*
HILL	25 Dec 1711	HURFORD	11 Sep 1751
HILL	27 Jul 1712	HURFORD	15 Apr 1844
HILL	14 Nov 1714	HURFORD	6 Apr 1897
HILL	14 Jul 1717	HUSSEY	8 May 1911
HILL	24 Sep 1724	HUSSEY	1 May 1920
HILL	4 Apr 1733	HUSSEY	2 Mar 1933
HILL	6 Jul 1753	HUSSEY	1 May 1937
HILL	25 May 1755	HYLL	3 Jan 1644
HILL	20 Mar 1756	HYNDHAM	7 Jul 1630
HILL	2 May 1756	HYNDHAM	16 Jul 1630
HILL	2 Jan 1757	HYNDHAM	15 Aug 1630
HILL	18 Jan 1795	HYNDHAM	6 Apr 1631
HILL	19 Feb 1797	HYNDHAM	10 Apr 1631
HILL	22 Mar 1801	H...WOOD	5 Sep 1729
HILL	4 Sep 1814	IBBETSON	18 Mar 1975
HILL	9 Sep 1827	INGERIME	9 Jan 1630
HILL	11 Feb 1837	INGGARMAN	9 Mar 1693
HILL	21 Apr 1842	INGGRUM	21 Jun 1686
HILL	28 Apr 1844	JAMES	24 Dec 1682
HILL	25 Apr 1852	JAMES	15 Mar 1690
HILL	2 Feb 1952	JAMES	28 Aug 1692
HILL	13 Aug 1969	JAMES	11 Dec 1697
HILTON	19 Apr 1924	JAMES	13 Aug 1699
HILTON	9 Apr 1929	JAMES	31 Jan 1725
HOBBS	3 Jun 1834	JENNINGS	10 Jun 1882
HOBBS	7 Dec 1834	JETSON	25 Apr 1700
HOBBS	3 Sep 1843	JEWELL	20 Apr 1829
HOCKESTON	31 Mar 1695	JEWELL	22 Nov 1841
HOCKING	19 May 1989	JOHNSHING	1 Apr 1711
HOCKSLIN	4 Sep 1743	JONES	3 Dec 1749
HOLCOMBE	22 Sep 1793	JONES	17 Mar 1872
HOLLAND	12 Apr 1868	KAMPE	8 Nov 1695
HOLMES	29 Jul 1838	KEMP	2 Aug 1893
HOLMES	4 Sep 1842	KERSLAKE	24 Oct 1705
HOPSLAND	18 Dec 1736	KERSLAKE	14 Mar 1790
HOSEGOOD	10 Apr 1757	KERSLAKE	16 Aug 1795
HOSEGOOD	9 Jun 1771	KERSLAKE	22 Jul 1804
HOSEGOOD	9 Jun 1771	KERSLAKE	7 Dec 1842
HOW	17 Dec 1891	KIDLEY	4 Jan 1999

Burial Registers Index

KIDLEY	6 Aug 2014	LONGMAN	15 Dec 1881
KNIGHT	26 May 1759	LOVEL	22 Feb 1857
KNOWLES	23 Feb 1755	LOVELL	19 Jun 1844
LAB	25 Nov 1590	LOVELL	2 Jul 1853
LAMPREY	17 Jun 1855	LOVELL	22 Oct 1873
LAMPREY	10 Apr 1859	LOVERIDGE	4 Feb 1936
LAMPREY	29 Apr 1866	LOWMAN	21 May 1627
LANGE	30 Oct 1726	LUCAS	26 Aug 1781
LARANCE	22 Jan 1808	LUCAS	17 Dec 1791
LAURENCE	5 Aug 1810	LUCAS	6 Apr 1800
LAWRENCE	13 Nov 1599	LUCAS	21 Apr 1805
LITTLEJOHN	24 Jul 1854	LUCAS	7 Oct 1810
LOCK	28 Jul 1695	LUCAS	28 Feb 1813
LOCK	29 Oct 1696	LUCAS	3 Jan 1819
LOCK	29 Oct 1699	LUCAS	30 Dec 1821
LOCK	13 Apr 1700	LUCAS	25 Apr 1830
LOCK	12 Apr 1717	LUCAS	11 May 1839
LOCK	14 Aug 1723	LUCAS	28 Jun 1845
LOCK	15 Jun 1755	LUCAS	20 Aug 1856
LOCK	29 Mar 1798	LUCAS	12 Apr 1860
LOCK	22 May 1802	LUCAS	17 Oct 1874
LOCK	5 Jul 1828	*LUCKFELL*	24 May 1767
LOCK	29 Nov 1862	LUCKIS	5 Feb 1836
LOCK	3 Jun 1866	LUCKIS/LUCAS	4 Aug 1848
LOCK	26 Aug 1868	LUTLY	4 May 1729
LOCKE	17 Feb 1634	LYDDON	23 Mar 1893
LOCKE	7 Sep 1636	LYNHAM	Oct 13 1911
LOCKE	14 Jan 1659	MANLY	31 Mar 1715
LOCKE	10 Nov 1659	MARKS	22 Oct 1864
LOCKE	3 Nov 1663	MARKS	19 Apr 1884
LOCKE	28 Nov 1694	MARKS	27 Aug 1885
LOCKE	12 Mar 1706	MARKS	26 Jul 1901
LOCKE	30 Jun 1723	MARSHELL	6 Aug 1674
LOCKE	21 Dec 1724	MARTIN	11 Jun 1732
LOCKE	16 Feb 1731	MARTYN	14 Nov 1725
LOCKE	18 Nov 1738	MARTYN	26 Jul 1730
LOCKE	21 Sep 1740	MATTHEWS	8 Feb 1934
LOCKE	7 Jun 1761	MAY	10 Jun 1792
LOCKE	27 Jan 1763	MAY	11 Sep 1796
LOCKE	20 Nov 1768	MAY	19 Mar 1797
LOCKE	18 Dec 1768	MAY	30 May 1813
LOCKE	18 Feb 1770	MAY	15 Oct 1815
LOCKE	10 Jun 1772	MAY	22 Sep 1816
LOCKE	13 Nov 1774	MAY	9 Mar 1828
LOCKE	11 Nov 1781	MAY	26 Oct 1834
LOCKE	10 Jun 1787	MAY	8 Mar 1835
LOCKLEY	14 Jan 1722	MAY	22 Aug 1836
LONGMAN	15 May 1852	MAY	2 Nov 1853
LONGMAN	31 Oct 1860	MAY	21 Feb 1858
LONGMAN	11 Apr 1879	MAY	28 Feb 1858

MAY	3 May 1858	MORSE	22 Jun 1672
MAY	6 Jun 1858	MORSE	1 Dec 1676
MAY	7 Mar 1885	MORSE	5 Jun 1684
MAY	21 Mar 1912	MORSE	7 Sep 1684
MCCANCE	27 Jan 1949	MORSE	4 Oct 1684
MEARS	29 Oct 1921	MORSE	25 Feb 1685
MEERS	23 Oct 1922	MORSE	6 Jun 1686
MILLS	17 Nov 1687	MORSE	25 Jul 1686
MILLS	5 Feb 1692	MORSE	29 Dec 1686
MILLTON	28 Nov 1685	MORSE	1 May 1692
MILTON	3 Apr 1838	MORSE	1 May 1709
MILTON	22 Sep 1839	MORSE	18 Apr 1722
MILTON	13 Feb 1848	MORSE	27 May 1744
MILTON	1 Apr 1848	MORSE	4 Jan 1754
MILTON	14 Apr 1850	MORSE	21 Apr 1758
MILTON	17 Aug 1851	MORSE	2 Apr 1766
MILTON	4 Oct 1857	MORSE	14 Apr 1770
MILTON	13 Jun 1863	MORSE	29 Dec 1775
MILTON	23 Sep 1866	MORSE	31 Oct 1779
MOGFORD	13 Feb 1853	MORSE	6 Jun 1812
MOON	12 Aug 1849	NEEDS	14 May 1820
MOON	17 Dec 1854	NEEDS	4 Jan 1824
MOON	17 Jun 1866	NEEDS	4 Mar 1838
MOON	26 Mar 1871	NEEDS	13 Apr 1838
MOON	25 Jan 1874	NEEDS	9 Dec 1838
MOON	18 Apr 1875	NEEDS	28 May 1839
MOON	16 Oct 1880	NEEDS	27 May 1866
MOON	31 Oct 1885	NEEEDS	14 Apr 1830
MOON	28 Dec 1895	NEWMAN	28 Dec 1864
MOON	30 Apr 1904	NEWMAN	13 Jan 1880
MOON	26 Mar 1906	NEWMAN	12 Jul 1882
MOON	22 Jun 1907	NEWMAN	3 Apr 1883
MOON	3 Feb 1916	NEWMAN	16 Jul 1883
MOON	19 Oct 1923	NEWMAN	2 Dec 1891
MOORE	3 Mar 1838	NEWMAN	23 Jun 1920
MOORE	6 Jan 1893	NEWMAN	9 Jul 1933
MORAL	25 May 1735	NEWMAN	22 Apr 1947
MORLE	9 Feb 1645	NORMAN	1 Oct 1676
MORLE	20 Sep 1695	NORMAN	27 Dec 1678
MORLE	27 Apr 1700	NORMAN	30 Mar 1690
MORLE	9 Jun 1700	NORMAN	24 Apr 1791
MORLE	26 Jun 1700	NORMAN	10 Jun 1798
MORLE	1 Jul 1700	NORMAN	26 Sep 1813
MORLE	12 May 1728	NORMAN	11 Nov 1827
MORRELL	9 Apr 1592	NORRIS	13 Nov 1584
MORRELL	7 May 1904	NORRIS	5 Dec 1599
MORRELL	23 Jul 1907	NORRIS	21 Mar 1639
MORRELL	10 Sep 1911	NORTH	2 Jul 1970
MORRELL	24 Feb 1945	NORTHAM	9 Apr 1919
MORRIS	26 Aug 1623	NORTHAM	28 Dec 1944
MORRIS	23 Sep 1827	NORTHAM	9 May 1966
MORRISH	7 Oct 1984	NORTHAM	28 Mar 1968
MORSE	21 Jan 1664	NOTT	4 Feb 1791

Burial Registers Index

NOTT	16 Nov 1873	PERRY	14 Nov 1714
NOTT	5 Jun 1884	PERRY	14 Jul 1717
OLAND	29 Jun 1755	PERRY	7 Sep 1729
OLAND	25 May 1760	PERRY	6 Jul 1753
OSEMOND	15 Dec 1642	PERRY	20 Mar 1756
OSEMOND	16 May 1643	PERRY	30 Apr 1758
OSMOND	22 Nov 1845	PERRY	21 Jan 1760
OSMOND	20 Jun 1858	PERRY	14 Jun 1761
PAINE	15 Feb 1678	PERRY	5 May 1765
PAINE	9 Apr 1831	PERRY	23 Aug 1766
PALFREY	9 Dec 1905	PERRY	1 Jun 1777
PALFREY	12 Mar 1919	PERRY	22 Mar 1801
PALFREY	13 May 1925	PERRY	Oct 30 1802
PALFREY	3 Mar 1934	PERRY	22 May 1803
PALLMAN	21 May 1721	PERRY	29 Dec 1810
PALMER	20 Jan 1702	PERRY	2 Jan 1811
PALMER	8 Dec 1832	PERRY	11 Nov 1811
PARR	17 Nov 1822	PERRY	20 Nov 1814
PARR	11 May 1856	PERRY	10 Mar 1816
PARR	12 May 1866	PERRY	14 Mar 1819
PARR	12 Sep 1885	PERRY	25 Aug 1822
PARR	12 Mar 1986	PERRY	25 Feb 1827
PARR	25 Jun 1996	PERRY	26 Apr 1829
PASCHE	24 Apr 1737	PERRY	21 Jan 1832
PATCH	2 Mar 1698	PERRY	3 Nov 1832
PAUL	23 Sep 1866	PERRY	30 Mar 1833
PAVEY	1 Jan 1822	PERRY	1 May 1834
PAVEY	14 Jun 1831	PERRY	22 Jun 1834
PAVEY	22 Mar 1834	PERRY	20 Sep 1835
PAVEY	18 Oct 1851	PERRY	28 Jul 1839
PAYNE	17 Mar 1707	PERRY	15 Jun 1848
PEACE	18 Jul 1684	PERRY	13 Jan 1854
PEARCE	20 Jul 1685	PERRY	27 Apr 1860
PEARCE	19 Jan 1690	PERRY	23 Mar 1876
PEARCE	4 Apr 1756	PERRY	2 May 1884
PEARSE	7 Jul 1695	PERRY	10 Dec 1987
PEARSE	16 Aug 1696	PHILIPS	3 Mar 1776
PEARSE	8 May 1709	PHILIPS	28 Sep 1783
PEARSE	10 Sep 1769	PHILLIPS	17 Oct 1938
PEARSE	18 Feb 1770	PONSFORD	22 Apr 1947
PEARSE	7 Jul 1771	PRESCOTT	5 Jun 1913
PEARSE	3 Oct 1773	PRESCOTT	3 Sep 1993
PEASE	4 Mar 1715	PRESCOTT	25 Mar 1994
PEPPERELL	5 Jan 1916	PRESCOTT	21 Jul 1999
PERCE	25 Nov 1664	PRESCOTT	12 Jun 2002
PERCY	4 Apr 1733	PRESTON	10 Apr 1971
PERRY	17 Nov 1706	PROUT	23 Dec 1664
PERRY	25 Mar 1711	PULLIN	2 Apr 1688
PERRY	25 Dec 1711	QUICK	31 Mar 1734
PERRY	27 Jul 1712	QUICK	6 Jul 1740

QUICK	2 Apr 1749	RIDWOOD	1 May 1681
QUICK	30 Apr 1749	RIDWOOD	4 Jun 1687
QUICK	12 Aug 1750	RIDWOOD	2 Aug 1691
QUICK	13 Jan 1751	ROBERTS	2 Mar 1817
QUICK	2 May 1756	ROBERTS	25 Apr 1850
QUICK	8 Aug 1760	ROBERTS	19 Dec 1868
QUICK	15 Feb 1801	ROSSITER	8 Sep 1850
QUICK	18 Mar 1804	ROW	28 Nov 1662
QUICK	15 Mar 1807	RUSSELL	19 Oct 1857
QUICK	24 Oct 1819	SAIER	12 Jun 1768
QUICKE	27 Jan 1691	SANDER	7 May 1587
RADFORD	2 Dec 1827	SANDER	13 Jul 1596
REDWOOD	16 Dec 1683	SANDER	29 May 1602
REDWOOD	25 May 1700	SANDER	8 Oct 1614
REDWOOD	9 Mar 1700	SANDER	14 Aug 1623
REDWOOD	30 Jan 1702	SANDER	14 Aug 1623
REDWOOD	4 May 1706	SANDER	8 Sep 1623
REDWOOD	24 May 1713	SANDER	15 May 1639
REDWOOD	16 Jul 1721	SANDERS	7 Jul 1743
REDWOOD	20 May 1722	SANDERS	24 Jan 1779
REDWOOD	24 Jun 1722	SAUNDER	11 Jan 1643
REDWOOD	18 Aug 1722	SAYER	7 Aug 1639
REDWOOD	5 Jul 1724	SAYER	15 May 1791
REDWOOD	27 Apr 1729	SAYER	21 Feb 1802
REDWOOD	11 Aug 1731	SAYER	6 Jun 1819
REDWOOD	25 Nov 1741	SAYER	1 Apr 1831
REDWOOD	19 May 1765	SCOT	23 May 1729
REDWOOD	4 Dec 1765	SCOT	5 Aug 1739
REDWOOD	4 Dec 1765	SCOTT	13 Feb 1666
REDWOOD	12 Sep 1776	SCOTT	13 Feb 1666
REDWOOD	21 Mar 1779	SCOTT	30 Jan 1708
REDWOOD	19 Jun 1789	SCOTT	15 Nov 1835
REDWOOD	2 Apr 1797	SHACKELL	24 Jul 1599
REDWOOD	17 Apr 1808	SHAPCOTT	26 Oct 1834
REDWOOD	25 Dec 1819	SHAPLAND	4 Jun 1820
REDWOOD	17 Oct 1830	SHAPTON	25 Dec 1761
REDWOOD	June 1867	SHAPTON	7 Nov 1779
REDWOOD	17 Jan 1874	SHAPTON	8 Oct 1786
REDWOOD	5 May 1879	SHARLAND	20 Nov 1610
REDWOOD	12 Mar 1882	SHARLAND	13 May 1612
REDWOOD	6 Feb 1886	SHARLAND	20 Jan 1675
REDWOOD	1 Jan 1888	SHARLAND	17 Feb 1677
REDWOOD	12 Sep 1893	SHARLAND	20 Oct 1680
REDWOOD	2 Dec 1916	SHARLAND	1 Dec 1687
REDWOOD	14 Aug 1940	SHARLAND	15 Dec 1688
REDWOOD	31 Jul 1949	SHARLAND	6 Mar 1741
REDWOOD	15 Apr 1950	SHARLAND	12 May 1782
REDWOOD	25 Nov 1993	SHARLAND	10 Feb 1799
REDWOOD	30 Jun 2006	SHARPE	7 Nov 1698
RESTORICK	21 Aug 1855	SHARPE	19 Jun 1702
RIDGEWAY	26 Dec 1869	SHARPE	24 Jan 1708
RIDGEWAY	24 Jul 1873	SHARPE	26 Oct 1711
RIDWOOD	6 Feb 1680	SHARPE	27 Nov 1719

Burial Registers Index

SHATTOCK	3 May 1893	STANLEY	6 Nov 1844
SHATTOCK	24 Feb 1970	STEEPFIN	17 Aug 1661
SHEPPARD	9 Jul 1593	STEEPHIN	14 Sep 1663
SHOPLAND	11 Nov 1911	STENNER	18 Jan 1905
SHOPLAND	15 Mar 1928	STEPHEN	14 Nov 1591
SHOPLAND	8 Oct 1965	STEPHEN	17 Feb 1596
SHOPLAND	25 Feb 1978	STEPHEN	3 Apr 1596
SHORLAND	6 Sep 1579	STEPHEN	20 Jan 1599
SHORLAND	14 Feb 1580	STEPHEN	6 Feb 1600
SHORLAND	3 Feb 1585	STEPHEN	19 May 1618
SHORLAND	14 Mar 1585	STEPHEN	20 Apr 1643
SHORLAND	20 Apr 1586	STEPHEN	27 Mar 1645
SHORLAND	3 Aug 1589	STEPHENS	24 Jul 1696
SHORLAND	21 Nov 1592	STEPHENS	23 Apr 1715
SHORLAND	14 Jan 1592	STEPHENS	17 May 1723
SHORLAND	7 Nov 1598	STEPHENS	16 Sep 1737
SHORLAND	10 Jan 1604	STEPHENS	10 May 1763
SHORLAND	18 Jun 1605	STEPHENS	23 May 1784
SHORLAND	21 Dec 1605	STEPHENS	12 Nov 1786
SHORLAND	7 Oct 1616	STEPHENS	24 Aug 1856
SHORLAND	1 May 1623	STEPHENS	8 Feb 1857
SHORLAND	22 Jun 1623	STEPHENS	25 Feb 1858
SHORLAND	9 Feb 1629	STEPHENS	5 Nov 1864
SHORLAND	25 Sep 1630	STEPHENS	2 Dec 1872
SHORLAND	9 Aug 1647	STEPHENS	8 Sep 1880
SHORLAND	21 Mar 1663	STEPHENS	4 Nov 1890
SHORLAND	17 Nov 1664	STEPHENS	4 Mar 1911
SHORLAND	26 Jan 1665	STEPHENS	8 Nov 1911
SHORLAND	26 Feb 1726	STET	19 Dec 1742
SHORLAND	6 Aug 1749	STEVEN	3 Aug 1590
SHORLAND	23 Dec 1753	STEVEN	21 May 1659
SHORLAND	22 Jul 1759	STEVENS	13 Nov 1882
SHORLAND	23 Dec 1849	STEVENS	11 Sep 1885
SHORLLAND	28 May 1721	STEVENS	8 Jun 1893
SHORT	24 Jan 1597	STILL	6 Aug 1775
SLOMAN	12 Jan 1834	STILL	13 Feb 1780
SMITH	11 May 1889	STITT	11 Mar 1783
SMITH	30 Aug 1995	STONE	25 Aug 1579
SMITH	19 Jan 1997	STONE	2 Aug 1590
SNOW	2 Jul 1882	STONE	4 Jan 1593
SNOW	10 Jan 1886	STONE	30 Aug 1609
SPACKMAN	25 Oct 1912	STONE	26 Nov 1609
SPRAGUE	29 Jan 1865	STONE	29 Oct 1617
SPRAGUE	28 Sep 1879	STONE	12 Jan 1635
SPRAGUE	30 Jul 1899	STONE	12 Feb 1642
SPRAGUE	29 Apr 1905	STONE	15 Jun 1648
SPRAGUE	1 May 1906	STONE	Nov 1649
SQUIRE	12 Nov 1830	STONE	21 Feb 1655
SQUIRE	25 Jan 1831	STONE	13 Mar 1655
STALEINGS	22 Apr 1589	STONE	17 Jun 1656

STONE	14 Jun 1662	SULLY	25 Jan 1877
STONE	17 Jan 1665	SUTTON	12 Mar 1731
STONE	22 Sep 1667	TALBOT	28 Jul 1861
STONE	5 Nov 1668	TALBOT	31 Dec 1878
STONE	5 Mar 1670	TALBOT	15 May 1885
STONE	14 Mar 1671	TALBOT	6 Mar 1902
STONE	30 Apr 1676	TALLBUT	2 May 1684
STONE	20 Feb 1676	TANNER	7 Jun 2006
STONE	25 Jul 1677	TARR	1 Apr 1883
STONE	16 Sep 1678	TARR	7 Sep 1902
STONE	20 Aug 1681	TAYLOR	27 Jan 1751
STONE	17 Jul 1681	TAYLOR	16 Jan 1757
STONE	12 Sep 1685	TAYLOR	6 Oct 1765
STONE	12 Sep 1685	TAYLOR	29 Nov 1775
STONE	27 Jan 1685	TAYLOR	16 May 1790
STONE	25 May 1690	TAYLOR	13 Jul 1794
STONE	23 Feb 1690	TAYLOR	26 Jun 1796
STONE	22 Mar 1690	TAYLOR	18 Dec 1825
STONE	20 May 1693	TAYLOR	23 Dec 1927
STONE	27 Aug 1693	THOMAS	2 Jun 1611
STONE	15 Mar 1695	THOMAS	10 Dec 1621
STONE	4 Jun 1699	THOMAS	13 Feb 1926
STONE	27 Sep 1702	THOMAS	3 Sep 1927
STONE	3 Mar 1705	THOMAS	18 Feb 1965
STONE	8 Sep 1706	THOMAS	1 Sep 1995
STONE	6 May 1716	THORN	4 Feb 1827
STONE	19 Apr 1719	THORNE	28 Jun 1600
STONE	18 Jul 1723	THORNE	29 Oct 1722
STONE	30 Aug 1732	THORNE	11 Dec 1723
STONE	26 Dec 1734	THORNE	17 Mar 1726
STONE	2 Apr 1736	THORNE	27 Jan 1729
STONE	30 May 1736	THORNE	10 Apr 1730
STONE	23 Nov 1746	THORNE	19 Mar 1733
STONE	2 May 1749	TOOTLE	7 Mar 1885
STONE	1 Mar 1772	TOOZE	14 Mar 1830
STONE	18 Jan 1778	TOOZE	30 Aug 1884
STONE	16 Jul 1779	TOOZE	10 Jul 1908
STONE	21 Dec 1783	TOOZE	26 Jul 1908
STONE	16 Jan 1946	TOOZE	8 Jun 1935
STONE	30 Jul 1954	TOTTERDELL	10 Feb 1956
STRONG	9 Nov 1859	TOTTERDELL	4 Oct 1985
STUCKLY	14 May 1699	TOTTLE	20 Nov 1842
STUCKLY	10 Aug 1699	TOTTLE	15 Dec 1861
STUEKLY	4 Jul 1731	TOTTLE	22 Aug 1875
STUKELEY	12 Jul 1789	TOTTLE	5 Oct 1895
STUTE	15 Feb 1767	TOTTLE	27 Jan 1896
STUTT	8 Jul 1810	TOZE	9 Nov 1823
SULLEY	20 Nov 1791	TROAKE	2 Mar 1897
SULLEY	13 Jul 1794	TROAKE	26 Mar 1901
SULLEY	1 Nov 1795	TRUDE	1 Nov 1915
SULLY	26 Mar 1609	TRUDE	17 Feb 1943
SULLY	16 Jun 1754	TUCKFIELD	24 Jun 1759
SULLY	11 Oct 1755	TUCKFIELD	7 Oct 1759

Burial Registers Index

TURNER	25 Aug 1838	WEBBER	9 Mar 1683
TURNER	1 Jan 1940	WEBBER	21 Jun 1730
TURNER	5 Jun 1841	WEBBER	17 Feb 1740
TWOOZE	28 Mar 1863	WEBBER	3 Nov 1782
TWOZE	11 Jan 1634	WEBBER	9 Jul 1815
TWOZE	23 Feb 1862	WEBBER	10 Jan 1858
TWOZE	15 Feb 1877	WEBBER	15 Apr 1886
TWOZE	2 Aug 1863	WEBER	8 May 1664
UNKNOWN	8 Dec 1697	WEBSTER	18 Mar 1791
UNKNOWN	25 Jan 1729	WEBSTER	13 Aug 1799
VENN	2 Nov 1872	WEBSTER	Oct 17 1812
VICKERY	1 Nov 1898	WEBSTER	11 Apr 1819
VICKERY	5 Aug 1913	WEBSTER	5 Apr 1830
VICKERY	18 Mar 1915	WEBSTER	18 Jan 1834
VICKERY	3 Aug 1918	WEBSTER	5 Apr 1834
VICKERY	24 Mar 1958	WEBSTER	19 Jun 1856
VICKERY	3 Apr 1958	WELCH	31 Jan 1741
VICKERY	d. 3 Apr 2002	WELCH	21 Feb 1741
VICKERY	d. 22 Dec 2002	WELLAND	17 Aug 1718
VOWLER	11 Jan 1756	WENE	21 Feb 1587
WADDLETON	19 Feb 1837	WENE	19 Sep 1601
WARD	16 Oct 1765	WENSLEY	10 Nov 1868
WARD	21 Sep 1783	WENSLEY	1 Jul 1871
WARD	11 Apr 1790	WENSLEY	10 May 1872
WARE	19 Jan 1909	WENSLEY	5 Jan 1873
WARE	30 Jan 1953	WENSLEY	25 Apr 1874
WARREN	19 May 1902	WENSLEY	24 Mar 1877
WATERMAN	1 Feb 1611	WENSLEY	11 Mar 1885
WATERMAN	29 May 1625	WENSLEY	15 Aug 1885
WATERMAN	16 Jan 1662	WENSLEY	18 Apr 1955
WATERMAN	13 Mar 1686	WENSLEY	26 Feb 1959
WATERMAN	11 Aug 1717	WEST	22 Jun 1853
WATERMAN	9 Oct 1737	WESTCOTT	23 Dec 1890
WATKINSON	20 Dec 1986	WESTCOTT	18 May 1891
WATKINSON	d. 29 Jun 2007	WESTCOTT	15 Mar 1892
WATTERMAN	27 Apr 1718	WHITE	31 May 1865
WATTS	22 Apr 1808	WHITE	20 Sep 1876
WAYETT	3 Jan 1768	WHITE	15 Jul 1887
WEALAND	16 Aug 1578	WHITE	10 Nov 1892
WEALAND	25 Nov 1581	WHITE	12 Nov 1900
WEALAND	31 Jan 1587	WIATE	16 Nov 1737
WEALAND	20 Aug 1597	WIEAT	29 Jan 1685
WEALAND	21 Oct 1610	WIETT	12 May 1695
WEALAND	20 May 1611	WILLCOKE	17 Sep 1678
WEARE	7 Jan 1611	WILLKINS	12 Dec 1708
WEBBER	3 Aug 1590	WILMOTON	2 Jul 1643
WEBBER	27 May 1595	WINE	18 Apr 1624
WEBBER	15 Dec 1613	WOLLAND	23 Apr 1724
WEBBER	3 Jun 1625	WOLTERMAN	20 Oct 1649
WEBBER	25 Jun 1644	WOOD	21 Aug 1757

WOOD	31 Dec 1769	WYATT	13 Mar 1702
WOOD	15 Sep 1770	WYATT	18 Jun 1705
WOOD	17 Oct 1779	WYATT	16 Oct 1796
WOOD	6 Nov 1785	WYEAT	12 Jul 1789
WOOD	25 Apr 1813	WYETT	7 Apr 1633
WOOD	27 Mar 1814	WYETT	28 Sep 1636
WOOD	16 Oct 1859	WYETT	28 Oct 1637
WOOD	8 Jun 1887	WYETT	5 Jul 1639
WOODBERRY	10 May 1866	WYETT	8 Oct 1665
WOODBURY	7 Dec 1879	WYETT	18 Oct 1732
WOODBURY	10 Mar 1893	WYLBROKE	19 Feb 1670
WOODBURY	3 Jan 1911	WYNN	15 Jul 1827
WOOLLAND	14 May 1726	WYNN	23 Sep 1827
WYAT	29 May 1706	WYNN	17 Oct 1845
WYAT	4 Jul 1731	WYNN	8 Aug 1846
WYATT	25 Mar 1691	YARDE	24 Aug 1962
WYATT	10 Aug 1699	YARDE	23 Aug 1972
WYATT	20 Oct 1700	YEOENS	6 Jul 1746

1750   [Devon Heritage Service: 3083A/PR/1/1]

BIBLIOGRAPHY AND SOURCES

Absent Voters' List 1919
Alumni Oxonienses 1715-1886 Joseph Foster, Parker & Co, Oxford 1888
A Map of the county of Devonshire Benjamin Donn [1765]
Army Roll of Honour, Soldiers Died in the Second World War, 1939-1945
    CD version produced by Naval & Military Press in association with
    TNA (The National Archives), Kew
Comparative Account of the Population of Great Britain, 1831
Crockford's Clerical Directory
Directory & Gazetteer of the County of Devon [1857] M Billing
Domesday Survey
The Eccesiastical Historian Oliver, 1846
Electoral Rolls 1918-1925
Highways and Tithes Payments – Hockworthy West Side [26 Sep 1832]
The History of Devonshire Richard Polwhele, 1793
History of the Devonshire Regiment, Volume III (1914-1919), compiled by
    W J P Aggett, published by the Regiment, 1995
The Huntsham Book published by The Huntsham Society, 2005
Kelly's *Directory* [1897] [1906] [1939]
Registers of the Commonwealth War Graves Commission, Maidenhead
Soldiers Died in the Great War, published by the War Office, 1919
War Diary, 2nd Battalion, The Gloucestershire Regiment, 1915 period
White's *History, Gazetteer and Directory of Devon* [1850][1878]

NEWSPAPERS

Exeter & Plymouth Gazette 23 Apr 1920
Exeter Flying Post 25 May 1820
Taunton Courier 8 Nov 1865
Wellington Weekly News 18 July 1863
The Western Times 14 Feb 1896, 13 Oct 1916, 19 Apr 1929

WEBSITES (selected)

Ancestry	Find My Past
British Newspaper Archive Google	Free BMD
Commonwealth War Graves Commission	Google
Family Search	TNA (The National Archives)

DEVON HERITAGE SERVICE

The Hockworthy parish archives held in Exeter in the care of the Devon Heritage Service were deposited in five tranches between 1979 and 2003. They have kindly agreed to the Burial Registers being transcribed and reproduced at *Appendix G [p.113]*. Devon parish registers are currently being digitised and eventually will be available to all on the *findmypast* website. Documents consulted were:

Parish Registers
3083A/PR/1/1	Baptism, Marriages and Burials	1557-1750
3083A/PR/1/2	Baptisms and Burials	1750-1812
3083A/PR/1/3	Baptisms	1813-1885
3083A/PR/1/4	Baptisms	1885-1995
3083A/PR/1/5	Marriages and Banns	1755-1993
3083A/PR/1/6	Marriages	1813-1837
3083A/PR/1/7	Marriages	1839-1978
3083A/PR/1/8	Burials	1813-1999

Churchwardens Papers
3083A/PW/1/a/1	Rate and Account Book	1844-1937

Vestry Papers
3083A/PV/1/1	Minute Book	1883-1942

Miscellaneous Papers
DEX/4/a/TM	Tithe Map	1842
DEX/4/a/TM/210	Tithe Apportionments	8 March 1842
2514D/1/311	Wesleyan Preaching Room, Staple Cross	1883
3083A/PF/1/1/1	Church House grant	20 Jun 1525
3083A/PZ/3/1	Church Visitors' Book	1938 - 1993
3082A/add2/PB/11	*London Gazette* Creation of United Benefice of Holcombe Rogus and Hockworthy	31 Jan 1922
4386A/PX/5	Parish Meeting Minute Book	1894-1961
4386A/PX/6	Letters to Major J N A Daniell about the history of Hockworthy	1978-1981
4386A/PZ/1-2	Exercise book, photocopies and notes by Major J N A Daniell about the history of Hockworthy	c.1980
676C/EFA1	Church of England school Log Book	1869-1950

GENERAL INDEX
Bold = illustration

Adams, Revd John 103
Aldridge, Edith May 28, 29
  Lena 40
Arnald, Revd 3, 102
Ash, Abel **38**
  Betty **39**
  Caroline 38, 98
  Elizabeth **38**, 39
  Emma **38**, 57
  James **38**
  Jane **38**, 98
  Joan **39**
  Mr 105
  Robert **38**, 39, 98
  William **38**, **39**
Ashbrittle 21, 22, 29, 53, 55, 60,
  61, 63, 70, 72, 88, 90, 95, 98
Atkins & Co 9
At Wyll, Revd Walter 102
Auton, Herbert James **39**
  Nora Mary **39**, 45
Avery, Bessie 25
Baker, Maud 96
Bampton 40, 69, 79, 99
Barker, Revd Henry 103
Barne, Revd Charles 103
Barnett, Beatrice 84
Baron, Revd Noel 103
Barton, Revd Edward 103
Bathealton 59
Bell, Joe 72
  Phyllis Adah 72
Bells **4**, 5, 48
Berry, Violet 28
Besley, Anne 42, 71
Bilbie, Thomas **4**, 5
Bishop's Faculty **6**, 7
Bishop of Colombo 13
Bishop of Exeter 5, 7, 13, 102, 104
Blackmore, Mary 16

Blade, Revd Susan ix, 103
Blake, Florence 18
Bowerman, Sarah **40**, 62
  William **40**, 62
Bowring, Revd Thomas 103
Bray, Jonathan 109
Brewer, Ellen 40
  Eva 40
  Francis **40**
  Lena 40
Britton, Revd Thomas H 103
Brock, Hilda 23
Brompton Ralph 44
Brompton Regis 67
Broomfield, Elizabeth 20, 41, 90
  Emma 20, **41**
  Frank 20, 41
  Henry **41**, 90
  Johannah 41
  Sarah Ann 41
Browne, Peter Finlay **42**
  Rachel 42
Bucknell, Anne 42, 71
  Arthur **43**
  Arthur Besley 42
  Eliza **42**
  Hannah **43**
  Jacob 43
  John **42**, 43
  John Broome 42
  Mary Ann 68
  Sarah 11, **43**
Burials Registers 113
  Index 151
Burlescombe 5, 41, 46, 53, 82
Burnell 29
  Jane 53
  John 53
  Mary 53
Burnett, George 44

Henry 'Harry' **44**
Lilian Rose **44**
Sarah 44
Burston, Walter **15**, 17
Butt, George **44**
  Hannah **44**
Cadyho, Revd William 102
Canonsleigh 3, 5, 102
Capron, Revd Christopher 103
Carr, Charles 21, 98
  Edith Fanny 21, 98
  Ernest Victor **21**
  Ethel Lilian 21
  Florence 21
  Gilbert Henry **21**
Catford, Dorothy 7
  John, Revd 7, 103
Cawsey, Emily 28
Canonsleigh 3, 5, 102
Chamberlayn, Revd William 102
Chidgey, Alice Ruth 22
  Charlotte 22
  Thomas H **21**, 22
  William **21**, 22
  William J 22
Chimney Down 3, 83, 98
Church Patrons 102, 103
  Registers of birth,
  deaths and marriages 11
  Wardens 109
Clark, Enid 94
  Paul 94
Clarke, Revd Thomas 103
Clayhanger 26, 40, 61
Cleeve, William **45**, 97
Clergy 102, 103
Cloete, Revd Richard 103
Cockram, Alfred 'Dickie' **45**
  Alice 17, 22, 39, 45
  Dickie **45**
  Dora **45**
  Elizabeth 23
  Elizabeth Bessie 22
  Frederick 17, 22, 39, 45
  Frederick John **15**, 17
  Margaret Jane 'Dora' **45**
  Nora 39, 45

Sydney 17, **21**, 22, 23, 39
  William Henry **15**, 17
Coles, Annie May 25
  Florence 21
Collins, Frances 'Fanny' 70
Colman, William 119
Colombo, Bishop of 13
Comins, John, Revd 103
  William, Revd 103
Cooksley, Jane 38
Cottrell, Florence Emma 89
  James **46**, 89
  Mary 46
  William Walter **46**
Court Hall 7, 110
Cove 21, 96
Covyntre, Revd Richard 102
Cowan, Harold 53
  Marcella 53
  Marjorie 'Bobbie' 53
Cowan-Douglas, Hugh 72
  Phyllis Adah 72
Crook, Daisy C 22
  Eli 22
  Lawrence F **21**, 22
  Lydia 22
Curates 103
Curtis, Amy 84
  Fred 84
Daniell, Major John 'Jack' N A
  9, **46**, 109, 166
  Mary vii, ix, 46
Darby, Edward **4**, 5, 47, **48**, **49**,
  105, 109
  Frank **21**, 22
  Jane **48**
  Louis 22, **49**
  Loveday **48**
  Mabel 22
  Mildred 22, **49**
  Susannah 47
  William **47**, 109
  William Edward **48**, 49
Dart, Charlotte 50
  Ellen 28, **50**, 63, 89
  John 50
  Rosina 28, 50, 89

General Index

Samuel 28, **50**, 89
Dartmouth 75, 76, 77
Davey, Ann 69
  Davies, Revd John 103
Davis Company 7, 13
Day, Eliza Jane 44
de Berneville Henry 3, 102
  Roger, Revd 102
de Bynnewill, Hugo 5
de Chevithorne, Walter 3, 102
de Claville, Walter 3
de Kerdyf, Revd John 102
de Menestoke, Revd John 102
de Molendinis, Revd Reginald 102
Dester 24, 55
  Anne 23, **51**
  Cecil Bates **51**
  Ethel Jane 23, **51**
  John Montague **21**, 23, **51**
  Lilian Ann 'Nancy' **51**
  Mary Grace **51**
  Maud Blanche **51**
  Montague Howse **51**
  William 23, **51**
  William Staple **51**
Devon Heritage Centre
  vii, ix, 11, 46, 115
Dicken, Revd Edmund 103
Dinham, Agnes 53
  Albert **53**
  Charles **53**
  Jane 53
  Mary 53
  Mary Ann 53
  Phyllis I M 30
  William 53
Dinnicombe, Frances 69
Disney, Florence 80
Doble, Charles 53
  Douglas 53
  John vii, 11, 53, 109
  Marcella **53**
Domesday Book 3
Dunn, Daisy C 22
  Harriet **55**
  Jesse **54**

John **54**
Mary **54**, 55
Susan 54
William **54**, **55**
Durnford, Catherine 75
  Harriet 75
East Anstey 64, 96
Eivers, Alice **92**, 93
  James 93
Ellis, Revd 102
Elvy, Lavinia 9, 109
English Heritage 11, 43
Evans, Helen 62
Exeter, Bishop of 5, 7, 13, 102, 104
Exeter and Plymouth Gazette 15
Exeter Flying Post 47
Faculty 7, **8**, 104-6
Falls, Flavia 55
  Janet Margaret **55**, 56, 83
  John Blyth 55
  Thomas 55
Farley, Fred **56**
  Kay **56**
Farms 110, 111
Farrington, Diana x
Fellowes, Anne 55, **56**
  Thomas Balfour 55, **56**
  Thomas Butler, Sir 56
Ferris, Edith 23
  Edward Tom **57**
  Elizabeth **57**, 71
  Emma 38, 57
  John **38**, **57**, 71
  Mark **57**
  Martha Sarah **57**
  Sarah 38, **57**
  Tom **57**
Fewings, Tiverton 44, 50, 81, 96
Filmer, Dawn 59
  George Henry **59**
Flower, Barbara E G 89
Follett, Charles **60**
  Clara 60
Forgan, Albert Jesse 20
  Edith 20
  Tom 20

Fowler, Mary 92
  Mary Ann 59
  Robert **59**
Foxford, Elizabeth 19
Frost, Frances 57
  Henry 57
  Mary **57**
  Sarah 'Sally' 57
Fudge, Paul 44
Gale, Revd Keith 103
Gamlin, Elizabeth 59
  John **59**
  Mary Ann 55, **59**
  Robert 55
Goddard, Albert 61
  Bessie 60
  Clara 60
  Edwin **60**
  Edwin George 60
  Emily 61
  Emma 60
  Ethel 23
  Eveline **60**, 61, 68, 94
  Frances Ellen 60
  Gilbert James 60, **61**, 109
  Jean 60, 94, 100
  Jessie 70, 71
  John 60, 70, 71
  Louis **60**, 61, 68, 94
  Malcolm 60, 94
  Mary 60
  Mildred 'Millie' Ruth **61**
  Sarah **60**
  Tom 61
Goffin, George 61
  Mary **61**
  Sarah 61
  William **61**
Goodall, David 109
  Delia 91
Goodhind, Gladys May 24
Govier, Robert 109
Goss, Eva Ellen 27
Grant, R 84, 85
Greedy, Francis 62
  Sarah 40, 62
  William James 40, **62**

Greenway, Catherine 75
  Charles D 9, 75, 104, 105, 107
  George C 75
  Harriet 75
Griffin, Florence 64
  James 64
  Laura Mary 64
Guscott, Hilda M 28
Gypsies 83, 98
Hall, Anne 51
  William Henry 51
Hamilton, Helen 62
  Kathleen Munro **62**
  Stephen Heysham 62
Hancock Brewery 86
Hardacre, Margaret Jane 'Dora' 45
Hardman, John 9,
Harry, Revd Thomas 102
Haselford, Revd John 102
Harvey, Eddie 62
Harwood, Elizabeth 87
Hawkins, Edith 23
  Elizabeth 22, 23, 50, **63**
  Freddie **63**
  James 23, 63
  John **21**, 22, 23
  Mary 23
  Nellie **63**
  Obed J 109
  William 63
  William James **23**
  William Thomas **63**
Hayne, Revd John 103
Heard, Jane 49
  Mildred 'Millie' Ruth 49, 61
  Richard 49
Hedgeland, Cecil Charles **21**, 23, 63
  Fanny Mabel 23, **63**
  Frederick Charles 23, **63**
  Hilda 23
  Violet Gwendoline 63
Heywood, Albert Tom 64, 65
  Christine May **65**
  Edith Louise **65**
  Laura Mary 64
  Louisa 64, 65
  Merlin John 9, 64, 109

General Index

Nina Mildred **65**
Phyllis Mary 'Molly' 9, **65**, 108
Hicks, Henry 19
  Nelly 19
Hill, Betty **66**
  Edith 68
  John 66
  Martha 71
  Thomas 66
Hilton, Alice 23, 66
  Charles Herbert **21**, 23, 66
  Geoffrey **66**
  James 23, **66**
Hobbs, Bertha 23
  Frances 96
  Louisa 23
  Mary Jane 23
  Rosa 23
  William 23
  William George **21**, 23
Hockford Waters 3, 110
Hocking, Edgar John 67
  Winifred Alice **67**
Hockworthy School 11, 25, **85**, 91
Holcombe Rogus 5, 16, 22, 23, 29,
  42, 53, 64, 71, 73, 92, 97
Honiton 25, 85
Hopkins, Revd Henry 103
How, Beatrice Elizabeth **88**
  Catherine 67, 69, 78, 79
  Charles 53, **67**, 79, 88, 109
  Charles John 67
  Charlotte 53, **67**, 79, 88
  Charlotte Isabella 78, 88
  Frances Catherine **67**
  Gertrude Mary **88**
  Harriet 67
  Isabella 67
  John 67
  William James 67, 78, 88
Howe, Gerald 59
Huntsham 19, 39, 40, 41, 45, 48,
  53, 60, 61, 62, 86
  Estate 49, 68, 69, 78, 85, 89, 94, 98
Hurford, Bessie 27
Hussey, Eveline 60, 68

Frank 60, **68**
Mary Ann **68**, 97, **100**
Maurice 68, 97
William Robert **68**
William White **68**, **100**
Incorporated Society for Promoting
  the Enlargement, Building and
  Repairing of Churches and Chapels
  7, 108
Incumbents 102, 103
Jennings, Jane 78
John, Revd 102
Jones, Revd Joseph 32, 103
Kemp, Catherine 67, 69, 78
  Frances 69
  Frank 67, **69**, 78
  John Wallis 69
Kerslake, Beatrice 84
  Frank 84
  Susan 84
Kidley, Alfred 20
  Freda May 20
  Rhoda Ann 20
  Samuel Frederick Gerald **15**, 20
  Walter 20
Kittisford 48, 54
Knollis, Revd The Hon Francis 103
Lamprey, Ann 69
  James 69
  Samuel **69**
  Susan **69**
Langford Budville 20
Lea 3, 111
Lee, Freda 20
  Harriet 29
Lewis, George, Revd 103
  Gladys May 24
  John 17, **21**, 24
  Mary 17, 24
  Sidney 17, 24
  Walter **15**, 16, 24
Lock, Ann 70
  Bessie 70
  Frances 'Fanny' 70
  John 70
  Maria **70**

Mary 70
Matilda 70
Thomas **70**
Locke, Edward, Revd 103
  Jonathan 109
  Richard 109
  Thomas 109
Longman, Alice 71
  Anne **70**, 71
  Elizabeth **71**
  Ethel 71
  Jessie 70
  John 70
  Martha 70
  Samuel **70**, 71
  William **71**
Lovell, Mary 46
Lucas, Anne 42, 71
  Elizabeth 57, 71
  Henry 42, 57, **71**, 109
  Martha 57, 71
  Mary 55
  Thomas 55
Luscombe, Revd Epworth 103
Manning, Mary 46
Manning & Knight 65
Maps 33-37
March, Revd Ivor 103
Marke, May 24
Marks, Elizabeth 59
  John **59**
Marshall, Katherine 93
  Sidney James 93
Masland, Joseph 44
Max, Hannah Rose 42
  Randy 42
May, Emma 60
McCance, Joseph Bell **72**
  Phyllis Adah 72
Meers, Frances 24
  Laura 24
  Reginald **21**, 24
  William 24
Mellen, John 93
  Katherine **92**, 93
Mewett, Alexander George **15**, 18
  Alfred 18, 24

Emily 18, 24
Florence 18
Irene 18
Reginald 18, **21**, 24
Walter **15**, 18,
Milton, Ann 72
  Charles **72**
  John 72
Milverton 38, 39, 69
Moon, Mary **73**, 90
  Samuel **73**
Morebath 40, 50, 70, 91
Morrell, Ann 50
  Elizabeth 50, 63
  Ellen 50, 63
  William 50
Morrish, Derek John **73**
Morse, Elizabeth 7
Mundy, Alison 42
Musgrave, Revd William 103
Mylles, Edward 117
Naish, Emma 57
Nelson, Revd Arthur 103
Newberry, W 86
Newman 7, 9, 11, 24
  Alice Susanna **77**, 107
  Caroline 75, **76**, 77, 107
  Caroline Durnford **77**, 107
  Charles, Revd 13
  Frances Elizabeth **77**, 107
  Frances Emma **77**
  Herbert Roope **76**, 107
  John **75**
  Nora 75, **76**, 107, 109
  William 75
  William Frederick, Revd 75, 76, **77**, 103, 107
  William Frederick Wyndham 75, **76**, 77, 107, 108, 109
  William James, Revd 9, **75**, **76**, 77, 103, 104, 105, 107
Nicholashayne 62, 72
Norman Conquest 5
  Font 9
Norman, Revd Roger 102
Norris, Revd John 32, 103
North, Bridget 82

General Index

Northam, Almira 25, 81
  Annie May 25
  Elias Eli **21**, 24, 25
  Ethel 24
  Frederick 18, **21**, 24, 25
  Gilbert George **15**, 18, 24, 25
  Henry **21**, 24, 25
  Isabella 18, 24, 25
  Ivy D 25
  Jessie 25
  John 25
  Leslie W D 25
  May 24
  Roderick 25
  Ruby 25
  Sue 83
  William 18, 24, 25
  William J **21**, 24, 25
  Walter **21**, 25, 81
Oakford 17, 22, 45, 64, 94
Ordnance survey x, 5
Organ **8**, 107
Osmond, Geo. 107
Ottery St Mary 99
Page, Revd Walter 102
Paige, John 70
  Martha 70
Palfrey, Catherine 67, 69, **78**, 79
  Elizabeth 79
  Francis James H **79**
  George 67, 69, 78, 79
  Herbert C **79**
  James 79
Parr, Florence 80
  Frederick John **80**
  Frederick Richard 80
  Mary **80**
  Geoffrey 80
Patrons, Church 102, 103
Pavey, Henry 81
  Henry Allen **81**
  Joseph 81
  Mary **81**
  Susannah 47
  William **81**
Pearce, Hilda Betty 25, 86
  Mildred 25
Peart, Revd Humphrey 103
Penn, Lilian Rose 44
  Stanley Harold 44
Penpaly, Revd John 102
Pepperell, Almira 25, 81
  John Weeks 81
  Sarah Mary **81**
Perkins, Ralph 106
Perry, Adra 82
  Alice Ruth 22
  Bridget 82
  Elizabeth 82, 93
  Hannah 82
  James 82
  Joan Ada 'Ann' 83
  John 82, 109
  Maria 82
  Mary **82**
  Roy, Revd 103
  Thomas 82
  William **82**
Petty, Revd Brian 103
Poor House 11, 72
Post Office 62, 97
Prescott, Alice 85
  Amy 84
  Bessie 25, 27
  Betty 25
  Edith 27
  Edward 'Ted' **21**, 25, **26**, 27
  Emily 84
  Eva Ellen 27
  Frederick James **26**, 27
  Gilbert Victor **21**, 25, **26**, 27
  Henry 'Harry' **21**, 25, **26**, 27
  James **26**, 84, **85**
  John 'Jack' **21**, 25, 27
  Keith 19, 84
  Lucy 19, 25, **26**, 27
  Mildred 25
  Miss F 26
  Miss O *[Olive]* 26
  Percy **15**, 19, 25, **26**, 27, **84**
  Reginald **26**
  Robert How **21**, 25, **26**, 27

Susan **84**
  William 19, 25, 27
  William J 19, **26**
Preston, Ruby 25
Pring, Hannah 42
Pugin, A W N 9
Quick, Maria 70
Quilter, Phyllis 72
  Ted 72
Raddington 19
Redhode, Revd William 102
Redwood, Alice 27, 28, 67, 84, 86
  Anthony 'Tony' 27, 86
  Arthur Henry **21**, 28
  Bessie **60**
  Betty 25, **86**
  Emily 28
  Ernest **21**, 27, 28
  Frances Ellen 60
  Herbert 86
  Hilda Betty 86
  Hilda M 28
  Hugh 27
  Jesse **21**, 27, 28, 78
  John **21**, 27, 28, 60, 67, 84, 86
  Lionel Jack 25, 67, **86**
  Martha 28
  Mary Ann 27
  Vera **67**, **86**, **100**
  Violet 28
  William 28
  Winifred Alice 67
Reed, Ruby Winifred 94
Richards, Elizabeth 64
  John 64
  Louisa 64
Roberts, Elizabeth **87**
  Henry 87
  John **87**
Robins, Marjory 109
Rockett, Charles 67
  Charlotte 67
  John 67
Rodgment, Anne 70, 71
Roman Fort 69
Sage, Revd Thomas 102
Salisbury, Alice 27, 86

Sampford/Moor/Peverell
  11, 22, 28, 39, 41, 60, 61, 87
Sanders, Frederick 104
Saunders, Revd Lloyd 103
Sayer, Sarah 60
Seccombe, Revd John 102
Sharpe, Revd John 32, 103
Shattock, Alfred 109
  Charles George 88
  Charlotte Isabella 67, 78, 88, 99
  Herbert 89
  Mary Jane 88
  Mary Maria 89
  Robert 50, 88
  Robert White 67, 78, **88**, 99, 109
  Robert William 88
Shepherd, Ann 20
  Edith 27
  Walter 20
  William 20
Shopland, Alice Jane 89, 91
  Florence Emma 89
  James 28, **88**, 91, 109
  Mary Ann 28, **88**, 91
  Mary Maria 89
  Rosina Charlotte 28, 50, **89**
  Samuel **21**, 28, 50, 88, **89**, 91
Shorland, Peter 117
Simms, Florence 80
Smith, Andrew J Bay **89**
  Barbara E G **89**
Snell, Mary 80
Snow, Lily Laura 78
Sprague, Elizabeth 20, 41, 73, **90**
  Mary **90**
  Robert 41, 73, **90**
  Simon **90**
Stallenge Thorne 3, 111
Staple Cross 3, 111
Staple Cross pub 28, 111
Stawley 46, 48
Stephens, Emma 60
  Nicholas 109
Stevens, Elizabeth 78
  John 90
  Sarah 90
  William Edward **90**

General Index

Stone, Alice Jane 89, **91**
  Caroline Amy **91**
  Charlotte 67
  Delia 91
  George Henry 91
  Richard 119
  William Albert 45, 89, **91**, 109
Sully, Mary 73
Sweet, Ann 48
 Jane 48
 William 48
Talbot, Albert Jesse **92**, 93
  Alice 92, 93
  Edith 93
  Elizabeth 20, **92**, 93
  Frederick Mark **92**, 93
  Jesse 20, **92**, 93
  John **92**, 93
  Katherine 92, 93
  Lewis John **92**, 93
  Mabel Annie **92**, 93
  Mary **92**, 93
Tanner, Peter Treherne **94**
  Sylvia **94**
Tarr, Elizabeth 41
  Emma 41
  Henry 41
  Mary 96
Taunton 7, 24, 41, 42, 51, 55, 82, 93
Taunton Courier **13**
Taylor, Elsie 30
The Huntsham Book 47, 66
Thomas, Derek 94
  Enid 94
  Frederick **15,** 19, 23, 28
  Jean 60, 94
  John 94
  Lionel *[see Walter Lionel]*
  Louisa 19, 23, 28
  Nelly 19, 94
  Ruby Winifred **94**
  W **21**, 28
  Walter 28
  Walter Lionel 60, **94**, 109
  William 19, 23, 28
Thorne, Revd Thomas

32, 103, 117
Tiverton 3, 28, 44, 49, 50, 51, 57, 59, 64, 65, 70, 72, 73, 81, 96
Toms, John **6**, 7
Tooze, Edith May 28, 29
  Eliza 29
  Elizabeth 95
  F **21**, 29
  Frank 29
  Frederick 29
  Grace 29
  James 'Jim' **21**, 29
  John 'Jack' **21**, 29
  Laura 24
  Mark **21**, 28, 29
  Mary 29, **95**
  Samuel 29, **95**
  Selina 29
  Thomas 95
  William 95
Trace Bridge 27
Trevor, Revd Fred 103
Troake, Albert John **15,** 19
  Elizabeth 19
  John 19
  Mary 19
Turk's Head pub 20
Turner, Nora 75, 76
  Phyllis Adah 72
  William Berrow 76
Twose, William **95** *[see Tooze]*
Twysden, Aileen Frances Mary 55
  Anne Evelyn Frances 55, 56
  James Stevenson 55
  Janet 55
Uffculme 97
Uplowman 19, 42, 47, 50, 54, 63, 68, 88
Upton 79
Venn, Robert 60
  Sarah 60
Vickery, Albert **96**
  Alice 96
  Ann 72
  Benjamin 96
  Edward 96

Elizabeth 29
Frances 96
Harriet 29, 55
James **96**
John 29, 96
Lucy 19, 96
Mary **96**
Maud **96**
Robert Thomas **21**, 29
Sarah Ann 41
Stella Frances **96**
Thomas **96**
Vera Florence **96**
William 41, 96
Vowles of Bristol 8, 9
Vyvyan, Revd Charles 103
Walker, Greta 97
Ware, David Alfred **21**, 22, 30, 97
    Elizabeth 30, **97**
    Elsie 30
    Harold Edgar **21**, 30, 97
    Henry, Revd 103
    Phyllis I M 30
    Thomas 30, **97**
Waterslade 3, 111
Watkinson, Geoffrey **97**
    Greta **97**
Watts, Beatrice 84
    Edmond, Revd 103
Webster, Godfrey 109
Wellington 3, 6, 7, 39, 46, 53, 65
Wellington Weekly News 69, 72
Wensley, Caroline 38, 98
    Hannah **98**
    James 38, 98

    William **98**
Westebeare, Revd John 102
Western Times **26**, 40, 66, 99
Westlake, Fanny Mabel 63
Weymouth, Almira 81
Wheaton, Mary Ann 99
Whitaker, Caroline 76, 107
White, Alfred 109
    Emma **99**
    Florence 64
    Harriett **98**
    Henry 98
    J 109
    Mary **99**
    Mary Ann **99**
    Mary Jane 88
    Thomas **99**, 109
    W H 109
Whytyng, Revd Thomas 102
Wills, Revd Joshiah 103
Wilson-Todd, Lady Aileen Frances 55
    Sir William Henry, Bt 55
Winter, Hannah 98
Wiveliscombe 3, 19, 70, 71, 86, 98
Wood, David 99
    Ethel Lilian 21
    Fanny Ann **99**
    Mary 99
Woodbury, Ethel 24
Wright, Ivy D 25
Wyndham, Frances Emma 77
Yarde, Andrew Joseph 'Jack' 56
    Minnie Hannah 56
Yem, Revd Simon 102

NUMERICAL INDEX
TO
GRAVE PLOTS ON CHURCHYARD PLAN

A-1	LOCK		B-1	WOOD
A-2	HEYWOOD		B-2	HUSSEY
A-3	REDWOOD		B-3	HUSSEY
A-4	PERRY		B-4	LUCAS
A-5	VICKERY		B-5	BUCKNELL
A-6	BUTT		B-6	BUCKNELL
A-7	COTTRELL		B-7	BOWERMAN
A-8	NO NAME		B-8	BURNETT/PENN
A-9	HILTON		B-9	VICKERY
A-10	DARBY		B-10	GREEDY
A-11	DARBY		B-11	LAMPREY
A-12	DARBY		B-12	HEDGELAND
A-13	DARBY		B-13	BREWER
A-14	TALBOT/MELLEN/EIVERS		B-14	NO NAME (BREWER)
A-15	TALBOT		B-15	PERRY
A-16	COCKRAM		B-16	TANNER
A-17	WENSLEY		B-17	PAVEY
A-18	FERRIS		B-18	DART
A-19	HILL		B-19	CLEEVE
A-20	FERRIS/FROST		B-20	DUNN
A-21	EARLEY		B-21	DUNN
A-22	NO NAME		B-22	DUNN
A-23	NO NAME		B-23	LONGMAN
A-24	ROBERTS		B-24	LONGMAN
A-25	ROBERTS		B-25	STONE
A-26	ROBERTS		B-26	LONGMAN
A-27	MILTON		B-27	LONGMAN
A-28	TWOSE		B-28	LONGMAN
A-29	TOOZE		B-29	LONGMAN
A-30	GAMLIN/MARKS /FOWLER		B-30	HOW
			B-31	SHOPLAND
A-31	ASH		B-32	SHOPLAND
A-32	ASH		B-33	SHATTOCK/HOW
A-33	STEVENS		B-34	KEMP

B-35	PALFREY		D-1	HEYWOOD
B-36	PALFREY		D-2	GODDARD
B-37	PALFREY		D-3	PRESCOTT
B-38	McCANCE		D-4	REDWOOD
B-39	BROOMFIELD		D-5	PRESCOTT
B-40	SPRAGUE		D-6	PRESCOTT
B-41	NO NAME		D-7	FILMER
B-42	BROOMFIELD		D-8	HOCKING
B-43	DINHAM		D-9	DANIELL
B-44	WARE		D-10	PERRY
B-45	DESTER		D-11	HEYWOOD
B-46	DESTER		D-12	PARR
B-47	WHITE		D-13	NEWMAN
B-48	NEWMAN			
B-49	NEWMAN		E-1	MORRISH
B-50	NEWMAN		E-2	WATKINSON
B-51	NEWMAN		E-3	STONE
			E-4	AUTON
C-1	GOFFIN		E-5	DOBLE
C-2	MOON		E-6	SMITH
C-3	PEPPERELL		E-7	HEYWOOD
C-4	DARBY			
C-5	GODDARD/FOLLETT/REDWOOD			
C-6	WHITE			
C-7	HAWKINS			
C-8	THOMAS			
C-9	GODDARD			
C-10	HAMILTON			
C-11	FELLOWES			
C-12	FALLS			
C-13	BROWNE/MAX			

ENVOI

Now fades the glimmering landscape on the sight
And all the air a solemn stillness holds.
. . .
Far from the madding crowd's ignoble strife
Their sober wishes never learned to stray;
Along the cool sequestered vale of life
They kept the noiseless tenor of their way.

From an
*Elegy written in a Country
Churchyard*
Thomas Gray
1750